LIBERTY AND POETIC LICENCE
NEW ESSAYS ON BYRON

LIVERPOOL ENGLISH TEXTS AND STUDIES, 42

LIBERTY AND POETIC LICENCE

NEW ESSAYS ON BYRON

EDITED BY
BERNARD BEATTY, TONY HOWE,
AND CHARLES E. ROBINSON

LIVERPOOL UNIVERSITY PRESS

First published 2008 by
Liverpool University Press
4 Cambridge Street
Liverpool
L69 7ZU

British Library Cataloguing-in-Publication data
A British Library CIP record is available

ISBN 978-0-85323-589-7 hb

Typeset by XL Publishing Services, Tiverton
Printed and bound by Biddles Ltd, King's Lynn

Contents

Preface — vii

Abbreviations — viii

Introduction
BERNARD BEATTY — I

Byron Tests the Freedom of Southwell
PETER COCHRAN — 10

The Bride of Abydos: The Regime of Visibility and the Possibility
of Resistance
TOM MOLE — 20

'A Very Life in Our Despair': Freedom and Fatality in *Childe Harold's
Pilgrimage*, Cantos III and IV
MICHAEL O'NEILL — 37

Byron, Manfred, Negativity and Freedom
PETER GRAHAM — 50

Manfred's Quarrel with Immortality: Freeing the Self
KATHARINE KERNBERGER — 60

The Language of Freedom and the Reality of Power in
Byron's *Mazeppa*
GABRIELE POOLE — 72

Marino Faliero: Escaping the Aristocratic
ALAN RAWES — 88

Byron, 'Inkle and Yarico', and the Chains of Love
ANDREW M. STAUFFER — 103

'I Have a Means of Freedom Still': Aesthetic Dialectic in *Sardanapalus*
JONATHON SHEARS   117

Byron, Milton, and Doctrines of Christian Liberty:
Cain and *Paradise Regained*
JOAN BLYTHE   132

Byron's Afterlife and the Emancipation of Geology
RALPH O'CONNOR   147

Byron and Grammatical Freedom
GAVIN HOPPS   165

Byron, Napoleon, and Imaginative Freedom
JOHN CLUBBE   181

Slaves of Passion: Byron and Staël on Liberty
JONATHAN GROSS   193

Uncircumscribing Poetry: Byron, Johnson, and
the Bowles Controversy
TONY HOWE   206

Free Quills and Poetic Licences: Byron and the Politics
of Publication
TIMOTHY WEBB   219

Index   233

Preface

The road to publication for this volume has been long and winding. The editors would like to thank everyone involved, especially the contributors, for their patience. A particular debt is owed to David Leyland for his practical help in the early stages of editing, and we would like to acknowledge, too, the assistance of Rebecca Saleem. Our gratitude also goes out to all at Liverpool University Press, and especially to Anthony Cond, for his encouragement and optimism.

Abbreviations

Unless otherwise stated, all quotations from Byron's poetry are taken from *Lord Byron: The Complete Poetical Works*, ed. Jerome J. McGann (Oxford: Clarendon Press, 1980), abbreviated throughout as *CPW*; all quotations from Byron's letters are taken from *Byron's Letters and Journals*, ed. Leslie Marchand, 13 vols (London: John Murray, 1973–1994), abbreviated throughout as *BLJ*; all references to Byron's other prose are taken from *Lord Byron: The Complete Miscellaneous Prose*, ed. Andrew Nicholson (Oxford: Clarendon Press, 1991), abbreviated as *CMP*.

Introduction

BERNARD BEATTY

This liberty is a poetic licence.

(Don Juan, I, 120)

The dustjacket of this volume shows Eugène Delacroix's painting of François de Bonnivard in prison. It is an unsurprising choice for a book with this title. Nor is it surprising that the painter of *Liberty Leading the People* should produce an image of imprisonment based on a poem by Byron. We all know, as it is likely that Delacroix did, the opening lines of the sonnet that Byron prefixed to *The Prisoner of Chillon*:

> Eternal Spirit of the Chainless Mind!
> Brightest in dungeons, Liberty! Thou art.

Byron is the poet of liberty. This is not a critic's postulation but the judgement of the nineteenth century, and he seems to invite and revel in it. This volume offers confirmation that the phrase still rings true in the twenty-first century.

Neither we nor Byron, however, would say of the 'Sonnet on Liberty': 'Why Man the Soul of such writing is it's [*sic*] licence.'[1] We know at once that it is *Don Juan* that is now being talked about. Would it be too sweeping a statement to say that the works of the poet which find their centre in the spirit of *Childe Harold's Pilgrimage* are concerned with liberty and its antitheses, and those which find their centre in the spirit of *Don Juan* are concerned with licence and its constraints? I think we could say that this was a helpful preliminary assumption – and it is one that many of the writers in this volume share – but that it is no more than that. The Venice of *Beppo* is a city of carnival licence compared to the London world to which it is addressed, but the licence operates within agreed constraints. The judgement offered on George III and even Robert Southey in 'The Vision of Judgement' is, in the end, much more charitable than Southey's judgements on Byron; but it is still a judgement and the licentious Wilkes, licentious no longer, is moved to pity for his old adversary. The poem invited the attentions of the Censor, of course, but it is a more Christian poem than Southey's absurd projection of his political prejudices onto the cosmos, and it is not in league with anarchy.

This volume is designed to expand but also to critique these preliminary assumptions about liberty and licence as we have begun to do here. In so doing, it is following the tracks that Byron left for us. One of his most striking traits was his ability to adhere unswervingly to certain clear convictions and principles such as liberty – hence his disdain for the 'Lake School' poets who had, in his view, swerved from theirs – while at the same time being far more aware than most of the ambiguities, intricacies, secret connexions, dead ends, and historical twists and turns, that shape the bewildering but sustaining paradoxes inherent in any attempt to understand life or establish clear value judgements that will apply to myriad circumstances.

For instance, Delacroix assumes, not unreasonably, that Bonnivard, celebrated in the sonnet, is the subject of *The Prisoner of Chillon*. Without Byron, Delacroix would never have chosen Bonnivard as his subject. But the poem, despite its Preface, does not seem in the least concerned to activate the resonances naturally attaching to such a figure of fortitude in the face of injustice. Milton – another poet for whom liberty was a central value, and whom Byron admired as such – would most certainly have sought these out. Even Sir Walter Scott, less keen on liberty, would have carefully reconstructed the intricacies of Swiss politics and the fact that Calvin arrived in Geneva in the year of Bonnivard's release. Byron not only does not do this, though he makes a casual nod to the possibility that he might have done some of this in the 'Advertisement' to the poem, but he does not even align his prisoner with the liberal Romantic valuation of liberty placed unassailably in the heart and mind, and which is so wonderfully articulated in the sonnet prefixed to the poem. On the contrary, the frame of mind that the prisoner ends up with is so far from either of these that he confesses:

> It was at length the same to me,
> Fetter'd or fetterless to be.

The nameless prisoner does not sound like Bonnivard nor like one of the 'sons' of liberty who, the sonnet tells us, when they 'to fetters are consign'd', extend 'Freedom's fame … on every wind'. Manifestly *The Prisoner of Chillon* tells a very different tale from *Fidelio*. Equally, it is clear that liberty is not always 'Brightest in dungeons'. Should we conclude, then, that Byron falters in his belief in liberty? Or, perhaps, might we hazard that only someone passionately attached to liberty would be so interested in tracking its extinction in a consciousness ostensibly devoted to it? We might compare this supposition with Shelley's addiction to deconstructing those ideal images of love to which he is so passionately attached. The author of *Julian and Maddalo* certainly had an ambiguously troubled sense of Byron's attitude to liberty.

The word 'licence' causes us similar problems. 'Licence' is, customarily, the unacceptable face of liberty. It is so for St Paul, worried that his demolition of the claims of the law might be construed as an invitation to absolute licence. Literally, the word means to be allowed or authorised to do something. Licence, provided it is of the right kind (from the Archbishop of Canterbury, in this case), will authorise Byron's marriage in Seaham as readily as, in the extended sense of the word, it will authorise Byron's sexual abandon when he first arrives in Venice. Joan Blythe reminds us elsewhere in the volume that Milton, lover of liberty but not of Comus's licence, was official *censor deputatus* to Cromwell and may have lost his job for licensing a translation of a Socinian catechism. Poets are customarily allowed more licence than other writers so there is, it seems, some connection between poetry and licence but Byron's poetic 'licence' is, in Southey's eyes, intimately connected with satanic licentiousness. The French Revolution's Tree of Liberty is a value for Byron, who wishes to see 'Freedom's stranger-tree grow native' in Spanish soil (*Childe Harold's Pilgrimage*, I, xc), and for the young Wordsworth, but for others it was seen as presiding over the sexual and judicial licence of the Reign of Terror.

Equality is associated more readily with liberty than with licence. The French Revolution rests upon the identity of the two, but Marino Faliero, champion of his own and his people's liberty, distinguishes sharply between them ('not rash equality but equal rights'). Sardanapalus, on the other hand, initially associates liberty with licence or something very close to it. So does *Don Juan*. But only up to a point.

Those early readers who did not much like *Don Juan* tended to associate its poetic licences of rhyme and diction with the poem's ostentatiously sustained study of a variety of extra-marital sexual relations in differing social worlds. There is no real equivalent to either of these in any other poetry of the time. For most of these critics, both kinds of licence – poetical and sexual – were evidence of what was also wrong with Byron's political defence of liberty. Byron did not quite see it that way. He insisted that *Don Juan* was a moral poem. The form of *Don Juan*, however apparently novel and improvised, follows Italian, English, and Scottish practice. Byron tells us so by producing a version of Pulci's *Morgante Maggiore. Don Juan* rhymes, often outrageously, but normally strictly and its metre is much more orthodox than that of Southey's *Thalaba* or Coleridge's 'Christabel'. In the same way, Byron is at some pains to tell us that his sexual frankness is much less extreme than Smollett's or Fielding's or Sterne's. His licence is licensed – by which he means that it has 'precedents'. It also has limits. Shelley describes love-making but Byron does not. Indeed when the first occasion in the poem arrives where he might do so, he asks the reader whether he may 'take a liberty' and then explains that this liberty 'is a poetic licence'. Byron's jokes are clever and pertinent. It is worth unpicking this one for it is, of course, the source of this present volume's title and it is also a clue to its character.

To 'take a liberty' is a phrase that belongs to courteous behaviour, when someone uses it as an excuse for an insufficiently accommodated request. The formula, as in the poem, is 'may I take the liberty of doing so and so?' It expects the answer 'yes'. But the formula may have sexual overtones as in 'may I take the liberty to sit beside you, hold your hand, etc.?' When it is used descriptively about someone who does this, it is nearly always negative and, again, often implies sexual presumption. If we say that someone 'took the liberty to do something' we are likely to be criticising them. If we say that someone 'took a liberty', the implication is probably sexual. This is not the sense here. Byron's request confirms him to be a courteous narrator who is aware of social forms. The modern phrase 'the implied reader' is not quite right for him. By preference, and certainly in the ottava rima poems, Byron as narrator talks to an explicitly addressed reader. Keats does not, and indeed does not 'narrate' at all in Byron's deliberated sense. Byron is politely asking this reader to allow him to take the liberty of moving a few months forward in the story without relating what happens in between. He does so out of a larger courtesy. He will not describe the love-making of Juan and Julia, as he will not, later, describe consummation with Haidée, Dudu (except via the device of a dream that will signal that it takes place), Catharine, or Fitz-Fulke (in the latter case we cannot, for once, be sure that it has taken place at all though we presume so). The 'liberty' that he takes therefore is one that enables him to tell the story as he pleases – that is to say he is claiming 'poetic licence' – but its other purpose is to avoid a description of love-making which could not be accommodated within the polite norms of communicating with an equally polite stranger – the reader – that he never wholly abandons. So he takes a narrative liberty in order to avoid sexual licence and, with consummate wit, points out that this is a 'poetic licence'.

So far so good. But if we ask where the narrator, with so much delicate concern for the reader's feeling, actually takes us to, we find that he takes us to the rudest section in the canto. Julia is hiding Juan in her bed while she delivers a tirade to her unfortunate husband in defence of her chastity. Byron now uses his customarily courteous acknowledgement of omission to quite different purpose. It becomes a comedian's shared risqué joke with an audience complicit in his knowingness:

> He had been hid – I don't pretend to say
> How, nor can I indeed describe the where –
> Young, slender, and pack'd easily, he lay,
> No doubt, in little compass, round or square.
> (*Don Juan*, I, 166)

This is about as licentious as Byron gets in *Don Juan* though we are aware of the narrator's roving eye earlier on:

> the black curls strive, but fail,
> To hide the glossy shoulder, which uprears
> Its snow through all; – her soft lips lie apart,
> And louder than her breathing beats her heart.
> (*Don Juan*, I, 158)

This is perhaps the sort of erotic warmth that the Reverend Mr Becher might have reproved in Byron's Southwell days. It is 'licence' of a different sort to the narrator's poetic licence. Peter Cochran gives us several examples of it, both heterosexual and homosexual. But Byron clearly calculates that neither the farce of Juan's hiding and discovery, nor his warm drawing of Julia's panting charms, breaches the magic line of which he is always aware. He will give us a comic picture of Juan and Julia in bed, but not an erotic one, yet he will remind the reader, through his engagingly enthusiastic but not quite prurient description of Julia's attractive body, why Juan is in bed with her in the first place. Even here, it is important to emphasise that it is not only her body but her energetic spirit, evidenced in her improvised tirade, that attracts both reader and Juan to the body which it animates.

These calculations are to be admired, surely, and they indicate how sharp and how persistent Byron's thinking is about liberty and licence in art and in life. We would have to go back via Fielding to Chaucer to find a similar ability to mediate between bawdiness and delicacy in sustained narrative.

It would have been better, perhaps, for the editors to have added an illustration of Julia in bed (energetically haranguing her suspicious husband while certain lumps suggest the hidden presence of Juan to the informed eye) as a companion picture to Delacroix's picture of Bonnivard in chains for the jacket of this book. The picture of Julia would be an icon of liberty as well as of licence and the two illustrations together would suggest the play of Byron's thinking on the subject. We did not do so because there are not, so far as we know, any illustrations of this scene in the various illustrated editions of Byron common in the nineteenth century. It was too licentious a scene for the Victorians though the intrinsically more risqué one of the clothed Haidée beholding the naked body of Juan washed up on the beach and relishing in the midst of her concern, as Andrew Stauffer reminds us, 'so white a skin' (an unconscious precursor of Manet's mingling of clothed and erotic unclothed in *Déjeuner sur l'herbe* which so shocked its first viewers) is a common subject for illustrators. What must have appalled Victorian readers of canto I is not only the assault on marital values but that any reader is bound to be cheering for the magnificently deceitful wife rather than the peevishly deceived husband. Yet it is equally important that the reader does not protest when Julia is caught out, dethroned, and ends up, like Bonnivard, imprisoned, but in a convent. Byron preserves all kinds of balances. We might say that this, too, is what liberty is for him.

As we have seen, Byron was acutely aware of a tradition of writing that had often made these delicate calculations between licence and decorum. He consciously stood within this and invoked it as defence when attacked. This tradition of texts was, as he well knew, now becoming unreadable in the new breed of mixed company that only allowed grosser dividing lines between decorum and vulgarity, but the tradition was not, in his view, fundamentally licentious at all.[2] It was the hypocrisy and anaemic prurience of his contemporaries that he wished to pillory rather than in any way implying acceptance of the view that the tradition is corrupt and corrupting. We can find a parallel argument in the customary invocation of political tradition to defend present liberties against attack. This was used, especially by Whigs, to defend English liberties against George III's political ambitions. 'Liberty' here, as in Gray's 'Progress of Poesy' (completed six years before George came to the throne), looks for home-grown precedents in Anglo-Saxon law, the Magna Carta, the 1688 'Revolution' and so on. If some new practice was condemned as revolutionary or destructive, then this tradition could be and was invoked to justify its customary nature. So it was by Richard Price who argued in November 1789 that the French Revolution was only a version of 1688, but Burke, famously, denied that it worked in this case. The liberty offered by the French Revolution, though it often used the same Classical Republican references as English Whigs to justify its actions and its preferred form, presented itself in practice as more unprecedented than this. No one accused the Anglo-Saxons or the Runnymede Barons or the Seven Bishops of 1688 of being in league with 'licence', but *The Anti-Jacobin* takes for granted the connection between the French Revolution's proclamation of liberty and unbridled licence, and makes much fun of it. Byron read it more enthusiastically than he read the radical journal *The Examiner* and yet he could never wholly condemn the Revolution without condemning liberty itself. The problem for him is made more acute by the figure of Napoleon who is the embodiment of the Revolution in the sense of ensuring that radical changes cannot be reversed (despite Metternich and the temporary Bourbon restoration), but who rules in a more authoritarian fashion than Louis XVI or George III ever could. Similarly Napoleon brings revolutionary change to many other nations but also seeks to bind them to his imperial rule. Byron was, as John Clubbe insists, 'obsessed' with Napoleon, but once again he has to try and find a magic line, a decorous line increasingly unrecognisable to his contemporaries, through these contrarieties.

So, too, do the contributors to this volume, some of whom we have already named. We can neither simply take Byron as, say Verdi or Mazzini,[3] take him – as the unqualified apostle of the libertarian ideals of Romantic nationalism – but neither can we endlessly deconstruct him or follow his own deconstructions into a morass of indeterminacies as though this is definitive too. We can say simply that Byron loved freedom and we can mean something by it. Indeed we must do so. Literary criticism needs to be capable of asserting simple 'Truths that you will not read in the Gazettes' (*Don Juan*, IX, 10) as well as insisting, as Gabriele Poole does in his delineation of multiple freedoms in *Mazeppa*, upon the infinitely complex ways that truth has to 'navigate o'er fiction' (*Don Juan*, XV, 88).

The essays in this volume come at this complex but central topic in a variety of ways. A number of them supply some historical context and historical extension of Byron's multi-faceted concern for freedom into Ireland, Greece or even geology which, according to Ralph O'Connor, was freed up from Biblical literalism by Act II of *Cain*. Others are directly concerned with a range of Byron's texts. That several of these are concerned with his plays (excluding *Manfred*) is a sign that these now form both a natural part of Byron studies and the major source for determining Byron's political attitudes. Alan Rawes' focus is on Byron's ambiguous relation with aristocracy in *Marino Faliero*; Jonathon Shears argues that *Sardanapalus* celebrates a realisable aesthetic freedom rather than political autonomy. Other essays (Katharine Kernberger, Peter Graham) focus in various original ways on the relation between will and freedom, so fundamental to Byron's thinking about the energies of the self, especially in *Childe Harold's Pilgrimage*, *Manfred*, and *Cain*. Tom Mole examines the interrelation of Byron's gaze with his acute sense of being gazed at. Our earlier argument tended to associate liberty with politics and licence with sexuality, but Julia is an emblem of liberty and of power as much as of licence, and, as Mole argues with respect to *The Bride of Abydos*, sexuality can occasion an exercise of power.

Byron, as we saw earlier, can ask his reader's permission to omit details from his story. Two essays, Peter Cochran's and Timothy Webb's, explore the political dimensions of Byron's omissions and sense of omission. Webb's account of Byron's 'pragmatic' relationship to what he includes and excludes from this text dovetails with Michael O'Neill's sensitive account of how Byron's simultaneous freedom and restriction in the represented act of writing *Childe Harold's Pilgrimage* emerges from his uncanny compulsion 'to hear the inflections of both sides of a question'. Gavin Hopps ties this in with Byron's grammatical freedom in the act of writing which is a form of poetic licence that embodies a wider sense of freedom.

The volume ends deliberately with Timothy Webb's direct exploration of the relation between publication and freedom but precedes this by a number of essays that depend upon Byron's relation to someone else (Napoleon, Mme de Staël, and Dr Johnson). Jonathan Gross argues that Byron agrees with Mme de Staël that liberty 'is impossible without being freed from erotic constraint'. Tony Howe argues that Byron 'read Johnson as an opponent of circumscribed poetry' and a precedent for his own war against the stultifying constrictions of cant. In this way, liberty and licence can be traced from beginning to end of this collection of essays.

One of the most cheering things about contemporary interest in Byron is the intelligent interest given to the whole range of his work by a considerable number of young scholars. This was not the case two or three decades ago. It is not surprising, then, that essays by well-established and respected names form only just over half of the content of this volume. We think and hope that the volume works as a whole and that it augurs well for the future of Byron studies. We hope that you will think the same.

Notes

1 *BLJ*, 6, 208.
2 It is true that Byron acknowledges that Pope and Sterne and Restoration literature are sometimes indecent, but the general lines of his defence, especially his invocation of Fielding's example, is to assert the legitimate inclusions of the diction and references of these writers within a polite but liberal tradition.
3 Mazzini is a brilliant but simplifying expositor of Byron. Verdi's political attitudes are not very complicated but he is attracted to the darkness of Byron's imagination as in his version of 'The Two Foscari' as well as to Byron's liberal nationalism.

Byron Tests the Freedom of Southwell

PETER COCHRAN

This essay will examine the sequence of four juvenile books – two private and two public – which Byron published from Newark between 1806 and 1808. Although the books have been subject to at least two interesting critical analyses – by Jerome McGann in *Fiery Dust*, and by Germaine Greer in the 2003 *Newstead Byron Society Review* – I feel that concentration exclusively on the third and most famous book, *Hours of Idleness*, and neglecting to see it in the context of its three fellow volumes, causes some interesting points to be missed. The books raises questions about what Byron at first wanted to print in Southwell; about how free he found himself to be, firstly in Southwell and later in the world at large; and about how, finally, other pressures, both social and emotional, forced him to censor himself.

The first of the four volumes, *Fugitive Pieces*, contains thirty-eight poems, and was printed privately and anonymously by S. and J. Ridge of Newark; it was ready for distribution by October 1806.[1] It contains seventeen heterosexual love poems of one kind or another,[2] one ('The Cornelian') almost overtly homosexual, one poem about Newstead Abbey, seven translations from Latin or Greek, four poems satirical of school and university life, six personal poems, and two ('On the Death of Mr Fox' and 'An Occasional Prologue') which fit into none of these categories.

The book is a product of Byron's life at Southwell in a way that none of the following three are: it is in fact a Southwell document, 'printed', as Byron's preface says, 'for the perusal of a few friends to whom [the poems] are dedicated'. In it, Byron portrays himself as writing ripostes to his friends' verses in books (p. 12); he acts in their private theatricals (p. 39); he is friends with the young menfolk, with whom he shares problems of the heart (pp. 46 and 54); practising with his pistols, he narrowly misses two young ladies of the place (p. 61). If such casual and harmless pieces would be instantly decodable by Southwell gossips, what of the amatory ones? The question seems to have given Byron pause.

Perhaps a result of this proximity and accountability, three and a half of the poems in *Fugitive Pieces* were, at the last minute, deemed by Byron unprintable, and form the reason why only four copies of the book survive: he recalled the entire print run (as Willis Pratt conjectures, one of a hundred copies)[3] and burned most of it. The 'inappropriate' poems are 'To Mary', 'To Maria ——', 'To Caroline', and the last six verses of 'To Miss E. P.' The poems 'To Mary' and 'To Caroline' imply that Byron had made love to at least two women at Southwell – and that he had indeed, in the case of 'Mary', become surfeited with the passion:

> No more with mutual love we burn,
> No more the genial couch we bless,
> Dissolving in the fond caress;
> Our love o'erthrown will ne'er return.
>
> Though love than ours could ne'er be truer,
> Yet flames too fierce themselves destroy,
> Embraces oft repeated cloy,
> *Ours* came *too* frequent, to endure.

It is surprising that only these two were cut – if we take the names and blanks in the titles at face value, it would appear that the eighteen-year-old Byron had had liaisons (of differing degrees of intensity) with approximately nine women of Southwell,[4] 'a town', he wrote, 'whose inhabitants are notorious for officious curiosity'.[5] On being sent a copy of the book, Byron's Anglican friend the Reverend J. C. Becher protested in verse:

> Say, Byron! Why compel me to deplore
> Talents designed for choice poetic lore,
> Deigning to varnish scenes, that shun the day,
> With guilty lustre, and with amorous lay?
> Forbear to taint the Virgin's spotless mind,
> In Power though mighty, be in Mercy kind,
> Bid the chaste Muse diffuse her hallowed light,
> So shall thy Page enkindle pure delight,
> Enhance thy native worth, and proudly twine,
> With Britain's honours, those that are divine.[6]

But Byron did not need such holy advice. He himself told John Pigot that Pigot would 'perceive them' (the poems) 'to be *improper* for the perusal of Ladies', and added that 'of course none of the females in your family must see them'.[7] He told Edward Long that 'Mary' was 'a Mrs. Cobourne' and that 'Caroline' was Mary Chaworth-Musters' mother-in-law: natural doubt has been cast on his veracity.[8] Whether from fear of censure from his

Southwell friends, or from a modest sense of having gone too far, or from the desire not to have too much of his private life in print, even though encoded – or from all three – Byron found himself unable to be as frank about his Nottinghamshire sex life as he had initially intended. 'To Mary', 'To Maria ———', and 'To Caroline' never saw print again while he lived.

I assume that it was on grounds of facetiousness and blasphemy that the end section of the poem to Elizabeth Pigot was cut:

From this we suppose, (as indeed well we may,)
That should Saints after death, with their spouses put up more,
And wives, as in life, aim at absolute sway,
All Heaven would ring with the conjugal uproar.

Distraction and discord would follow in course,
Nor MATTHEW, nor MARK, nor St. PAUL, can deny it,
The only expedient is general divorce,
To prevent universal disturbance and riot.

Another factor in the decision to 'pull' *Fugitive Pieces* can be seen by examining its text as printed, and the alterations Byron made to it in the Morgan copy.[9] The text is clearly the product of inadequate proof-reading, and is riddled with misprints: at line 29 of 'On Leaving Newstead', 'and' is printed 'aud'; in the note to 'On the Death of a Young Lady', 'he preferred' is 'be preferred'; at line 18 of 'To Caroline', 'meets' is 'mets' … and so on. In the Morgan copy, several missing letters are inked-in. The book's indecency may have been the ostensible motive for its withdrawal, but the banal fact of its unprofessional presentation, and the fact that it did not as yet embody Byron's final thoughts, may have been motives just as strong, though harder to boast about. Confessing that a book is rude raises a smile among your friends: confessing that it it is incompetently printed doesn't. Byron had been too impatient about his first book: not for him Horace's advice to 'keep your piece nine years'.

The next Newark volume, *Poems on Various Occasions* – Byron's second thought – contains forty-eight poems. It was privately and anonymously printed by the Ridges between 23 December 1806 and 13 January 1807. It is, as Byron wrote to John Pigot, *'vastly* correct, & miraculously *chaste'*.[10] Names which might give offence in Southwell are altered – 'Julia' becomes 'Lesbia', and so on. Love and marriage are no longer subjects for mirth, as they were to be years later in *Beppo* and *Don Juan*. Of the new poems, one is on Newstead Abbey, only six are love poems, two are translations from the Latin (one, a very short version of the Nisus and Euryalus episode from

Aeneid IX, is another celebration of male love); and three are personal.[11] The poems are divided into three sections, the first with no heading, the second and third headed respectively 'Translations and Imitations' and 'Fugitive Pieces'. Seventeen of them are not seen again: when putting his next book together – his first public book – Byron abandons them.

One new poem offers an answer to the Southwell censors, specifically to the Rev. Becher, whom it quotes:

> Far be't from me, the 'virgin's mind' to 'taint',
> Seduction's dread, is here no slight restraint:
> The maid, whose virgin breast is void of guile,
> Whose wishes dimple in a modest smile;
> Whose downcast eye disdains the wanton leer,
> Firm in her virtue's strength, yet not severe;
> She, whom a conscious grace shall thus refine,
> Will ne'er be 'tainted' by a strain of mine.
> But, for the nymph, whose premature desires
> Torment her bosom with unholy fires,
> No net to snare her willing heart is spread,
> She would have fallen, tho' she ne'er had read.[12]

In an unpublished poem, Byron is more scathing about Becher:

> if a little parson joins the train,
> And echos back his Patron's voice again –
> Though not delighted, yet I must forgive,
> Parsons as well as other folks must live: –
> From rage he rails not, rather say from dread,
> He does not speak for Virtue, but for bread;
> And this we know is in his Patron's giving,
> For Parsons cannot eat without a *Living*.[13]

And our sense that there was something fraudulent about Becher is reinforced by the knowledge that, of the four surviving copies of *Fugitive Pieces*, one of them is his.

That there was something fraudulent about Byron too is a thought worth remaining with. It was, it seems, all very well to corrupt young Southwell ladies in *reality*; but in *ink*, a gentleman knew the limits of decorum to be more strict.

The heterosexual love interest remains substantially less in *Poems on Various Occasions* than it had been in *Fugitive Pieces*. A major addition in this second book is *Childish Recollections*, which compensates for the loss of the earlier love poems, giving an implicit reason for their being cut, namely the nineteen-year-old Byron's sexual satiety:

> Farewell! ye nymphs, propitious to my verse,
> Some other Damon, will your charms rehearse;
> Some other paint his pangs, in hope of bliss,
> Or dwell in rapture, on your nectar'd kiss,
> These beauties grateful to my ardent sight,
> No more entrance my senses in delight.[14]

Rather than celebrate, or regret, or joke about women, the new Byron of *Poems on Various Occasions* laments the passing of innocent boyhood love:

> For ever to possess a friend in thee,
> Was bliss, unhop'd, though not unsought, by me;
> Thy softer soul was form'd for love alone,
> To ruder passions, and to hate unknown;
> Thy mind, in union with thy beauteous form,
> Was gentle, but unfit to steer the storm;
> That face, an index of celestial worth,
> Proclaim'd a heart, abstracted from the earth.
> Oft, when depress'd with sad, foreboding gloom,
> I sat reclin'd upon our favourite tomb,
> I've seen those sympathetic eyes o'erflow
> With kind compassion for thy comrade's woe;
> Or, when less mournful subjects form'd our themes,
> We tried a thousand fond romantic schemes,
> Oft hast thou sworn, in friendship's soothing tone,
> Whatever wish was mine, must be thine own.[15]

Childish Recollections is, as Jerome McGann writes, 'the most ambitious piece published in B[yron]'s early poems'.[16] The vulnerable nostalgia for schoolboy innocence which Byron displays both in it, and in the Nisus and Euryalus translation, may have been inspired in part by his new attachment to John Edleston, the Trinity choirboy. On 5 July 1807 he wrote about Edleston to Elizabeth Pigot:

> I certainly *love* him more than any human being, & neither *time* or Distance have had the least effect on my (in general) changeable Disposition. – In short, We shall put *Lady E. Butler*, & Miss *Ponsonby* to the *Blush*, *Pylades* & *Orestes* out of countenance, & want nothing but a *Catastrophe* like *Nisus* & *Euryalus*, to give *Jonathan* & *David* the 'go by'.[17]

Poems on Various Occasions was printed, so Byron claimed, 'merely for the perusal of a friendly Circle'.[18] So far he had printed his works privately and anonymously. But in March 1807 he announced to William Bankes:

> Contrary to my former Intention, I am now preparing a volume for the Public at large, my amatory pieces will be expunged, and others substituted, in their place ... This is a hazardous experiment, but want of better employment, the encouragement I have met with, & my own Vanity, induce me to stand the Test, though not without *sundry palpitations*. – The Book will circulate fast enough in this County, from mere Curiosity.[19]

Hours of Idleness, a Series of Poems, Original and Translated contains thirty-nine poems and was published by Ridge – publicly, under Byron's name, at last – in the final week of June 1807.[20] The book is divided into three sections as before, but shows a great broadening of subject-matter: no longer is it an expression of Byron's relationship with Southwell. The love poems are down in number, from the seventeen in *Fugitive Pieces*, to ten. There are the two poems on Newstead Abbey; ten translations from Greek and Latin, including Byron's version of the Nisus and Euryalus episode, expanded from eighteen lines to a sensational 406; one Ossian imitation, which also celebrates male bonding; *Oscar of Alva*; two poems on school and university; and a multitude of poems either personal (though not erotic) or miscellaneous. *Childish Recollections* reappears – but slightly muted: both the intimate passages quoted previously are cut.

The Virgil translation, being of a classical writer, *most* of whose 'songs are pure' as Byron later puts it in *Don Juan*, must have been above suspicion in Southwell; but the male-for-male passion it celebrates remains intense (Byron told Edward Long that it was 'the best in point of Versification I have ever written'):[21]

> 'But thou, my generous youth, whose tender years,
> Are near my own, whose worth, my heart reveres,
> Henceforth, affection sweetly thus begun,
> Shall join our bosoms, and our souls in one;
> Without thy aid, no glory shall be mine,
> Without thy dear advice, no great design;
> Alike through life esteem'd, thou godlike boy,
> In war my bulwark, and in peace my joy.'[22]

Hours of Idleness sold well and received at least eighteen reviews,[23] of which Byron noticed at least seven,[24] one of them being of course the one by Henry Brougham in the *Edinburgh Review*, which led to *English Bards and Scotch Reviewers*.

The fourth volume, *Poems Original and Translated*, contains thirty-eight poems and is, strictly, a second edition of *Hours of Idleness*. To have a second edition seems to have been Ridge's concept,[25] but once Byron accepted the idea he worked hard at revision. The book was published at Newark in March 1808,[26] and is divided into three sections like its predecessors.

The important *Childish Recollections*, already cut internally in *Hours of Idleness*, is now, however, deleted completely – owing, Byron said, to his reconciliation with Dr George Butler, the new Headmaster of Harrow, who had been pilloried in the poem as the pedant Pomposus. On 11 February 1808 Byron wrote to Ridge:

> You must *go back* and *cut out* the whole *poem* of *Childish Recollections*. Of course you will be surprised at this, and perhaps displeased, but it must be *done*. I cannot help it's detaining you a *month* longer, but there will be enough in the volume without it, and as I am now reconciled to Dr. Butler I cannot allow any Satire to appear, against him, nor can I alter that part relating to him without spoiling the whole. – You will therefore omit the whole poem.[27]

He is being disingenuous, for there are only three references to Butler/Pomposus[28] in the final version of *Childish Recollections*, and deleting or re-fashioning them would not be hard, and would not unbalance the work at all. Byron's major attacks on Pomposus are in the earlier poem 'On a Change of Masters, at a Great Public School', which only appears in the first two books, and in an eighteen-line fragment[29] existing on a separate manuscript. There seems to have been some unspoken inhibition on Byron's part which made it hard for him to see his vulnerable recollections of boyish love before the public. Having removed the more passionate of his earlier heterosexual poems, he now – without being frank about the reason, as was not the case with his former decision – removes the more passionate of his nostalgic homo-social poems.

For whatever reasons, the confessional urge which made up one of the motives behind Byron's need to publish his juvenile work, was thus twice defeated. It seems as if he did not wish to appear before the public in so exposed a manner.

Southwell itself was in part to blame. By June 1807 Byron was styling it '*your cursed, detestable* & *abhorred* abode of *Scandal, antiquated virginity*, & universal *Infamy*, where ... I care not if the whole Race were consigned to the *Pit* of *Acheron*, which I would visit in person, rather than contaminate my *sandals* with the polluted Dust'.[30]

'Oh Southwell, Southwell', he writes a fortnight later, 'how I rejoice to have left thee, & how I curse the heavy hours I have dragged along for so many months, amongst the *Mohawks* who inhabit your *Kraals*.'[31]

But what Byron said of Southwell in 1807, he would be saying by 1816 of England as a whole; and it was not until he reached the distance and safety of Venice, and discovered ottava rima, that the confessional mode which came most naturally to him (confession, of course, *without* contrition, and certainly *without* atonement) would find its happiest vehicle, and its most apt audience – albeit in a style infinitely more sophisticated and crafty than the style which had been available to him in Nottinghamshire. There he had attempted to express himself without inhibition; but had discovered that it was not possible: factors both within himself and within Nottinghamshire prevented it. But by 1822 he was writing,

> I love the Sex, and sometimes would reverse
>   The Tyrant's wish, "that Mankind only had
> One Neck which he with one fell stroke might pierce;"
>   My wish is quite as wide, but not so bad,
> And much more tender on the whole than fierce,
>   It being (not *now* but only while a lad)
> That Womankind had but one rosy mouth,
> To kiss them all at once from North to South.
>
> Oh enviable Briareus! with thy hands
>   And heads, if thou had'st all things multiplied
> In such proportion! – But my muse withstands
>   The giant thought of being a Titan's bride,
> Or travelling in Patagonion lands;
>   So let us back to Lilliput, and guide
> Our hero through the labyrinth of love
> In which we left him several lines above.
> (*Don Juan* VI, 27–8)[32]

It was a bold idiom undreamed of in the shadow of the Minster at Southwell.

Notes

1   The four known copies of *Fugitive Pieces* are in the British Library (Rev. J. T. Becher's copy: Ashley 2604); at Newstead Abbey (John Pigot's incomplete copy, wanting pp. 17–20 ['To Mary'] and pp. 59–66 ['To A—, Doubtless, sweet girl', and the translations from Catullus, Domitius Marsus, and Tibullus]; in the Pierpont Morgan Library New York (Byron's copy with revisions: 15799); and at the University of Texas (corrected copy, perhaps Elizabeth Pigot's).

2 Two poems – 'The Tear' and 'Reply to Some Verses of J. H. Pigot, Esq. on the Cruelty of his Mistress' – are signed, seemingly by oversight: *Fugitive Pieces*, pp. 43–8.

3 Willis W. Pratt, *Byron at Southwell* (New York: Haskell House, 1973), p. 39.

4 E—— (p. 3), —— (p. 6), Caroline (p. 7), Maria (p. 10), Mary (p. 17), A Lady, who presented the Author a Lock of Hair (p. 31), Julia (p. 36), A—(p. 59), and one of the 'Ladies passing near the Spot' where he was 'discharging his Pistols in a Garden' (p. 61).

5 *BLJ*, I, 105.

6 *BLJ*, I, 181, n.1, quoted Pratt, *Byron at Southwell*, p. 38.

7 *BLJ*, I, 97.

8 *BLJ*, I, 116 and n.

9 See Alice Levine and Jerome J. McGann (eds), *Lord Byron Vol. IV. Miscellaneous Poems*, in *Manuscripts of the Younger Romantics* (Garland, 1988), pp. 11–80.

10 *BLJ*, I, 103.

11 Copies with MSS addenda are at the BL (Dept of Printed Books C.28.b.9); Texas; Princeton Taylor; and Harrow.

12 'Answer to Some Elegant Verses, Sent by A Friend of the Author, complaining that one of his descriptions was too warmly drawn' (*Poems on Various Occasions, Hours of Idleness*). See also three further poems at *CPW*, I, 17–22 and 25–8.

13 *CPW*, I, 26.

14 *Poems on Various Occasions* only: *CPW*, I, 158. Byron gives Edward Long a 'key' to the poem at *BLJ*, I, 109–10.

15 *Poems on Various Occasions* only: *CPW*, I, 167.

16 *CPW*, I, 382.

17 *BLJ*, I, 125. Compare *Antony and Cleopatra* IV.xiv.50–4.

18 *BLJ*, I, 103.

19 *BLJ*, I, 112.

20 There is one spurious printing of larger size – see *Athenaeum* 28 May 1898; T. M. Blagg, *Newark as a Publishing Town* (Newark: 1898), pp. 20–35. Second edition, Galignani Paris, 1819 (but Galignani's text is *Poems Original and Translated*); Piracies, Sherwin and Co., 1820; Benbow, 1822 (but this text is also *Poems Original and Translated*); Galignani Paris, 1822; Stevenson and Smith Edinburgh, 1824; Glasgow, 1825. MSS are at New York Berg (mottoes only); Texas (draft preface only); a transcript by Teresa Guiccioli is at the Keats–Shelley Memorial House, Rome: there is a microfilm at the Keats House London.

21 *BLJ*, I, 118.

22 'Nisus and Euryalus', 163–70. Byron minimises the age gap which Virgil stresses ('te vero, mea quem spatiis propioribus aetas / insequitur, venerande puer', *Aeneid* IX, 275–6).

23 *The Annual Review* (1808) by Lucy Aikin; *The Anti-Jacobin Review* (December 1807); *Le Beau Monde* (September 1807); *The British Critic* (October 1807); *The Critical Review* (September 1807) by John Higgs Hunt; *The Eclectic Review* (November 1807: mentions Rochester); *The Edinburgh Review* (January 1808) by Henry Brougham: reprinted *The Analectic Magazine* (June 1814) as offprint (1820) *The Literary and Scientific Repository* (1820), *The Polar Star* (1830);,and *The Chautauquan*

(March 1911); *The Gentleman's Magazine* (supplements 1807 and March 1808); *The Literary Panorama* (November 1807); *Monthly Literary Recreations* (July 1807); *The Monthly Mirror* (January 1808); *The Monthly Review* (November 1807) by George Edward Griffins; *The Poetical Register* (1811); *The Portfolio* (March 1809); *The New Annual Register for 1807* (1808); *The New Monthly Magazine* (February 1819); *The Satirist* (October 1807, June/August 1808) by Hewson Clarke; and *The Universal Magazine* (September 1807).

24 See W. S. Ward, 'Byron's Hours of Idleness and Other than Scottish Reviewers', *Modern Language Notes* 59 (1944), pp. 547–50.

25 See *BLJ*, 1, 137–8.

26 Then in 1812, 1814, and 1820. One counterfeit (see Texas exhibition, 1924, pp. 93–7). It was pirated accurately as 'Second edition of Hours of Idleness', by Galignani of Paris in 1819; by Sherwin and Co. in 1820 (four editions); in Paris 1820, 1822; and by William Benbow in 1822. It was reviewed in *The Satirist* (August 1808) by Hewson Clarke.

27 See *BLJ*, I, 155.

28 *CPW*, I, 161, lines 89–92.

29 *CPW*, I, 172–3.

30 *BLJ*, I, 123.

31 *BLJ*, I, 127.

32 For an interesting gloss of these stanzas, see the conclusion of Joshua D. Gonsalves, 'Byron – In-Between Sade, Lautréamont, and Foucault: Situating the Canon of "Evil" in the Nineteenth Century', at *Romanticism on the Net: Lord Byron's Canons*, Issue 43, August 2006.

The Bride of Abydos: The Regime of Visibility and the Possibility of Resistance

TOM MOLE

'All convulsions end with me in rhyme', Byron wrote to Thomas Moore, 'and, to solace my midnights, I have scribbled another Turkish story' (*BLJ*, 3, 184). The connection Byron made between *The Bride of Abydos* and his own emotional life has proved compelling, not least because the 'convulsions' are so numerous and well documented. After the end of his turbulent affair with Lady Caroline Lamb, and her departure for Ireland in September 1812, Byron began an intrigue with Lady Oxford. They met at the Hampden Club in June 1812, and Byron accompanied the Oxfords to Cheltenham in September. He stayed with them at their country home, Eywood, in November and again in December 1812 and March 1813. The Oxfords were planning a trip abroad, however, and Byron accompanied Lady Oxford to Portsmouth on 13 June 1813, from where she sailed with her husband on 28 June, ending the affair. After this Byron became involved with his half-sister Augusta Leigh while pursuing Lady Frances Wedderburn Webster. Augusta socialised with Byron in London in July 1813 and he visited her at the beginning of August. By mid-August he was writing to Lady Melbourne that he wanted to take Augusta abroad with him (*BLJ*, 3, 87, 93), and telling Thomas Moore that he was in 'a far more serious, and entirely new, scrape' (*BLJ*, 3, 96). Byron and Augusta were together at Six Mile Bottom in December 1813, and at Newstead Abbey in January 1814. Meanwhile, Byron pursued Lady Frances, under the nose of her imperceptive husband, while visiting the Websters at Aston Hall in September and October 1813 and during their visit to Newstead later that month. He finally 'spared her' and the Websters left for a tour of Scotland in November (*BLJ*, 3, 146).[1] In the midst of these emotional entanglements, Byron started writing *The Bride of Abydos* at the beginning of November 1813, and published it on 2 December.[2]

Byron himself, with his habitual knack of tracing his poems back to fascinatingly obscure emotional springs, was the first to identify this series of events as the poem's primary interpretative context. Before he had finished the first draft, he wrote to Lady Melbourne, 'my mind has been from late and later events in such a state of fermentation that as usual I have been obliged to empty it in rhyme – & am in the very heart of another Eastern tale' (*BLJ*, 3, 157). When William Gifford read the poem in manuscript, Byron wrote, quoting Pope:

> It was written – I cannot say for amusement nor 'obliged by hunger and request of friends' but in a state of mind from circumstances which occasionally occur to 'us youth' that rendered it necessary for me to apply my mind to something – any thing but reality – and under this not very brilliant inspiration it was composed.

> (*BLJ*, 3, 161)

For later readers, that context has been difficult to avoid. It was endorsed by Jerome McGann in his edition of Byron's *Complete Poetical Works*, when he noted that '[t]he impetus that set B[yron] writing *Bride* was his recollections of his love for Augusta, on the one hand, and of his more recent "platonic" affair with Lady Frances Wedderburn Webster on the other' (*CPW*, 3, 435). Partly as a result of this apparently solid link between amorous tangles and poetic production, *The Bride of Abydos* has been marginal to the modern revaluation of Byron's tales. Recent criticism, moving away from the tendency to read these poems as camouflaged autobiography or psychoanalytic evidence, has viewed them in the context of British imperialism, or as allegories of domestic politics.[3] This essay brings insights from these new approaches to bear on *The Bride of Abydos,* alongside theories of gender and the gaze; but rather than linking the tale too forcefully to a single issue or event, I address Byron's abstract political thought, analysing the relation between a macro-politics of social control and a micro-politics of resistance or disruption.

Byron's affair with Lady Oxford was not only an amorous diversion. It was also an important episode in his political education.[4] Byron described her as 'a woman, who, amid all her fascination, always urged a man to usefulness or glory' (*BLJ*, 3, 229). '[S]he always pressed me on senatorial duties, and particularly in the cause of weakness', he recalled (*BLJ*, 3, 229). Byron's three speeches in the House of Lords had been full of fiery rhetoric, but had failed to establish his parliamentary career.[5] By November 1813 he declared himself 'sick of parliamentary mummeries' and, refusing William Baldwin's request that he present a petition, withdrew from parliamentary politics (*BLJ*, 3, 206). But he still dedicated *The Bride of Abydos* to his political mentor Lord Holland, in a gesture that was partly a farewell to active politics and partly a renewed declaration of his political allegiances. The Hollands and the Oxfords had introduced Byron to a Whig elite that was, in Malcolm Kelsall's words, 'in crisis'.[6] The Whigs defended a legacy from the Glorious Revolution of 1688 that aimed for a balance of power between the Sovereign and the people. They hoped that the Prince Regent would create a Whig government in 1811, but he failed to do so. As a result, the Whigs had to content themselves with marginal gains and quotidian politicking; more substantial reforms were only to appear with the disintegration of the Whigs and the emergence of modern liberalism in the 1820s and 30s.[7] Byron would play a role in that later shift through his involvement with *The Liberal*, but in 1813 he had lost any illusions about being instrumental in rapid, prompt and far-reaching political change in Britain. For this reason, we should pay attention not only to *The Bride of Abydos*'s depiction of revolutionary *kairos*, but also to its concern with satisfactory ways of 'making do' in political *chronos*.

The gaze, as both a pathway of desire and a vector of coercion, is an important vehicle for the poem's analysis of the circulation of power and the possibilities of resistance. In *The Bride of Abydos*, looking can arouse desires and produce pleasures. Selim and Zuleika, the cousins whose love is thwarted by Zuleika's murderous father Giaffir, gaze longingly at one another. Their love thrives on exchanging furtive glances or gazing into each other's eyes. While Selim 'gazed … through the lattice grate' (1. 255), 'to him Zuleika's eye was turned' (1. 257). Looking for him to reciprocate her gaze and confirm their mutual devotion, she 'watch'd his eye', but 'it still was fixed' (1. 268). When Selim comes out of his reverie, 'the soul of that eye' flashes 'through the long lashes round it' and their gazes can finally meet (1. 338–9). The lovers' eyes express their attachment and their unblinking constancy. Zuleika pledges to 'do all but close thy dying eye', as though not even death could break their mutual gaze (1. 404). Their love affair is a lattice of interlocking glances, looking to meet and be reciprocated.

But looking more often arouses resentment and produces dangers. Leander is invoked at the start of Canto 2 because his gaze is dangerously preoccupied:

> He could not see, he would not hear,
> Or sound or sign foreboding fear;
> His eye but saw that light of love,
> The only star it hail'd above.

(2. 12–15)

Dazzled by Hero's light at the centre of his infatuated tunnel vision, Leander swam to a watery death that Selim's death echoes. Wading in the shallows, Selim is shot down by Giaffir's fatally accurate eye when he looks back for Zuleika:

> Ah! Wherefore did he turn to look
> For her his eye but sought in vain?
> That pause, that fatal gaze he took,
> Hath doom'd his death, or fix'd his chain.

> (2. 563–6)

A misplaced gaze in this poem can be fatal, laying Selim open to the all too effective gaze that Giaffir directs down the sights of his musket, closing Selim's eyes forever. Meanwhile, in a telling metonym, Zuleika's eye

> was closed –
> Yea – closed before his own!

> (2. 619–20)

The Bride of Abydos, then, is concerned with the dangers of looking and the risks of being looked at.

A politics of the gaze is systemic in Giaffir's regime, and deeply inscribed in Islamic society as the poem represents it. Zuleika affirms that

> To meet the gaze of strangers' eyes
> Our law, our creed, our God denies.

> (1. 429–30)

Giaffir paranoiacally controls who can look at whom, and who is watched by whom, in an effort to secure his power. He has 'Slaves, tools, accomplices – no friends' (2. 332), living in a totalitarian society of universal mistrust, beset by deception, power struggles, and fear. This regime uses gender identities as a mechanism of social control. The harem is, in the poem's Orientalist imagination, an important way of structuring looking to reify gender in support of power.[8] Neither quite a prison nor quite a refuge, the harem keeps women away from prying eyes while preventing them from looking out and returning the gaze of a seducer. The 'massy doors' (1. 240) of its architecture are reinforced by the surveillance of the guards 'who watch the women's tower' (1. 80). More than an architectural structure, the harem is a power structure based on the regulation of the gaze: a blind spot which renders women literally and figuratively invisible, and a Foucauldian institution materialising the power of the tyrant who can call them into his sight at any moment.[9] Because the Moors so carefully oversee them, the women can be overlooked in all matters of social importance. 'All that thy sex hath need to know' Giaffir tells Zuleika, is 'thy father's will' (1. 216, 215). The veil extends the harem's jurisdiction beyond its walls, structuring looking without the corresponding physical structure. Women who cannot be seen clearly and cannot freely look are denied agency by the surveillance of others.[10] The women of the harem are subject to a Foucauldian panopticism, which enforces discipline by submitting its subjects to a constant and inescapable surveillance.[11] No transgression passes unobserved. The gaze of power in this disciplinary technology coerces the subjects' bodies into docility, quashing insurgence. Giaffir's command of his womenfolk is maintained, as in the panopticon, by dictating the terms of concealment and visibility. The women are care- fully watched by their guards in order to make sure they are not watched by anyone else:

> Woe to the head whose eye beheld
> My child Zuleika's face unveil'd!

> (1. 38–9)

Comparable practices of coercion operate on men in the poem. When describing the constraints Giaffir places on Selim, Byron elaborates an understanding of gender identity as performative and culturally circum- scribed. Arguing for an understanding of gender as performative, Judith Butler asserts:

> Gender ought not to be construed as a stable identity or locus of agency from which various acts follow; rather gender is an identity tenuously constituted in time, instituted in an exterior space through a *stylised repetition of acts*. The effect of gender is produced through the body and hence must be understood as the mundane way in which bodily gestures, movements, and styles of various kinds constitute the illusion of an abiding gendered self.[12]

Although Butler intends her theory to open new possibilities for political praxis, she is careful to include a qualified and sophisticated account of the nature of political agency, to which I shall return.[13] Since gender is a 'strategy of survival within compulsory systems' which 'regularly punish those who fail to do their gender right', she insists on 'the situation of duress under which gender performance always and variously occurs.'[14] Performativity therefore describes the manner in which subjects are compelled to stabilise a gender identity, but also the manner in which gender may be subverted, queered or troubled. This dual aspect of gender performativity provides a useful way to understand Selim's shifting masculinity and his relation to Giaffir's robustly patriarchal regime.

Whilst subjects in the poem shore up a gender identity by repeatedly performing certain gender-specific actions before an audience, their performances are not free choices. In Giaffir's regime the body and its performances signify all personal worth for men. The attributes of the manly body, such as strength, martial skill, and horsemanship, must be proven by display in battle or competition. For this purpose, Giaffir maintains an elaborate system of spectacular military exercises.[15] He leaves his couch to

> witness many an active deed
> With sabre keen, or blunt jerreed
>
> (1. 237–8)

With his 'Maugrabee' (mercenaries) and 'Delis' (cavalrymen), Giaffir performs martial arts (1. 235–6). The 'javelin-darting crowd' display their prowess by

> cleav[ing] the folded felt
> With sabre stroke right sharply dealt[.]
>
> (1. 248–50)

These displays add up to a performance of masculinity, or what Butler would call 'a repetition and a ritual, which achieves its effects through its naturalisation in the context of a body'.[16] What isn't demonstrated as masculine must be feminine, femininity being conceived as non-male and therefore of extremely limited worth. Giaffir proscribes Selim from the theatre of 'mimic war', the arena where masculine roles are played out, and so underwrites his powerful inscription of Selim's body as feminine (1. 450). So while the body becomes the locus for performing gender identity, it is also subject to the coercive pressure of others gazes. Giaffir says to Selim, 'I mark thee – and I know thee too' (1. 120). Marking Selim cuts two ways: Giaffir keeps him under surveillance, scrutinising him for signs of rebellion, and tries to coerce the rebellion out of him, marking him down as effeminate, weak, and worthless, as if with a label or a brand.

'Vain were a father's hope to see / Aught that beseems a man in thee' taunts Giaffir (1. 83–4). But Giaffir's look, which claims to discover Selim's effeminacy, in fact coercively constructs it from a polemical reading of Selim's bodily performance. Giaffir's powerful gaze splinters Selim's body into a substandard assemblage of arms, eyes and hands, and reads these shards as effeminate. Having excluded Selim from 'the game of mimic slaughter' that Giaffir plays with his henchmen (1. 247), he taunts him with claims that he would rather lounge about in the garden

> when thine arm should bend the bow,
> And hurl the dart, and curb the steed[.]

(1. 85–6)

Selim's resentment at being excluded from these performances of masculinity boils over in Canto 2, where he complains that:

> Giaffir's fear
> Denied the courser and the spear –
> Though oft – Oh, Mahomet! how oft! –
> In full Divan the despot scoff'd,
> As if *my* weak unwilling hand
> Refused the bridle or the brand.

(2. 323–8)

Reading Selim's body for signs of masculinity, Giaffir surveys Selim's arm and finds it wanting: 'his arm is little worth' (1. 135). His eyes likewise fail to meet Giaffir's standards of masculinity:

> Would that yon orb, whose matin glow
> Thy listless eyes so much admire,
> Would lend thee something of his fire!

(1. 90–2)

Giaffir identifies Selim's body as boyish, claiming that he would only fear him if 'thy beard had manlier length' (1. 122), and he reads femininity in his hands, taunting,

> Go – let thy less than woman's hand
> Assume the distaff – not the brand.

(1. 99–100)

Listing the failings of Selim's 'listless' body, Giaffir enforces a standard of masculinity based on his claim that the body is inscribed with signs of the individual's gendered value. These elements apply to both women and men in the poem and, once again, the harem institutionalises a coercive gaze. The harem can only be penetrated at the cost of castration, whether literal for the eunuchs who traditionally attend on the women, or figural for Selim, who is emasculated by his association with the harem.[17] The fact that Selim has the harem's (phallic) 'grating key' mocks his supposed lack of virility, as he passes in and out of the harem without appearing as a sexual threat to its women (1. 67). Giaffir's gaze constructs Selim's effeminacy while it controls Zuleika's looks.

At the tale's pivotal moment, we are invited to look at Selim's body in a new way. Byron presents Selim's new performance of masculinity to the reader's gaze in twenty descriptive lines (2. 131–50).[18] He is now adorned not in the luxurious vestments that become a pacha's son, but in the simple clothes of a sailor. His ornamental dagger is replaced by a brace of pistols and a sabre which is for use and not for show, and he's armoured with a cuirass and greaves. 'High command' now '[speaks] in his eye, and tone, and hand', where before Giaffir read effeminacy and worthlessness (2. 147–8). When Selim reveals his alter ego, he transforms his body in the reader's eyes from a docile site of coercion to an eloquent site of resistance. Where Giaffir previously read his eyes and hands, they now speak for themselves, as Selim performs his gender differently. Selim's body, now actively signifying, performs for Zuleika's eyes the masculine identity that it was thought to lack when Giaffir's gaze rendered it docile.

Selim invests his transformation with great importance, claiming that the truth of his identity is now obvious to see:

I said I was not what I seem'd;
And now thou see'st my words were true.

(2. 151–2)

But his costume change, I contend, falls short of the kind of disruptive practice that Butler envisages precisely because it overestimates the agency available to Selim. Instead, it is part of a contained practice of resistance, a simulacrum of subversion that fails as soon as it becomes an open revolt. Giaffir's regime includes a number of safety valves, which allow it to continue operating by providing a tolerable outlet for his subjects' discontent. They are circumscribed spaces in which a temporary respite from the regime is available, but only within confines that prevent it becoming a threat. The first of these spaces is the cypress grove where Selim and Zuleika go early in the morning. Selim describes how, once they got there, the cousins seemed to have escaped the regime's surveillance, and felt such intense freedom that the whole world seemed to be theirs:

Before the guardian slaves awoke
We to the cypress groves had flown,
And made earth, main, and heaven our own!

(1. 68–70)

But this sense of freedom was fleeting, and when he 'heard the deep tambour' signal the start of Giaffir's divan, Selim returned to the court (1. 73). Once there, he reveals that the cypress groves are not in fact the liberated space that they at first appear, but are secured and kept under surveillance:

> none can pierce that secret bower
> But those who watch the women's tower.

(1. 79–80)

Giaffir warns Haroun that Zuleika must not be allowed this indulgence too often, but he is prepared to tolerate it (1. 101–4).

Such contained opportunities to experience a modicum of freedom are a recurrent feature of the poem, but their constrained nature is easy to overlook and uncomfortable to recognise. Selim's most impassioned hymn to freedom, and one of Byron's most lyrical treatments of liberty, in fact describes this kind of contained experience:

> 'Tis vain – my tongue can not impart
> My almost drunkenness of heart,
> When first this liberated eye
> Survey'd Earth, Ocean, Sun, and Sky,
> As if my spirit pierced them through,
> And all their inmost wonders knew!
> One word alone can paint to thee
> That more than feeling – I was Free!

(1. 343–50)

The stirring sentiments of that quotable passage can lead us to overlook the fact – as Selim himself is keen to overlook it – that he describes a moment of freedom that is contained within the dominant order and barely ruffles its operations. Selim's excursion takes place when he has been left under the guard of Haroun while Giaffir pursues a military campaign (2. 329–36). Having served Selim's father, and seen him murdered by Giaffir, Haroun knows Selim's secret history and is sympathetic to his plight (2. 276–302). He reluctantly allows Selim a strictly limited amount of liberty:

> His captive, though with dread resigning,
> My thraldom for a season broke,
> On promise to return before
> The day when Giaffir's charge was o'er.

(2. 339–42)

Selim enthuses about his experience, but he nonetheless submits once again to Giaffir's regime of visibility. These examples of safety valves in Giaffir's scopocracy suggest the extent to which the regime remains viable precisely through giving its subjects the carefully circumscribed and contained experience of liberty, or liberty's simulacrum.

The pirate cave, 'a grotto, hewn / By nature but enlarged by art', where Selim and Zuleika retreat, is another space in which the experience of temporary liberation can be contained by the dominant culture. Byron makes it clear that Selim and Zuleika have both been to the cave before, although apparently not together. It is an everyday resource which enables them to obtain a brief respite from Giaffir's society. Zuleika visits the cave to play her lute and read the Koran (2. 101–2) and Selim to meet with the band of pirates that he secretly leads (2. 382–3). Within the cave's confines, concealed from prying eyes, Zuleika and Selim gain a breathing space away from their usual constraints. They both use the opportunity to perform gendered actions that are normally denied them. Selim becomes a manly pirate and breaks the Muslim prohibition on wine (2. 127–8, 317–20) and Zuleika, looking up from her Koran, indulges in a heterodox speculation about the nature of heaven for women:

> And oft in youthful reverie
> She dream'd what Paradise might be:
> Where woman's parted soul shall go
> Her Prophet had disdain'd to show.
>
> (2. 104–7)

The cave is a paradoxically liberating confinement, one they are happy to take to in place of the confinements of wider society.[19] When Selim persuades Zuleika to meet him at night, he does not at first propose that they should elope. Instead he offers her this kind of limited liberation, within the circumscribed space of a walled garden:

> Then softly from the Haram creep
> Where we may wander by the deep:
> Our garden battlements are steep;
> Nor these will rash intruder climb
> To list our words, or stint our time.
>
> (1. 465–9)

Selim promises not an escape from Giaffir's structures of control, but a chance to avoid them temporarily. The garden battlements will keep intruders out, and Selim and Zuleika in.

Zuleika's impending marriage is the crisis which forces them to try turning their everyday tactics for living within Giaffir's regime into a revolutionary upheaval that will permanently overthrow it. When 'No more remains to win, and much to fear', Selim and Zuleika understand that they have become swept into revolutionary *kairos*: 'This hour bestows, or ever bars escape' (2. 445, 463). However, the experience of being allowed a modicum of freedom, or the simulacrum of freedom, within a space or time that can be circumscribed and contained by the dominant order, is not a preparation for revolt but an inoculation against it. Only a very limited audience – Zuleika and the pirates – sees Selim's transformation, and although it seems to be a threat to Giaffir, it may only be dressing up for a specific circle of friends. Selim 'ask[s] no land beyond my sabre's length' (2. 433). In fact, he fantasises a free future that appears as a whole series of tight corners. He will be 'girt by my band' (2. 412), but claims that

> My tent on shore, my galley on the sea,
> Are more than cities and Serais to me.
>
> (2. 390–1)

Selim wants to trade the walled-in spaces of city and caravanserai for the equally restrictive tent and boat. What works for Selim in the confines of cave, tent, boat, or pirate band won't work for the rest of those subjected to Giaffir's regime. The freedom that comes from confining oneself away from the gaze of power is shown to be freedom only within those confines, leaving the pirates in their cave to ponder victories to which Selim cannot lead them:

> The last of Lambro's patriots there
> Anticipated freedom share;
> And oft around the cavern fire
> On visionary schemes debate,
> To snatch the Rayahs from their fate.
> So let them ease their hearts with prate
> Of equal rights, which man ne'er knew;
> I have a love for freedom too.
>
> (2. 380–7)

The pirates see themselves as descendants of the Greek revolutionary Lambro Canzani (whom Byron mentions in a note to this passage), and imagine themselves liberating the Rayahs (those who pay the capitation tax, according to the note). But while Selim professes his love for this ideal, he dismisses the possibility of equality as only 'prate': the pirates, with their 'visionary schemes', may 'ease their hearts' but will never help the mass of their countrymen. The cave is a space that facilitates a fantasy of freedom, while ensuring a continuing reality of subjection.

Although Selim and Zuleika find temporary freedom in their liberating confinement, Byron warns that their response risks solipsism and produces a damagingly autistic autarky. The subjectivity that it consolidates makes sense only in its own terms, and cannot relate to the wider world. The fantasies of the cave cannot be realised in revolt. The cave temporarily provides both strategic cover (protecting against bullets) and existential safety (protecting against unwelcome gazes), but Selim doesn't survive for long once he leaves its confines. He looks back at Zuleika, hoping for a reciprocal glance that will confirm him in his alternative identity, but

> that fatal gaze he took,
> Hath doom'd his death, or fix'd his chain.

(2. 565–6)

Selim cannot always choose his spectators. He wants Zuleika for an audience, but when he leaves the cave he re-enters Giaffir's scopocracy, and gets cut down by the tyrant's gaze, which is 'too nearly, deadly aim'd to err' (2. 575). Retreating to the cave, playing at pirates and discussing 'visionary schemes' are shown to be simulacra of resistance that can be tolerated by the dominant order, so long as they stay within manageable confines. When they burst out of those confines, they are easily suppressed with overwhelming force.

But although he skewered the simulacrum of subversion, it does not follow that Byron was reconciled to a programme of political quietism in 1813. Whilst he was more pessimistic than he had been in, for example, 'Ode to the Framers of the Frame Bill', or 'Lines to a Lady Weeping' about attempts decisively to destabilise or renounce the dominant order, his political concerns were far from nugatory. Rather, his political interest had shifted towards those everyday practices of resistance that might enable subjects to live more satisfactorily in unsatisfactory political circumstances. Michel de Certeau refers to these practices as 'the clandestine forms taken by the dispersed, tactical, and makeshift creativity of groups or individuals already caught in the nets of "discipline."'[20] While most moments of potential subversion in *The Bride of Abydos* remain contained, Byron also makes clear that there are fissures of resistance within Giaffir's regime. Selim's claim that he could provide the spark to a tinder-box of revolution may be wishful thinking, but it still identifies pockets of discontent:

> Within thy father's house are foes;
> Not all who break his bread are true:
> To these should I my birth disclose,

His days, his very hours were few:
They only want a heart to lead,
A hand to point them to the deed.

(1. 270–5)

Selim's error is to imagine that, once he's reclaimed his 'true' masculinity, he will enjoy boundless political agency. Against that misplaced confidence, I would set Butler's understanding of agency for the gendered subject:

> There is no self that is prior to [gender] or who maintains 'integrity' prior to its entrance into this conflicted cultural field. There is only a taking up of the tools where they lie, where the very 'taking up' is enabled by the tool lying there.[21]

Gender cannot be renounced wholesale, but only disrupted, its protocols queered, its possibilities expanded. In Byron's tale, effective resistance to Giaffir cannot renounce the regime's structures of looking or constructions of gender, but only disrupt them.

One of the tale's most interesting moments of resistance concerns the politics of the gaze and suggests that a satisfactory practice of resistance can occur without overthrowing the dominant order, but by using the same tools with which it oppresses. *The Bride of Abydos* hints that, while structures of visibility can be technologies of coercion, the gaze can also become a weapon of resistance. When Giaffir taunts Selim with being the son of a slave (unaware that Selim knows himself to be the son of the pacha whom Giaffir murdered and supplanted), Selim inwardly boils with fury:

Thus held his thoughts their dark career;
And glances ev'n of more than ire
Flash forth, then faintly disappear.
Old Giaffir gazed upon his son
And started; for within his eye
He read how much his wrath had done;
He saw rebellion there begun.

(1. 112–18)

Selim looks rebelliously back at Giaffir, reflecting his wrath back at him. Looking, which is usually pressed into the service of Giaffir's regime, is here mobilised against it. The moment of resistance 'flash[es] forth' only to 'faintly disappear': its effect is temporary but real. This is a kind of resistance made possible not by escaping from the network of surveillance in which subjects find themselves caught, but by employing an element of the apparatus against itself in order to produce a space of comparative liberty *within* it. Selim's most effective, albeit temporary, tactic of resistance involves creatively deploying the same resource that Giaffir uses to dominate. Selim's subversive looking makes Giaffir start, and he redoubles his own surveillance, resolving to 'watch him closer than before' (1. 143).

Looking is the form through which Giaffir's tyranny maintains its control, but it is not his prerogative alone; vision does not belong exclusively to the dominant order. In Foucault's words, '[i]t's a machine in which everyone is caught, those who exercise power just as much as those over whom it is exercised.'[22] Because looking belongs to no one and serves no one in particular, it can be appropriated, at least temporarily, by the oppressed Selim, and mobilised against the despot Giaffir. For instance while Giaffir boasts that 'I mark thee – and I know thee too' (1. 120), Selim takes up the tools where they lie and turns them on their master:

> As sneeringly these accents fell,
> On Selim's eye he fiercely gazed:
> That eye return'd him glance for glance,
> And proudly to his sire's was raised,
> Till Giaffir's quail'd and shrunk askance –
> And why – he felt, but durst not tell.
>
> (1. 126–31)

Selim outstares Giaffir, the steadiness of his gaze revealing his strength, pride and rectitude. Giaffir, usually the tyrant of looking, cannot bear Selim's gaze, and shrinks. For Selim and Zuleika looking, like loving, is a kind of power or a kind of freedom available to those who are denied more tangible liberties. Selim's eye, which had previously been marked down as 'listless' and feminine, resists Giaffir's coercive reading of his body. While he is denied the chance to break Giaffir's lance, either in open battle or in military exercises, Selim can still break his gaze. He 'return[s] him glance for glance' and temporarily disrupts Giaffir's regime. The individual eye that observes Giaffir's tyranny and recognises its callousness is a silent accusation, bearing witness to oppression. When Selim dies, he has stopped looking, for a moment, in this resistant way, turning not full into Giaffir's face, but back to Zuleika. That backward glance is directed towards the cave, retreat, confinement, solipsism, and ineffectuality, and it costs Selim his life.

Although such a practice of resistance takes place within the governing system, it is not so easily contained by it, as Giaffir's uneasiness suggests. Byron's early and late interest in and contribution to revolutionary movements has tended to skew discussion of his politics away from moments of resistance such as this one, and towards an unfruitful debate over the efficacy of his revolutionary engagements with the Luddites, the Carbonari, or the Suliotes. We should not overlook his concern, in the middle of his poetic career, with more dispersed tactics of political resistance. In *The Bride of Abydos*, Byron is concerned both with the ways in which attempts at liberation can be contained and defused and with the effective practice of resistance in everyday life: with an activist looking-back that outstares the gaze of power but allows only a momentary gain.

Notes

1   For these events, see Leslie A. Marchand, *Byron: A Biography*, 3 vols (London: John Murray, 1957), I, 362–433 *passim*.

2   For details of the poem's composition and extant manuscripts and proofs, see *CPW* II, 431–4.

3   For a psychoanalytic reading, see Peter Manning, *Byron and his Fictions* (Detroit, MI: Wayne State University Press, 1978). For political contexts, see Daniel P. Watkins, *Social Relations in Byron's Eastern Tales* (Rutherford, NJ: Fairleigh Dickinson University Press, 1987). More recent, political readings begin with Edward Said, who mentions Byron a number of times in *Orientalism*, but without exception as part of a list of (two or more) writers. The only poem he mentions by name is 'The Giaour'. Edward Said, *Orientalism: Western Conceptions of the Orient* (London: Penguin, 1995), pp. 22, 31, 99, 101, 118, 167, 192. See also Nigel Leask, *British Romantic Writers and the East: Anxieties of Empire* (Cambridge: Cambridge University Press, 1992), pp. 13–67, Saree Makdisi, *Romantic Imperialism: Universal Empire and the Culture of Modernity* (Cambridge: Cambridge University Press, 1998), Marilyn Butler, 'The Orientalism of Byron's *Giaour*', in *Byron and the Limits of Fiction*, ed. by Bernard Beatty and Vincent Newey (Liverpool: Liverpool University Press, 1988), pp. 78–96, and Caroline Franklin, '"Some Samples of the Finest Orientalism": Byronic Philhellenism and Proto-Zionism at the Time of the Congress of Vienna', in *Romanticism and Colonialism: Writing and Empire*, ed. by Tim Fulford and Peter Kitson (Cambridge: Cambridge University Press, 1998), pp. 221–42.

4   The pioneering study of Byron's politics was D. N. Raymond, *The Political Career of Lord Byron* (New York: Henry Holt, 1924). For a more sceptical view, see Malcolm Kelsall, *Byron's Politics* (Brighton: Harvester, 1987). Neither of these books, however, discusses Byron's tales at length. Jonathan Gross identifies a new source for *The Bride of Abydos*, in the context of an exploration of Byron's liberalism. Jonathan David Gross, *Byron: The Erotic Liberal* (Lanham: Rowman & Littlefield, 2001) esp. pp. 55–78.

5   For the text of the speeches, see *Lord Byron: The Complete Miscellaneous Prose*, ed. by Andrew Nicholson (Oxford: Clarendon Press, 1991), pp. 20–45.

6   Kelsall, *Byron's Politics*, p. 2.

7   In addition to Kelsall, see David Erdman, 'Lord Byron and the Genteel

Reformers', *Publications of the Modern Language Association* 56 (1941), pp. 1065–94; Lord Blake, 'The Politics of Byron's Time', *The Byron Journal* 17 (1989), pp. 40–9; L. G. Mitchell, *Charles James Fox and the Disintegration of the Whig Party, 1782–1794* (Oxford: Oxford University Press, 1971); and Michael Roberts, *The Whig Party 1807–1812* (London: Macmillan, 1939, repr. F. Cass, 1965).

8   For an examination of the harem in Byron's writing, see Malcolm Kelsall, 'Byron and the Women of the Harem', in *Rereading Byron: Essays Selected from Hofstra University's Byron Bicentennial Conference*, ed. by Alice Levine and Robert N. Keane (New York: Garland, 1993), pp. 165–73.

9   It should go without saying that this is a misrepresentation of the harem's place in Islamic culture. Leslie P. Peirce describes it as 'a space to which general access is forbidden or controlled and in which the presence of certain individuals or certain modes of behaviour are forbidden. ... The word *harem* is a term of respect, redolent of religious purity and honour, and evocative of the requisite obeisance.' Leslie P. Peirce, *The Imperial Harem: Women and Sovereignty in the Ottoman Empire* (New York: Oxford University Press, 1993), pp. 4–5. Joseph Lew argues that 'Western empires, in reducing or fetishising "harem" as merely a collection of female bodies, facilitated the symbolic representation of ... empire building. What endangered polities ... might experience as dismemberment could [thus] be seen, through Western eyes, as "liberation".' Joseph Lew, 'The Necessary Orientalist? *The Giaour* and Nineteenth-Century Imperialist Misogyny', in *Romanticism, Race and Imperial Culture*, ed. by Alan Richardson and Sonia Hofkosh (Bloomington, IN: Indiana University Press, 1996), pp. 173–202 (p. 192).

10   Jerome Christensen connects the veil, agency, and the performance or imposition of gender in his comment that 'In *The Bride* the distinction between men and women hinges precisely on the ability to disguise oneself versus the necessity that one be veiled.' Jerome Christensen, *Lord Byron's Strength: Romantic Writing and Commercial Society* (Baltimore, MD: Johns Hopkins University Press, 1993), p. 116.

11   Michel Foucault, *Discipline and Punish: The Birth of the Prison,* trans. by Alan Sheridan (London: Penguin, 1991), esp. pp. 195–230.

12   Judith Butler, *Gender Trouble: Feminism and the Subversion of Identity* (New York and London: Routledge, 1999), p. 179.

13   Butler's sense of the subject's agency has often been overstated. In her more recent work, she notes: 'The misapprehension about gender performativity is this: that gender is a choice, or that gender is a role, or that gender is a construction one puts on, as one puts clothes on in the morning.' Judith Butler, *Bodies that Matter: On the Discursive Limits of 'Sex'* (London: Routledge, 1993), p. 94. Ten years after *Gender Trouble*'s first publication, Butler acknowledged 'Much of my work in recent years has been devoted to clarifying and revising the theory of performativity' (*Gender Trouble*, p. xiv).

14   Butler, *Gender Trouble*, pp. 177–8.

15   This aspect of the poem would have had particular resonance in Romantic Britain. The armed forces were expanding rapidly in response to the Napoleonic threat, and very large numbers of volunteer militia, distinguished by their fine uniforms, drilled regularly around the country. See Linda Colley, *Britons: Forging the Nation 1707–1837* (London: Vintage, 1996), pp. 297–337. Tim Fulford argues that the

period witnessed a protracted rethinking of the values of chivalric masculinity elegised by Burke. Tim Fulford, *Romanticism and Masculinity: Gender, Politics and Poetics in the Writings of Burke, Coleridge, Cobbett, Wordsworth, De Quincey and Hazlitt* (Basingstoke: Macmillan, 1999). John Tosh provides an overview of research in this area. John Tosh, 'The Old Adam and the New Man: Emerging Themes in the History of English Masculinities, 1750–1850', in *English Masculinities 1660–1800*, ed. by Tim Hitchcock and Michèle Cohen (London: Longman, 1999), pp. 217–38.

16 Butler, *Gender Trouble*, p. xv.

17 In fact the poem does not specifically mention eunuchs, although the Nubian Haroun does not seem to be considered a potential seducer, possibly because of his age or his dark skin.

18 On Byron's use of classical sources in this transformation, and the transformation that follows Selim's death, see Robert B. Ogle, 'The Metamorphosis of Selim: Ovidian Myth in *The Bride of Abydos* II', *Studies in Romanticism* 20, no. 1 (1981), pp. 21–31.

19 For a broader discussion of comparable themes, see Victor Brombert, 'The Happy Prison: A Recurring Romantic Metaphor', in *Romanticism: Vistas, Instances, Continuities*, ed. by David Thorburn and Geoffrey Hartman (Ithaca, NY: Cornell University Press, 1973), pp. 62–79.

20 Michel de Certeau, *The Practice of Everyday Life*, trans. by Steven Rendall (Berkeley: University of California Press, 1984), pp. xiv–xv.

21 Butler, *Gender Trouble*, p. 185.

22 Michel Foucault, *Power/Knowledge: Selected Interviews and Other Writings 1972–1977*, ed. by Colin Gordon (Brighton: Harvester, 1980), p. 156.

'A Very Life in Our Despair': Freedom and Fatality in *Childe Harold's Pilgrimage*, Cantos 3 and 4

MICHAEL O'NEILL

The emergence of creative freedom from Byron's existential and historical sense of fatedness in Cantos 3 and 4 of *Childe Harold's Pilgrimage* is the subject of distinguished attention in, among other places, Jerome J. McGann's *Fiery Dust*, with its discussion of how, for Byron, the soul must 'recreate itself under the influence of fresh experience', and Vincent Newey's *Centring the Self*, with its exploration of Byron's 'foregroundings of the power and limits of creation'.[1] What I wish to emphasise in this essay, through close attention to representative passages, is the intensity and virtuosity with which Byron snatches poetic victory out of the jaws of emotional defeat.

'There is a very life in our despair, / Vitality of poison' (3, 298–9); so Byron declares, at once flamboyant trailer of his bleeding heart and proleptic existentialist. He is also, and most importantly, a skilled poet, winning 'life' from 'despair' through the restless energy imparted by shifting caesurae and trampolining alliteration, and through the affecting appeal in 'our despair' to the readership with which he enjoys a bruised, ambivalent intimacy. Cantos 3 and 4 bear the impress of failure, personal and political, yet they discover 'freedom' in the process of immersing themselves in often destructive elements and telling the tale of doing so. In the lines just quoted, 'Vitality of poison' offers both a sardonic mirror-image of genuine 'vitality' and, so the snarling sub-text implies, the only 'vitality' that is possible. The lines seem themselves to confess that an appropriate response to the 'very life' they describe would be the Chamois Hunter's retort to Manfred's 'I live': 'This is convulsion, and no healthful life' *(Manfred,* II.i.42, 43). At the same time, the 'very life in our despair' does not wholly disengage itself from the poet's stirring commitment 'to create, and in creating live / A being more intense' (3, 46–7) earlier in Canto 3.[2]

'Vitality' was not Byron's first choice. The draft reads 'activity', and the change points up the self-thwarting nature of a 'Vitality' inseparable from 'despair'.[3] The ensuing image – 'a quick root / Which feeds these deadly branches' (3, 299–300) – elaborates the enfolding within one another of the creative and the destructive. 'Despair' is made equivalent to 'these deadly branches', 'these' implying our and Byron's familiarity with a condition in which a 'quick', or living, 'root' only nourishes what is 'deadly'. If 'deadly' means 'death-like', the stress is on 'like': that is, these 'deadly branches' are a form of (despairing) 'life'. The use of 'quick' anticipates a passage at the core of the third Canto: 'But quiet', Byron writes of Napoleon, 'to quick bosoms is a hell, / And *there* hath been thy bane' (3, 370–1), where 'quick' sustains the suggestion in 'Vitality of poison' of an over-energised and potentially self-destructive impulse.

The equivocal status of 'very life' builds on the complex implications of the preceding stanza (33), in which Byron makes an extended comparison between the broken heart and

> a broken mirror, which the glass
> In every fragment multiplies; and makes
> A thousand images of one that was,
> The same, and still the more, the more it breaks.

(3, 289–92)

The movement of these lines imitates a multiplying that is endless and yet 'The same and still the more, the more it breaks'. As often in *Childe Harold's Pilgrimage*, the writing teeters between the bitter and the residually affirmative. If the images, though multiply generated by the broken heart, are always the same, one might, negatively, sense entrapment by a fixed idea. More positively, one might detect a suggestion of the self's capacity to endure: the ship of the sovereign ego may be badly holed but it is still afloat.

Freedom for Byron lies in the capacity to hurl himself into different, seemingly final, but always, it emerges, finally provisional states. Indeed, it is arguable that Harold's misanthropy represents only one such state for Byron; Jerome McGann contends, for instance, that in Canto 3 'Byron as a character is still in the condition of becoming, whereas Harold is now fixed and determinate'.[4] The poetry, in its very form, thrives on the tension between 'the condition of becoming' and the 'fixed and determinate'. One might take a sideways look at *The Prophecy of Dante* to see why. In this poem Byron, or his persona, writes,

Many are poets but without the name,
For what is poesy but to create
From overfeeling good or ill; and aim
At an external life beyond our fate.

                                                                    (4, 10–13)

Any ventriloquising of a Dantean belief in a transcendent reality 'beyond our fate' gives way to trust in the linguistic creation that 'is poesy', a creation pointed up by the presence of rhyme. Just as the lines Romanticise Dante (via an echo of Wordsworth's *The Excursion*, 1, 77–91) by insisting on the pervasiveness of the poetic impulse and its link with 'feeling', whether its cause or object is 'good or ill', so the terza rima binds together 'create' and 'fate' in a rhyming partnership that speaks volumes about Byron's ambitions in *Childe Harold*. Throughout the poem, it is in creating that 'fate' can be overcome; it can also seem that 'fate' acts as a spur to as well as an antagonist of the impulse to create.

Nietzsche writes in *Ecco Homo*:

> My formula for greatness in a human being is *amor fati*: that one wants nothing other than it is, not in the future, not in the past, not in all eternity. Not merely to endure that which happens of necessity, still less to dissemble it – all idealism is untruthfulness in the face of necessity – but to love it.[5]

Byron may not love 'that which happens of necessity', but he needs the idea of necessity to prompt the poem's particular form of freedom, a form associated throughout Cantos 3 and 4, with 'create' and its cognate words. The poetry derives much of its force from its wrestling with a language of compulsion: 'Yet must I think less wildly' (3, 55), Byron writes, straight after the most memorable account in the poem of creativity and the 'Soul of my thought' to which it gives life (3, 51). In one manuscript 'Yet must I think less wildly' has below it the crossed-out 'I must not think and I must not':[6] almost a reduction to absurdity of Byron's compulsive relationship with compulsion. In the finished version of the stanza it is less that creativity meets its opposite than that creativity exposes as perilous any account of itself as purely exalted. The 'Soul of my thought' is such an exalted fiction, as is brought out by the ambiguity of 'of', a genitive that makes 'Soul' not only the essence, but also the product, of 'thought'. When, in stanza 7, Byron ricochets away from exaltation, 'thought' is no longer figured as the meditative hermit seeking 'refuge in lone caves, yet rife / With airy images' of stanza 5 (43–4), nor as the inspired-by-disenchantment mental traveller of stanza 6. The poem now represents thought as a process of anguished self-reflection ('I *have* thought / Too long and darkly', 3, 55–6), a process blamed for the poet's suffering, the 'whirling gulf of phantasy and flame' (3, 58) into which his mind has too often been transformed.

The turns and counter-turns of these stanzas are a feature of the poem. Here they manifest themselves through the persistent impulse to pivot on conjunctions such as 'yet' (lines 55 and 61) and 'though' (line 61). 'Something too much of this' (3, 8, 64), Byron declares, echoing Hamlet's switch mid-speech from praise of Horatio to letting his friend know of his plan (through the play-within-the-play) to make his uncle's 'occulted guilt' 'itself unkennel in one speech'.[7] Yet the attempted movement away from brooding on a state in which the poet's best hope is to 'feed on bitter fruits without accusing Fate' (3, 63) does not last long. Soon Byron discovers that his predicament is close to that of Harold whose 'occulted guilt' refuses either to 'unkennel' itself or to disappear: 'uncompell'd' (3, 104), even though 'his soul was quell'd / In youth by his own thoughts' (3, 103–4), Harold 'would not yield dominion of his mind / To spirits against whom his own rebell'd' (3, 105–6). The triple rhyme enacts the pressures being described and asserts Harold's status as a rebel, refusing to submit to compulsion, 'quell'd' only by his own thoughts.

What kind of freedom is being described here? It is a kind that is bound up with acute inner conflict and with a sense of relationship with others as a struggle for mental control. Such freedom is profoundly conflicted and conflictual. To quote Nietzsche again, 'The free man is a *warrior*. – How is freedom measured, in individuals as in nations? By the resistance which has to be overcome, by the effort it costs to stay *aloft*.'[8] But, again, Byron cannot be restricted by a gloss. Freedom, which takes on evident political and historical meanings in the poem, portrays itself, psychologically, as both a rebellion against dependence and a revolt against the constant pressure to be separate. That rebellion against dependence works, in part, as an attempt to display the self's superiority to the text that embodies its disparate impulses. The poetry's freedom involves a recognition that 'to stay *aloft*' may be impossible. As Jerome Christensen puts it, in a discussion of the opening of Canto 3, 'The Byronic text begins as the "I"'s insistence on a relative autonomy from the text that, subsequent to its separation from the social world of face-to-face encounter, is in fact the only vehicle by which the "I" can appear.'[9] But in that ability to make a version of the self 'appear', Byron restores a last-ditch control over 'the vehicle' which controls his attempt to control. Poetic control, as close to freedom as

Byron can come in *Childe Harold*, depends on his capacity to make the 'text', in Christensen's phrase, 'a vehicle'.

It may be the case that the line, 'And thus I am absorb'd, and this is life' (3, 689), is, in Christensen's witty view, 'by all odds the most unconvincing Byron ever wrote'. Just as wittily, the same critic speaks of the 'Wordsridgean doctrine of the "one life"' as being 'abbreviated with Byronic negligence' in the line.[10] And yet, as with other attempts to evoke absorption in nature as an escape from self-divided consciousness in Canto 3, the line's very unconvincingness is its dramatic justification. The line's meaning requires that it be voiced in an upbeat way, with vigorous emphases on 'this' and 'life'. But the mention of 'life' drags back into the reader's memory the less exalted 'very life' of 'our despair', and almost persuades the voice to falter, to admit a downbeat inflection, as though to say, 'And this is "life", this process of needing to escape from what I know only too well as "life".' The poem manages to capture the try-outs, the false starts, and the hopeful gestures that are inseparable from the self's imagining of freedom. Freedom here, as often in *Childe Harold*, is 'freedom from'.[11] Even a detail such as a description of a cloudless sky draws life from this impulse; so in Canto 4, Byron writes that

> Heaven is free
> From clouds, but of all colours seems to be
> Melted to one vast Iris of the West.

> (4, 238–40)

The lines depict what quickly becomes a symbolic cloudscape, for all Byron's insistence that the description 'is but a literal and hardly sufficient delineation of an August evening (the eighteenth)'.[12] That note suggests a further aspect of the search for 'freedom from': throughout, the poem's notes play against the text in fascinating ways, often to hint at the link between the experiential and fictive, but also, in doing so, to imply Byron's 'historical' freedom from the creation he is annotating. Here one is conscious of Byron's wish to free his poem from his own symbol-mongering.

In Canto 3, stanza 74, Byron anticipates a time when 'the mind shall be all free / From what it hates in this degraded form, / Reft of its carnal life' (698–700), trying out another version of Gnostic contempt for 'carnal life'. Giving the game away, though, are questions that seek to be rhetorical and assert the superiority of 'The bodiless thought' (3, 705), but come across as insinuating, rather, the poet's underlying lack of sureness about the truth of his assertions. This lack of sureness emerges openly in stanza 75, the famous or notorious rewordings of Wordsworthian nature worship:

> Are not the mountains, waves, and skies, a part
> Of me and of my soul, as I of them?

(707–8)

'You tell me', the reader wants to retort, and in a trice the game is up:

> But this is not my theme; and I return
> To that which is immediate.

(3, 716–17)

In allowing assertion to make clear its own unstable ground, Byron reduces our trust in his poetry as statement but simultaneously intensifies our regard for it as the vehicle for the untrammelled expression of extremely trammelled thought and feeling.

In Canto 3, stanza 88, Byron uses to expressive effect the iterative *b* rhyme of the Spenserian stanza, a form made subservient to his tortuous eloquence:

> Ye stars! which are the poetry of heaven!
> If in your bright leaves we would read the fate
> Of men and empires, – 'tis to be forgiven,
> That in our aspirations to be great,
> Our destinies o'erleap their mortal state,
> And claim a kindred with you; for ye are
> A beauty and a mystery, and create
> In us such love and reverence from afar,
> That fortune, fame, power, life, have named themselves a star.

(824–32)

Frequently there is a sense of tension, of a tug between a form that is associated with repose and melody and Byron's restless, ongoing, sideways-moving intelligence. Here, the rhyming soothes the argument between 'fate' and the urge to 'create': if we read our fate in the stars, that 'poetry of heaven', it is because they themselves

> create
> In us such love and reverence from afar.

The transcendent gesture speaks of human need; Byron mimics a stillness that bears witness to restlessness. The 'poetry of heaven' is projected onto the stars by an all too earthly poet.

Elsewhere, 'fate' and 'create' engage in a more familiar argument. At the start of Canto 4, where Byron states his conviction that 'The beings of the mind are not of clay' (4, 37) and aspires towards a transcendental assertion of the power of art, he writes that such beings

> create
> And multiply in us a brighter ray
> And more beloved existence.

> (38–40)

The rhythms enact the multiplying spread of verbal energy that assures us of this 'more beloved existence'. The stanza continues, though, by recalling all that opposes the impulse to create,

> that which Fate
> Prohibits to dull life, in this our state
> Of mortal bondage, by these spirits supplied
> First exiles, then replaces what we hate.

> (40–3)

The tables are turned on fate by the beings of the mind and what they create; yet their alternative universe is all too clearly a compensation for all that we hate. The 'very life in our despair', vividly apparent in the irresolutions, associative transitions, syntax, and rhythms of these Cantos, is only too aware of itself as called into being by, as a reaction against, 'dull life'.

In *Childe Harold* Byron's is the freedom less of the unmoved and all-moving Romantic Ironist than of the person condemned yet privileged, in the very quick of utterance, to hear the inflections of both sides of a question, to be impelled, above all to

> return
> To that which is immediate.

An example occurs in the account of Harold's star-gazing:

> Could he have kept his spirit to that flight
> He had been happy; but this clay will sink
> Its spark immortal, envying it the light
> To which it mounts, as if to break the link
> That keeps us from yon heaven which woos us to its brink.

> (3, 122–6)

Vincent Newey glosses the lines thus: 'Though respecting transcendental aspiration, Byron stresses the irreducible power of our earthly nature.'[13] In his own syntax and balancing of 'transcendental aspiration' and 'earthly nature', Newey mimics Byron's conceptual movement here. One might add to his account the assertion that Byron's style is attuned to the mental and emotional processes by which, nothing being one thing only, aspiration triggers off its 'envying' counterpart. The tenses establish a conflict between the conditional ('Could he', 'He had been') and the inevitable ('this clay will sink'), even as the final rhyme promotes the fragile 'link' that it recognises can be easily broken.

The use in Canto 3 of doubles and exempla, oblique versions of Byron that are at the same time warnings to himself and his readers, participate in the overall dance of freedom and fatality. Napoleon was unable to learn, so learned the hard way, that 'tempted Fate will leave the loftiest star' (3, 342). The phrase may strike the reader as a poetic flourish, but it is a flourish that gives a twist to the commonplace of tempting the fates. The effect is paradoxically to endow fate with free will, with a capacity for choice drawn from the very figure opposed by Fate and exercised by him in the practice of

> that untaught innate philosophy,
> Which, be it wisdom, coldness, or deep pride,
> Is gall and wormwood to an enemy.
>
> (3, 344–6)

Byron is fond of formulations that entwine choice and destiny: in Canto 3, stanza 42, the 'fire / And motion of the soul which will not dwell / In its own narrow being, but aspire / Beyond the fitting medium of desire' (371–4) compulsively drive beyond what is 'fitting', that is, appropriate and limiting. If this 'fire' and 'motion' express 'desire', what the 'soul' wants, the wish is also a compulsion,

> a fever at the core,
> Fatal to him who bears, to all who ever bore.
>
> (377–8)

Later, Byron laments that 'in a moment, we may plunge our years / In fatal penitence' (3, 662–3), where 'years' sheers away, with awareness of catastrophic consequence, from 'moment', while the active verb 'plunge' chafes against the hint of fatedness in 'fatal'.

Through all these sheerings off and chafings against, Byron's recompense is his deployment of an answerable style. Yet 'Art' is no collision-free domain for Byron; where it affects to be so, it prompts a divided response. 'Triumphal Art' (4, 445) provokes the jar of warring opposites. Although in great works of art such as the *Venus de' Medici* it is as if 'the gods become as mortals, and man's fate / Has moments like their brightest', 'the weight / Of earth recoils upon us!' (4, 463–4, 464–5); 'let it go!' (465), Byron cries. 'We can recall such visions, and create' (466) beautiful works of art from our recollections. Disillusion and fascination with art co-exist here, which is why I would qualify Robert Gleckner's contention, in connection with this passage, that 'To Byron art is, in the long run, an unsatisfactory substitute for reality, despite its purity'.[14] To put it like that is to ignore how, for Byron, 'art' and 'reality' entangle, live one another's life, die one another's death. In the passage just quoted, 'fate' accepts its kinship with the burdened 'weight', and it yearns towards its rhyming partner throughout *Childe Harold*, 'create'. Byron values the process of creating, and of responding to creation with an inner force of feeling; he satirises the critic whose 'connoisseurship' would 'describe the undescribable' (4, 471, 473); but, observing 'That what we have of feeling most intense / Outstrips our faint expression', he affirms, in a freshly rediscovered version of the sublime, that 'we ... dilate / Our spirits to the size of that they contemplate' (4, 1416–17, 1421–2) in the presence of St Peter's in Rome. Given the contest between 'fate' and 'creation', it is no accident that a climax of Canto 4 is the invocation of 'Nemesis' (1181). That Byron in exhibitionist mode converts 'curse' to 'Forgiveness' (4, 1207) is less striking than the fact that he wrests back for poetry a power associated with prophecy, as he proclaims 'The deep prophetic fullness of this verse' (4, 1205).

Elsewhere, freedom is gained in the writing as the writer laments its absence from his experience. Small things lead to great as the poet's 'everlasting centos of himself', in Hazlitt's hostile phrase, open up new tracts of imaginative territory'.[15] In stanzas 74 and 75 of Canto 4, Byron is conscious that a scene 'asks the lyric Roman's aid / For our remembrance' (666–7), but recoils from 'classic raptures' (671) because what he recollects is 'The drill'd dull lesson' (674). He might, however, be able to relish Horace's poetry had he been 'free to choose' (683) to read it. This seemingly meandering but adroitly handled passage anticipates, however, waywardly and almost comically (shades of *Nightmare Abbey* loom in the background), the later view of 'Our life' as 'a false nature' (4, 1126); it offers, by way of an unexpected and local detail, evidence of how lives can be thwarted, and has a wryness that foreshadows effects in *Don Juan*. Soon, Byron asserts,

> Alas, for Earth, for never shall we see
> The brightness in her eye she bore when Rome was free!
>
> (4, 737–8)

When the great address comes, the lines quoted by Shelley as the epigraph to his 'Ode to Liberty', 'Yet, Freedom! yet thy banner, torn, but flying, / Streams like the thunder-storm *against* the wind' (4, 874–5), the writing avoids a merely rhetorical use of catchphrases. The 'wind' against which it streams, so to speak, includes the disillusioned, though not cynical, account of the French Revolution that has preceded it. The reader is not obliged to agree with Byron's politics; but he or she needs to see that Byron has created a space where the illusion is generated, as Walter Scott put it, of 'an actual living man expressing his own sentiments, thoughts, hopes and fears'.[16]

As Harold stands in Canto 3 on the battlefield at 'deadly Waterloo' (155) – 'fatal' in one manuscript and, indeed, apostrophised as such at line 310 – Byron grimly acknowledges the fitness of the retribution paid by Napoleon, but mocks the idea that freedom has been served, especially given the post-Waterloo settlement:

> Fit retribution! Gaul may champ the bit
> And foam in fetters; – but is Earth more free?
> Did nations combat to make *One* submit;
> Or league to teach all kings true sovereignty?

(3, 163–6)

What contemporary history teaches Byron is the pervasiveness of contradiction in human affairs, working almost like a perverse principle. This is not to discount the possibility of integrity: Marceau appears in Canto 3, stanzas 56 and 57, as 'Freedom's champion' (549); but even here the praise is precisely nuanced to imply his virtue's rarity: he is

>   one of those,
> The few in number, who had not o'erstept
> The charter to chastise which she bestows
> On such as wield her weapons.

(3, 549–52)

If these lines anticipate Shelley's praise of the 'sacred few' (128) in *The Triumph of Life*, they anticipate, too, Shelley's fear in the same poem that 'Good and the means of good' (231) are frequently 'irreconcilable' (230).[17]

Freedom as a fully blown political abstraction is more evident in Canto 4. Byron sets it as the one thing resisting the all-engulfing, tidal pull of 'Destruction's mass' (4, 1476). Indeed, in the lament for the recently dead Princess Charlotte, he hears a voice 'from the abyss' (4, 1495) expressing grief for the Princess and he associates her with 'Freedom's heart' (4, 1516). Again, though, it is the staging by Byron of his own sombre vacillations (Charlotte has escaped through death a potentially disillusioning 'destiny' [1540]) that prevents the writing from seeming merely opportunist.

Hazlitt, quick to scent out inauthenticity in fellow travellers, writes that

'Byron, who in his politics is a *liberal*, in his genius is haughty and aristo-cratic'.[18] He also took a dislike in the same paragraph to a writer 'who obstinately and invariably shuts himself up in the Bastille of his own ruling passions'.[19] This is witty and deft, the allusion to the Bastille implying that Byron is, in poetic terms, both perpetrator of the injustice of the *ancien régime* and absurd victim of his own tyranny, his 'ruling passions'. But *Childe Harold* is more aware than Hazlitt's formulation allows. It sees the limits of the creative faculty: 'Of its own beauty is the mind diseased, / And fevers into false creation' (4, 1090–1), as Byron writes in the most passion-ately intelligent critique of Romanticism ever penned. And it recognises that it gazes out on Freedom as if through the bars of a prison, and achieves many of its most poignant yet unsentimental effects in so doing. Venice's loss of freedom may be elegised at the start of Canto 4. But Byron reveals that elegy is itself entangled in contradiction when he speaks in stanza 14 of the city in the past as 'all glory' (118), 'Her very by-word sprung from victory' (119), and clinches this presentation of 'free' Venice in the line, 'Though making many slaves, herself still free' (122). In an antithesis that makes a causal link between 'slaves' and 'free', Byron's language points up the poem's subliminal awareness that such freedom was already perilous, a question of civilisation's dependence on its own barbarism.

In her poem 'The Spirit's Mysteries' Felicia Hemans takes as her epigraph a passage from *Childe Harold*, Canto 4, stanza 23 (lines 202–7) in which Byron suggests the limits of stoical defiance, itself a reaction against the consciousness of suffering, which in turn takes on redoubled force after the Canto's opening celebration of the mind's power. The lines, as quoted by Hemans, are these:

> And slight, withal, may be the things which bring
> Back on the heart the weight which it would fling
> Aside for ever; it may be a sound –
> A tone of music – summer's breath, or spring –
> A flower – a leaf – the ocean – which may wound –
> Striking th'electric chain wherewith we are darkly bound.[20]

The logic of this and preceding stanzas is wildly associative and yet forms an unbreakable set of links: the mind's power shows itself in art and medi-tation; it is apparent in our ability to bear existence; existence must be spoken of in such terms because there is so much to bear; suffering is temporal and will end; and yet – and here the passage Hemans quotes begins. That 'electric chain wherewith we are darkly bound' proves that we are bound, and yet that we are bound darkly, mysteriously; if we are chained, the chain is electric, capable of communicating shocks that prove we are alive. A passage that suggests the mind's power is not absolute in that it cannot wholly subdue grief modulates into an assertion of the heart's unfathomable sensitivity and involuntary resources. Hemans turns Byron's lines into a reverential meditation on the fact that "Tis mystery all!' (30) and that

> we press upon the brink
> Haply of viewless worlds, and know it not.

> (31–2)

She is encouraged by our ignorance of origins and ends to believe in human greatness, using Byron as a point of departure for her own vision of freedom. Byron, by contrast, turns in his next stanza to the fact of such ignorance, as if in despair, and yet there is a characteristic, conflict-ridden vitality as he evokes 'The spectres whom no exorcism can bind' (214).

Appropriately, in his concluding address to the Ocean, Byron celebrates mutability and delights in its sublimity, in the Ocean's awesome, inhuman indifference to the fate of nations and civilisations. In one sense, this indifference finally establishes the bounds of human freedom. Human attempts to master Ocean are folly; the making of ships may let human beings 'the vain title take / Of lord of thee' (4, 1625–6), but, in fact, such omnipotence is a fantasy. Yet the very exposure of human pretensions acknowledges the need of human beings to 'aspire / Beyond the fitting medium of desire'. If freedom is the recognition of necessity, Byron's poetic recognitions throughout Cantos 3 and 4 are richly liberating. They spin round the belief that, in a deeply reflexive sense, 'There woos no home, nor hope, nor life, save what is here' (4, 945).

Notes

1   Jerome J. McGann, *Fiery Dust: Byron's Poetic Development* (Chicago, IL, and London: University of Chicago Press, 1968), p. 38; Vincent Newey, *Centring the Self: Subjectivity, Society and Reading from Thomas Gray to Thomas Hardy* (Aldershot: Scolar Press, 1995), p. 189. See also Robert F. Gleckner, *Byron and the Ruins of Paradise* (Baltimore, MD: Johns Hopkins University Press, 1967), p. 83, where Gleckner writes, 'as Byron sees in Canto 3, for the artist it is the act of creation itself that is his salvation'. M. G. Cooke, *The Blind Man Traces the Circle: On the Patterns and Philosophy of Byron's Poetry* (Princeton, NJ: Princeton University Press, 1969) argues that 'Byron's "art" means not the timeless product of cognitive and imaginative and emotional endeavor, but rather the complex temporal act of composition or

"creation"', pp. 42–3.

2   See Jerome McGann's related discussion of the movement from stanza 6 to 7, where he uses the word 'vitality' which I have been discussing: 'The problem is that only the thinnest line separates the vitality of the poet's projected "being more intense" from the "boiling and 'o'erwrought" confusion of a dark and wandering mind' (*Fiery Dust*, p. 79).

3   *Childe Harold's Pilgrimage: A Critical, Composite Edition*, ed. by David V. Erdman, with the assistance of David Worrall, Manuscripts of the Younger Romantics: Byron 6 (New York and London: Garland, 1991), pp. 204–5 (hereafter Erdman).

4   McGann, *Fiery Dust*, p. 83.

5   From *Ecce Homo*, in *A Nietzsche Reader*, selected and trans. with intro., R. J. Hollingdale (Harmondsworth: Penguin, 1977), p. 260.

6   See Erdman, pp. 176–7.

7   *Hamlet*, III.ii.67, 73, 74; quoted from *The Norton Shakespeare: Based on the Oxford Edition*, gen. ed. Stephen Greenblatt (New York: Norton, 1997).

8   'Twilight of the Idols', in *A Nietzsche Reader*, p. 271.

9   Jerome Christensen, *Lord Byron's Strength: Romantic Writing and Commercial Society* (Baltimore, MD, and London: Johns Hopkins University Press, 1993), p. 153.

10 Christensen, *Lord Byron's Strength*, p. 189.

11 The idea of 'freedom from' is discussed in Peter Graham's contribution to this volume.

12 Quoted in *CPW*, 2, 228.

13 Newey, *Centring the Self*, p. 182.

14 Gleckner, *Byron and the Ruins of Paradise*, p. 283.

15 'Lord Byron', in William Hazlitt, *The Spirit of the Age, or, Contemporary Portraits*, ed. by E. D. Mackerness (London: Collins, 1969), p. 116.

16 From Scott's unsigned review of *Childe Harold IV* in *The Quarterly Review*, April 1818 (publ. September), quoted from Theodore Redpath, *The Young Romantics and Critical Opinion 1807–1824* (London: Harrap, 1973), p. 238.

17 Quoted from *Shelley's Poetry and Prose*, ed. by Donald H. Reiman and Sharon B. Powers (New York: Norton, 1977). For further discussion of the complex relationship between Byron and Shelley, see Charles E. Robinson, *Shelley and Byron: The Snake and Eagle Wreathed in Fight* (Baltimore, MD: Johns Hopkins University Press, 1976).

18 Hazlitt, *The Spirit of the Age*, p. 115.

19 Hazlitt, *The Spirit of the Age*, p. 116.

20 Quoted, as is the text of Hemans's poem, from *Romantic Women Poets: An Anthology*, ed. Duncan Wu (Oxford: Blackwell, 1997).

Byron, Manfred, Negativity and Freedom

PETER GRAHAM

Even before English readers glimpsed the manuscript of his dramatic poem *Manfred*, Byron framed it negatively. Writing to Kinnaird, he begins defining his latest effusion with a denial – 'I have no tragedy nor tragedies.' He then goes on to deprecate the 'metaphysical drama' he has sent to his publisher John Murray. It is, says Byron:

> The very Antipodes of the stage and is meant to be so – it is all in the Alps & the other world – and as mad as Bedlam – I do not know that it is even fit for publication – the persons are all magicians – ghosts – & the evil principle – with a mixed mythology of my own – which you may suppose is somewhat of the strangest. – It has no pretense to being called a drama – except that it is in dialogue & acts.

(BLJ, 5, 194)

Thus Byron denies the generic nature that his 'Dramatic Poem' claims in its subtitle. As we shall see, his further comments on *Manfred* also repudiate or elide the principal literary influences on a work that is arguably one of the most diversely influenced of his creations.[1] Resembling the poet in kind but exceeding him in degree, the drama's protagonist says no at all levels, from the grammatical to the ontological. If not a practitioner of the utterance that Thomas Carlyle, who had Byron on his mind when formulating the phrase in *Sartor Resartus*, would later call the 'Everlasting Nay', Manfred is certainly master of naysaying in the here and now. In this essay I will focus on specific instances of the character's and the drama's relentless negativity, speculate on how negativity relates to freedom and, informed by the ideas of Isaiah Berlin and Benjamin Constant, offer some contingent reasons why both Byron and Manfred say 'no' as much as they do.

After *Manfred*'s publication and initial reviews, Byron sent Murray some thoughts on the critics' discussion of his work's resemblances to Dr Faustus. Again, his rhetoric and sentiments are in a decidedly negative vein:

> I *never read* – and do not know that I ever saw – the 'Faustus of Marlow' and had & have no Dramatic works by me in English – except the recent things

you sent me; – but I heard Mr. Lewis translate verbally some scenes of *Goethe's Faust* (which were some good & some bad) last Summer – which is all I know of the history of that magical personage. As to the 'Faustus of Marlow' – I never read – never saw – nor heard of it – at least thought of it – except that I think Mr. Gifford mentioned, in a note of his which you sent me – something about the catastrophe, – but not as having any thing to do with mine – which may or may not resemble it – for any thing I know – The Prometheus – if not exactly in my plan – has always been so much in my head – that I can easily conceive its influence over all or anything that I have written; – but I deny Marlow & his progeny – .

(*BLJ*, 5, 268).

The metaphysical drama that Byron, perhaps disingenuously, claims to be light on Goethe's influence and free of Marlowe's is, like the one play whose influence he does allusively acknowledge, Aeschylus's *Prometheus Bound*, all about defiance – refusal – naysaying. Its aptly named protagonist is Man-freed *from* things rather than *for* things, a freethinker whose nature inclines him to say 'no' much more than 'yes'. Even the most cursory look at the grammar and diction of Manfred's speeches will reveal that 'no' and 'not', as well as negative prefixes, suffixes, and constructions pervade his lines. When a sentence's grammar is positive rather than negative, what is being asserted is very often some sort of negation. Manfred's sprawling first two sentences, which are also the first lines of the drama, prove typical of what will be his dominant speech pattern:

MAN.   The lamp must be replenish'd, but even then
It will not burn so long as I must watch:
My slumbers – if I slumber – are not sleep,
But a continuance of enduring thought,
Which then I can resist not: in my heart
There is a vigil, and these eyes but close
To look within; and yet I live, and bear
The aspect and the form of breathing men.
But grief should be the instructor of the wise;
Sorrow is knowledge: they who know the most
Must mourn the deepest o'er the fatal truth,
The Tree of Knowledge is not that of Life.

(I.i.1–12)

Similarly, Manfred's last words offer an assertion phrased negatively: 'Old man! 'tis not so difficult to die' (III.iv.152).

Between these beginning and concluding speeches, we find a parade of negations stubbornly asserting Manfred's personal freedom: freedom from obligation, connection, need, or desire. When, in the drama's first scene, one of the conjured spirits asks what shape Manfred wishes them to take, he answers:

> I have no choice, there is no form on earth
> Hideous or beautiful to me.
>
> (I.i.184–5)

His valedictory utterance on the brink of the alpine abyss in Act I scene ii is

> – Farewell, ye opening heavens!
> Look not upon me thus reproachfully –
> Ye were not meant for me –
>
> (I.ii.107–9)

Moments later, he responds to the Chamois Hunter who has saved him with a less than grateful: 'Nay, grasp me not – ' (I.ii.113). His final words on parting with the hunter, who offers Manfred his prayers, are:

> I need them not,
> But can endure thy pity. I depart –
> 'Tis time – farewell! – Here's gold, and thanks for thee –
> No words – it is thy due. – Follow me not –
> I know my path – the mountain peril's past: –
> And once again, I charge thee, follow not!
>
> (II.i.70)

Manfred's very next line, which opens scene ii, begins with the words 'It is not noon' (I.ii.1); and his subsequent sentence starts 'No eyes / but mine now drink this sight of loveliness' (I.ii.8–9). His prosaic statements of fact, and even his tortured engagement with the world's 'loveliness', are pervasively negative.

Most negative of all are Manfred's introspective and philosophical monologues, which teem with negations from the syntactic to the ontological. A typical example is the soliloquy directly following his discourse with the Witch of the Alps. This meditation concludes with some thoughts on his dead sister Astarte, where the world's best blessings – love, life, and the giving and receiving of happiness – are negated by subjunctive verbs indicating conditions contrary to fact, and what's phrased in indicative verbs, Manfred's view of things-as-they-are, is laden with negative nouns ('sufferer', 'sins', 'thing I dare not think upon', 'nothing'):

> If I had never lived, that which I love

Had still been living; had I never loved,
That which I love would still be beautiful –
Happy and giving happiness. What is she?
What is she now? – a sufferer for my sins –
A thing I dare not think upon – or nothing.

(II.ii.193–8)

With a tortured but somewhat infuriating blend of brave willingness to shoulder all guilt and radical egocentricity that implicitly denies free agency to his sister, Manfred essentially wishes away his life and asserts that his own oblivion would have allowed Astarte to thrive, a dubious claim if their bond was as he characterises it. His subjunctively imagined vision of Astarte giving and receiving happiness is also intensely intransitive, end-stopped in mid-line. Manfred's syntax may not be grammatically broken in this monologue, but dashes unjoin words and ideas that could, metrically and intellectually, flow continuously. Implicit in the pauses signalled by those dashes are dark, unvoiced thoughts – which might be expected of a morbidly negative man whose worldview seems to be 'Give me oblivion or give me death' and whose world, whether as it actually is or as he perceives it, serves as a sympathetic backdrop to his overflowing feelings, so that as he avows the negative strength allowing him to 'act even what I most abhor/ And champion human fears. – The night approaches' (II.iii.204–5), whether that night is literal, figurative, or both.

But however morbid it may be, Manfred's negativity is the primary source of his power. On his next entrance, in scene iv of Act II, Manfred descends to the Hall of Arimanes. His first words to the dark prince's attendant spirits, who order him to bow down and worship Arimanes or 'dread the worst', are

I know it;
And yet ye see I kneel not.

(II.iv.35–6)

As he continues to defy Arimanes' attendants, Manfred's speeches remain negative in syntax, style, and substance alike. He reminds the infernal spirits that God made Arimanes 'not for worship' (II.iv.48) – and that 'without power, I could not be amongst thee' (II.iv.74–5). When asked what he seeks in the underworld, Manfred replies: 'Thou canst not reply to me' (II.iv.79). Only Astarte is able to do that, but when her phantom is conjured up Manfred's negativity continues:

Can this be death? There's bloom upon her cheek;

But now I see it is no living hue,
But a strange hectic – like the unnatural red
Which Autumn plants upon the perish'd leaf.
It is the same! Oh, God! that I should dread
To look upon the same – Astarte! – No,
I cannot speak to her…

(II.iv.98–105)

Throughout Act III, Manfred's speeches to the Abbot of St Maurice are particularly full of negatives, even by Manfred's standards. Refuting the priest's reminder that vengeance belongs to God and that penitence and pardon remain available, Manfred replies:

Old man! there is no power in holy men,
Nor charm in prayer – nor purifying form
Of penitence – nor outward look – nor fast –
Nor agony.

(III.i.66–8)

Again, Manfred gains freedom by naysaying as he obliterates the conventional religious reading of his dark deeds. In his unremittingly negative universe

no future pang
Can deal that justice on the self-condemn'd
He deals on his own soul.

(III.i.75–6)

Having resisted heaven's pardon, Manfred offers his final defiance to the dark spirits who come to drag him down to damnation. His speech is again a blend of negation and naysaying:

Back to thy hell!
Thou hast no power upon me, *that* I feel;
Thou never shalt possess me, *that* I know:
What I have done is done; I bear within
A torture which could nothing gain from thine:
The mind which is immortal makes itself
Requital for its good or evil thoughts –
Is its own origin of ill and end –
And its own place and time – its innate sense,
When stripp'd of this mortality, derives
No color from the fleeting things without,
But is absorb'd in sufferance or in joy,
Born from the knowledge of its own desert.

Thou didst not tempt me, and thou couldst not tempt me;
I have not been thy dupe, nor am thy prey –
But was my own destroyer, and will be
My own hereafter. – Back, ye baffled fiends!
The hand of death is on me – but not yours!

(III.iv.123–41)

In contrast to this resistance of supernatural power, his last act is a gesture of connection that involves ministering to human weakness. 'Give me thy hand', he says to the Abbot. The words and gesture lend themselves to various interpretations, but the Abbot's response to the handclasp, 'Alas! How fares it with thee?' (III.iv.150) evokes from Manfred the negatively phrased assertion so infamously omitted from the first edition: 'Old man! 'tis not so difficult to die'. As these words make clear, Manfred's dying gesture may display fellowship rather than alienation – but the fellowship enacted is contrarian in several ways. A dying man comforts a survivor. A younger man advises his elder. A sceptic instructs a priest in the ways of a good death. In short, Manfred's last act and last words negate the commonplace wisdom of church and world alike. His haughty negatives may seem to clank and rattle like the 'mind-forged manacles' in Blake's 'London' or the long, restrictive, self-imposed spiritual chains of Marley's ghost. Nevertheless, these naysayings serve as a declaration of independence.

But Man-freed's characteristics, actions, and feelings are those of a man whose condition of freedom is as negative as are his words. As the servant Manuel points out, Manfred 'nought resembles' his father: he has escaped not only from religious obligations, but from patriarchal burdens as well. He's also liberated from love's human bondage, now that his sister Astarte is dead – and if he has killed her, as he believes, he has done so not positively but negatively, by withering her heart. Deracinated from his family, Manfred is a Count who, as far as we can tell, has shed his political and social responsibilities. If we assume that the unspecified time of the metaphysical drama is 1816 (and we know that it is after 1806, due to a reference to the collapse of Mount Rossberg),[2] the protagonist even appears to be a newly freed Swiss citizen. The 1815 Congress of Vienna, which Byron despised for restoring Europe's crowned heads, did, however, strike a blow for democracy by abolishing the Helvetian Republic established when French revolutionaries overran Switzerland in 1798. This act allowed the Swiss nation to revert to being a loose alliance of cantons, guaranteed its neutrality in future European conflicts – and created a political context appropriate for Manfred's and Byron's preferred mode of freedom.

Free *from* much, Manfred is free *for* what? Because Byron's drama gives us Manfred's endgame, 'free to die and gain self-oblivion' might be the immediate answer – but Manfred's habitual behaviours, even and especially in his last days and last hours, suggest that in healthier times his freedom would also have been more a matter of *from* rather than *for*. Like Aeschylus's bound Prometheus, dramatised as the stubborn resistor of Zeus rather than as the benevolent giver of the gods' fire to humanity, Manfred asserts his existential freedom only negatively. He possesses remarkable strength of will – but a will limited, in the course of the drama, to thwarting supernatural powers small and large when they call on him to bend the knee. If he spoke in ottava rima pentameter rather than blank verse, Manfred might say in general what *Don Juan*'s Byronic narrator says of politics in specific: '– I wish men to be free, / As much from mobs as kings, from you as me.' Like the *Don Juan* narrator, Manfred might predict that being of 'no Party' he would 'offend all parties'.[3]

Offending all parties was something Byron took pride in doing at many points of his life, but being of no party was never sadder or truer for him than in 1816, as he was beginning *Manfred*. In the wake of scandal, separation, and financial crisis, Byron had turned his back on England and the English who had turned their backs on him. But he had not put old associations behind or formed sustaining new ties. Sometimes enduring and sometimes enjoying the early months of what would turn out to be life-long exile, he had compelling personal reasons to conceive of freedom as something essentially negative rather than positive when he wrote *Manfred* and such associated texts as his Alpine Journal, 'Prometheus', and 'Darkness'. Call it escape or call it alienation, for a man in Byron's storm-tossed boat, personal freedom in 1816 was bound to mean *freedom from*, not *freedom for* – and personal freedom of this sort would be bound to seem less than completely satisfying.

In the sphere of political philosophy, however, *freedom from* need not be dismissed as incomplete. Indeed, as Isaiah Berlin explains in his classic essay 'Two Forms of Liberty', there is a long tradition of sharply distinguishing negative freedom from positive freedom – and of assuming that the two sorts of freedom are incompatible rather than complementary. Negative freedom as Berlin characterises it (and as Byron cherishes it) involves not being limited by others. Because nearly all human beings are social creatures rather than hermits, this freedom is almost always constrained by competing values, including the freedom of other people.

The Chamois Hunter's injunction 'Hold, madman! – though aweary of thy life, / Stain not our pure vales with thy guilty blood' (I.ii.110–11), for instance, shows that Manfred's inclination to act out his freedom from any taboo against plunging suicidally into the Alpine abyss clashes with the interests of the people in the valley below, fellow humans who should be free from having to suffer the traumatic and messy consequences of Manfred's self-destruction. Manfred may have no living family, but nevertheless suicide in the form he contemplates would have social consequences in this corner of the Alps, where someone would have to discover, identify, clean up after, and dispose of Manfred's broken corpse.

The individual's pursuit of negative freedom involves resisting authority and interference of all kinds. In contrast, Berlin sees positive freedom, which derives from the wish to be one's own master, as an impulse often inflated into association with authority: 'some super-personal entity – a state, a class, a nation, or the march of history itself'.[4] Berlin further asserts that 'the "positive" conception of freedom as self-mastery, with its suggestion of a man divided against himself, has, in fact, and as a matter of history, of doctrine and of practice' led to a paradigm of split personality: 'the transcendent, dominant controller' seen as 'a more "real" subject of attributes than the empirical self' and thus fit to discipline and bring to heel the 'empirical bundle of desires and passions'.[5] Such self-mastery affirms and expresses the authority of 'super personal identity', not the autonomy of the individual. This insight about the nature of positive freedom goes far towards explaining Manfred's apparently perverse insistence on remaining alienated and isolated. We are repeatedly shown that Manfred possesses excellences that would make him a highly desirable member of almost any group, but he resists allying himself to a 'super personal identity' as stubbornly as he resists genuflecting to any extra-personal authority. The laconic Chamois Hunter is moved to offer the compliment 'You should have been a hunter' (I.ii.125); and one of Arimanes' attendant spirits notes, as the tortured Manfred masters himself on the departure of Astarte's phantom:

> Had he been one of us, he would have made
> An awful spirit.
>
> (II.iv.163)

Whatever rewards group affiliation might have brought him, though, Manfred remains committed to the lonely way of *freedom from*.

In emphasising the negativity of freedom in *Manfred*, Byron associates himself with a line of distinguished liberal thinkers, among them Locke, Mill, Tocqueville, and, most interestingly for a variety of reasons, the man of whom Berlin says 'No one saw the conflict between the two types of liberty better, or expressed it more clearly': Benjamin Constant.[6] Political philosopher, confessional novelist, and lover of Mme de Staël, Constant had published *Principe de politique*, his freedom-endorsing appraisal of France during the Revolutionary era, in 1815, shortly before he paid an extended visit to London.[7] The first months of his stay coincided with Byron's last months in his native land. Byron and Constant, who had met at a London dinner given by Lord Glenbervie in 1812, renewed their acquaintance in April 1816 through the offices of the Comte de Flahaut, the French soldier and diplomat who became the ambassador to Great Britain and the husband of Byron's loyal partisan Margaret Mercer Elphinstone. Constant paid his respects before Byron's departure for the continent. June of 1816 finds the two cosmopolitan liberals embodying a kind of geo-cultural chiasmus: Constant was established in London's Whig society, Byron's former base of operations, while Byron settled outside Geneva, in easy reach of Mme de Staël's salon at Coppet. During his residence in Switzerland Byron read Constant's novel *Adolphe* (written in 1806 but published in 1816), a *roman à clef* that, among other things, transparently fictionalised his affair with Mme de Staël much as Lady Caroline Lamb's scandalous novel *Glenarvon* (also published 1816) embodied and embellished the latter's liaison with Byron.

Although Constant's novel demonstrates that he resembled Lady Caroline in being ready to publish and publicise private relationships, his political writings show him to be like Byron in deploring any sort of authoritarian power that interferes with private freedom in the name of public goals, however desirable those goals might be in and of themselves. In *Principe de politique*, Constant regretfully claims that, at the end of the eighteenth century, French liberty involved 'active participation in collective power rather than the peaceful enjoyment of individual independence'.[8] From his vantage point as an advocate of negative freedom, the question of who holds power is less important than how far that power extends. Kings, directorates, mobs, and self-crowned emperors are all equally apt to trample on the rights of man: 'All the constitutions which have been given to France guaranteed the liberty of the individual, and yet, under the rule of these constitutions, it has been constantly violated.'[9] Among the non-French Europeans whose individual liberty would have been violated in the fashion Constant describes would be Manfred's Swiss countrymen, who lived under the Napoleonic constitution imposed on them in 1803 until the Congress of Vienna abolished the Helvetian Republic and, with it, the constitution. Thus only a year before Byron began writing *Manfred*, his most intense distillation of the negative power of human freethinking, Switzerland was freed – by a political act of negation.

Given the peculiar fertility of negative speech and thought when Byron deploys them, we should perhaps be unsurprised that the 'antipodes of the stage' can be so keenly dramatic and that a work 'mad as Bedlam' can be so sanely centred. Given the rich potential of *freedom from*, it should not be unexpected that Byron's self-uprooting should facilitate a phase of intense creativity. Nonetheless, it amuses the ironist's eye to survey *Manfred*'s sublime poetic landscape of mountains and metaphysics and discern through the transcendental fog delineations of such specific political and personal contingences.

Notes

1 For a concise account of the diverse works and authors influencing *Manfred*, see *CPW*, 4, 466–67. Among other studies, see also McGann's essay 'Byron and Wordsworth', in *Byron and Romanticism*, ed. by James Soderholm (Cambridge: Cambridge University Press, 2002), pp. 173–202; Samuel Chew, *The Dramas of Lord Byron* (Baltimore, MD: Johns Hopkins University Press, 1915), pp. 59–84; E. M. Butler, *Byron and Goethe* (London: Bowes and Bowes, 1956), pp. 29–37; and Travis Looper, *Byron and the Bible* (Metuchen, NJ: Scarecrow Press, 1978), pp. 124–30, 234–8.

2 See *CPW*, 4, 472 (note to I.ii.99).

3 *Don Juan*, IX, 25.

4 Isaiah Berlin, 'Two Concepts of Liberty', in *Four Essays on Liberty* (New York and London: Oxford, 1969), p. 134.

5 Berlin, 'Two Concepts of Liberty', p. 134.

6 Berlin, 'Two Concepts of Liberty', p. 163.

7 See Leslie A. Marchand, *Byron: A Biography*, 3 vols (New York: Knopf, 1957), II, 598–9, 606, 613–14, 642.

8 Benjamin Constant, *Political Writings*, trans. and ed. by Biancamaria Fontana (New York: Cambridge, 1988), p. 102.

9 Constant, *Political Writings*, p. 289.

Manfred's Quarrel with Immortality: Freeing the Self

KATHARINE KERNBERGER

When the figure of Astarte speaks to Manfred in the Hall of Arimanes, she promises him release from life: 'Tomorrow ends thine earthly ills' (*Manfred*, II.iv.152). She also creates one of the play's central ambiguities. She offers him the death he has long sought, but she does not clarify for him the meaning of death. Further, the adjective 'earthly' in Astarte's promise introduces a qualification, almost a prevarication: his *earthly* ills will end, but he has no guarantee that death will not extend his torment, carrying his painful consciousness of the past into eternity. In that case death will have been of no use to him. Since Manfred's pain is a mental one, derived from his sense of guilt over the death of Astarte, only an extinguishing of mind and thought, of all the details of memory that form the identity of the self, can deliver him from suffering. The liberation from the past that he seeks in death requires an annihilation of consciousness. If the mind is immortal, he has no hope for relief. Manfred needs to know what death will mean. Like Hamlet, he fears the 'dreams' that may exist even in death:

> To die, to sleep;
> To sleep: perchance to dream: Aye, there's the rub;
> For in that sleep of death what dreams may come,
> When we have shuffled off this mortal coil,
> Must give us pause. There's the respect
> That makes calamity of so long life.
>
> (*Hamlet*, III.i.64–9)

Will death bring release from memory of the past? Or will consciousness continue beyond the grave? Whatever we choose to call this aspect of man – mind, soul, consciousness, self – its status is the key to Manfred's fate.

Manfred sees man as 'Half dust, half deity, alike unfit / To sink or soar' (I.ii.40–1), an anomalous creature, suspended between the gods and the animals, participating in the qualities of both higher and lower beings: a 'creature of clay', as the spirits remind him, but endowed with the 'Promethean spark' that can lift him above his station. Many creeds and philosophies postulate such an inherent dualism in man – whether it is of mind–body or of higher and lower natures or of good and evil – and often they project that dualism outward onto the cosmos itself. Most of them assume that some part of man survives beyond the grave, to be punished or rewarded for its earthly conduct. Byron borrows features from three such traditions in constructing the cosmos Manfred inhabits: the Neoplatonic, the Zoroastrian, and the Christian. Act I introduces a spirit world that fits into the Neoplatonic scheme of a hierarchical Chain of Being stretching from the One on down to the phenomenal world; Act II brings on stage the evil spirits of the Zoroastrian scheme, while Manfred's two encounters with sympathetic mortals, the Chamois Hunter and the Abbot, insert the Christian view. Byron's syncretism leaves the work's actual cosmology and metaphysics open-ended, as he apologises in a letter to Murray, it is 'of a very wild – metaphysical – and inexplicable kind'.[1]

In the course of the play Manfred calls up all the powers he can command, asking each in turn for 'forgetfulness' of what has haunted him since 'that all-nameless hour' (I.i.24), when Astarte's blood was shed (though not by him) and Manfred could not 'staunch' it. Scene by scene he reveals glimpses of his mysterious past. If we examine Manfred's successive encounters with others – spirits and mortals – we see him assert his independence from all external judgement and turn towards death to free himself from his self.

When we first meet Manfred in his Gothic gallery at the Gothic hour of midnight, he is in quest of relief from thought and its demons:

My slumbers – if I slumber – are not sleep,
But a continuance of enduring thought.

(I.i.3–4)

He recites for us a catalogue of his knowledge (just as Marlowe's Faustus and Goethe's Faust do) and finds all his learning useless in his inner struggle against his guilt. The irony is clear: a man who has delighted almost solely in the pursuit of knowledge – in thinking rather than in feeling – has found that his knowledge has given him only sorrow, that 'The Tree of Knowledge is not that of Life' (I.i.12). Manfred insists, however, that to gain his knowledge and the power it gives him over the realm of spirits, he has not enthralled himself to any demonic force. He has acquired his mastery over those he summons from the invisible world

by superior science – penance – daring –
And length of watching

(III.iv.115–16)

His situation, then, does not parallel that of Faust. He has no debt to pay for his learning; his life is not forfeit to the devil. He is independent and unallied.

In Act I, scene i, Manfred summons the first group of spirits – six earthly demons that rule the elements of nature and therefore occupy the lowest reaches of the Neoplatonic Chain of Being.[2] Manfred's spirits come from the clouds, the mountains, the ocean, the earthquake, the wind, and the night. As their songs reveal, they control the powers associated with the natural phenomenon of the physical realm each spirit inhabits. The spirit of the wind, for example, says,

I am the Rider of the wind,
The Stirrer of the storm;
The hurricane I left behind
Is yet with lightning warm.

(I.i.100–4)

Along with these six embodiments of earthly forces, comes the ambiguous Seventh Spirit, the demon that rules Manfred's birth star. Being from beyond the sphere of the earth, from the realm of the stars, he represents a higher level of existence.[3]

Manfred asks these seven spirits whether they can grant him 'Oblivion, self-oblivion' (I.i.144). They respond that they can offer him 'subjects, sovereignty, the power / O'er earth' or its elements (I.i.140–1), but that they have no power over the human mind or psyche. They are also unable to answer his other question: 'Will death bestow it [oblivion] on me?' (I.i.148). Since they are immortal, they have no knowledge of death and are useless to him. As one of Byron's letters about the play explains, 'Almost all the persons – but two or three – are Spirits of the earth & air, or the waters, … [and] the hero is a kind of magician … [who] wanders about invoking these spirits – which appear to him – & are of no use.'[4]

Manfred, lashing out at their assumption of superiority, suggests the real root of his problem: his mind, his spirit, his 'Promethean spark', is as powerful as theirs. They agree with him that he may be no more subject to death than they are:

If, as thou say'st, thine essence be as ours,
We have replied in telling thee, the thing

Mortals call death has nought to do with us.

(I.i.161–3)

Manfred asks the invisible spirits to choose some visible form. The Seventh Spirit, guardian of Manfred's star, perversely takes the shape of a beautiful woman, presumably Astarte herself, and Manfred, confronted with the figure whose death torments him, faints. An unidentified voice forecasts his destiny. In the last two stanzas of the Incantation, the voice dooms Manfred to this fate:

> I call upon thee! and compel
> Thyself to be thy proper Hell!

(I.i.250–2)

This speech echoes Milton's Satan[5] and Marlowe's Mephistopheles[6] who both emphasise that Hell is not a place; it is a state of mind, an intellectual, not a physical place. Manfred carries around with him his own punishment and needs no external reminder of his transgression.

Because Manfred is convinced that he was responsible for the death of Astarte, who is surely intended to be his sister, he is cursed, 'by [his] brotherhood of Cain' (I.i.249). He believes he is fated, as Cain is according to some interpretations, to eternal life. Though he does not carry the visible mark of Cain on his forehead, he bears it as guilt within him, as his internal hell:

> Nor to slumber, nor to die,
> Shall be in thy destiny;
> Though thy death shall still seem near
> To thy wish, but as a fear;
> Lo! the spell now works around thee
> And the clankless chain hath bound thee.

(I.i.254–9)

'Nor to slumber, nor to die': Manfred, then, is like Ahasuerus the Wandering Jew, the Old Man in Chaucer's 'Pardoner's Tale', the Ancient Mariner; he has an invisible, 'clankless chain' that binds him to an unbearable life. While he has not sought, like Faust, to make himself eternal, he fears that he is a mortal no longer, but fated to an immortality of self-loathing.

As Act II begins, we expect the play to move the metaphysical search to another level. (Although Byron introduces the Christian worldview here, we will postpone consideration of the Chamois Hunter and his consolations until later.) But Manfred's summoning of the Witch of the

Alps in the second scene seems largely irrelevant. The Witch does not represent a power different in kind from the six earthly spirits of Act I, though she is above them and has control over them.[7] She seems merely an extension of their earth-bound powers. He rejects her offer of help. He wants only to gaze upon her beauty. Despite the irrelevance of the Witch to his quest, the scene allows him to confess more of his painful past.

Here we learn that he was alienated from his fellows. He fled human company and found joy in solitude and the study of death and the unknown, making his 'eyes familiar with Eternity' (II.ii.90). Only Astarte shared his thirst and talent for these matters:

> She had the same lone thoughts and wanderings,
> The quest of hidden knowledge, and a mind
> To comprehend the universe.
>
> (II.ii.109–10)

She was his equal, physically and intellectually, but he was not her equal morally. Her recognition of his inner nature broke her heart; she looked into his heart and, horrified by its faults, her own heart withered. We are not given a clear account of how she died because Manfred, speaking in phrases punctuated by starts and stops, gives incomplete evidence:

> I have shed
> Blood, but not hers – and yet her blood was shed –
> I saw – and could not staunch it.
>
> (II.ii.119–21)

In his flight from memory, he has searched for 'forgetfulness' in madness, fantasy, and many forms of death. But none of his efforts have allowed him to forget or to die.

Though the Witch cannot offer him death, 'that is not in my province', she professes that she can help him if he will 'swear obedience ... and do [her] bidding' (II.ii.250–1). Such a capitulation to a spirit he has commanded is unthinkable for Manfred, and he refuses. At this point Manfred turns to his last resource:

> I can call the dead,
> And ask them what it is we dread to be:
> The sternest answer can but be the Grave,
> And that is nothing.
>
> (II.ii.178–81)

There is a problem for Manfred inherent in the very notion of calling back the dead. If death extinguishes both body and soul, flesh and mind, there

is nothing spiritual to resurrect from the tomb. This sort of complete annihilation is what he desires death to be. If death erases consciousness and
identity, then the dead cannot really be brought back to converse with the
living. They might return as animated bodies, as ghouls or vampires, but
they cannot recover the whole person that lived before death.

Manfred gives a precis of his guilt at the end of the scene:

> If I had never lived, that which I love
> Had still been living; had I never loved,
> That which I love would still be beautiful –
> Happy and giving happiness. What is she?
> What is she now? – a sufferer for my sins –
> A thing I dare not think upon – or nothing.

> (II.ii.193–8)

His dilemma lies in this question: Is Astarte suffering for his faults? Is she
one of the damned or is she merely a body decomposing in the earth, no
longer sentient or knowing? He is responsible for her condition, whatever
it is, and can find peace only in resolving this mystery.

Up to this point the spirits he has invoked, including the Witch of the
Alps, are morally neutral: they control natural phenomena and have no
power over the human mind. As his problem is an internal one, based on
his own sense of guilt and not on any external crime, Manfred must turn
inward to alter his fate. I think it is significant that the poem offers no
explanation of how he arrives at Arimanes' court, penetrating to the heart
of darkness. As the first Destiny remarks,

> This man
> Is of no common order, as his port
> And presence here denote.

> (II.iv.51–3)

His mere presence in this realm is witness to his achievement. It might be
reasonable to see the supernatural or 'unnatural' order of beings he meets
there as internal features, as part of the evil principle within man.

We have passed from the concept of the Neoplatonic Chain of Being
to the Zoroastrian idea of the universe as the staging-ground of the battle
between light and dark, between good and evil. Both schemes presuppose
a hierarchy stretching throughout creation, and a duality which offers a
potential for mythic correspondence between the human and spiritual
dimensions, the microcosm and the macrocosm.

Arimanes, Byron's name for the Zoroastrian Ahriman, the Manichean

principal of darkness and evil, rules in balance with his twin and his opponent, Ormazd, the principal of light and goodness. With his attendant
spirits, Arimanes controls the same space governed by the six spirits in Act
I – the earthly sphere and the celestial spheres beyond earth. He is 'Prince
of Earth and Air!' He 'walks the clouds and waters' and holds in his hand
'the sceptre of the elements'. But his governance is not, like theirs, morally
neutral. He is responsible for the chaos in nature – tempests, thunder,
earthquakes, volcanoes, wild comets, and burned-out planets – and for the
disasters in the human sphere – pestilence, war, and death in all its forms.
The spirits around his fiery throne praise his dominion over pain:

> Life is his
> With all its infinite agonies.

> (II.iv.14–15)

He bends both the physical elements and human will and fate towards evil.

On the summit of the Jungfrau, his followers, the three Destinies, on
their way to the 'great festival', a sort of Manichean Walpurgis night to be
held in the Hall of their Master, exult in their destruction of human lives.
Nemesis joins them. This pagan deity who serves justice and punishes
crimes may be appropriate, given Manfred's sense of his guilt, but she is
not a usual part of the Zoroastrian universe. Here, as a servant of
Arimanes, she is malevolent rather than just. She complains that working
her evil has become increasingly difficult of late because intellectual daring
– freedom of thought – has begun to threaten the reign of evil:

> mortals dared to ponder for themselves
> To weigh kings in the balance, and to speak
> Of freedom, the forbidden fruit.

> (II.iii.69–71)

Nemesis and the Destinies 'mount [their] clouds' and set off through the
air to Arimanes' Hall.

Manfred, standing before Arimanes' globe of fire, refuses to bow his will
to the evil principal. He will not kneel before him, but asks that Arimanes
bow down *with him* to worship the higher power of the 'Maker', the 'over-
ruling Infinite' (II.iii.47), which may be Ormazd or his previous form, the
primeval being, Ahura-Mazda. Undeterred by the wrath of the spirits,
Manfred stands his ground and asks for their help in calling up the dead.
He fears no harm from them.

The first Destiny admits his equality in power with the servants of
darkness:

his sufferings
Have been of an immortal nature, like
Our own; his knowledge and his powers and will,
As far as is compatible with clay,
Which clogs the ethereal essence, have been such
As clay has seldom borne.

(II.iv.53–8)

At the root of Neoplatonism, Zoroastrianism, and Christianity lies the conception expressed here that 'clay', the flesh – physical, mortal, sinful – 'clogs' the spiritual part of man and divides him from the gods. Manfred's knowledge, powers, and will raise him above his mortal status into their ethereal sphere. The first Destiny declares, 'he's mine':

No other Spirit in this region hath
A soul like him – or power upon his soul.

(II.iv.69–72)

It is not clear on what basis she stakes her claim, or what her claim means. It *is* clear, however, that Manfred rejects her authority. He seeks 'Powers deeper still beyond', perhaps even beyond their reach: the dead, who might be subjects either of Arimanes or of 'the Maker'. Arimanes consents and Nemesis conjures up the phantom of Astarte, bringing her back from the grave:

Bear what thou borest,
The heart and the form,
And the aspect thou worest
Redeem from the worm.

(II.iv.92–5)

This evocation suggests that the body, at least, has decomposed and must be reconstituted to regain her form. If this is all that remains of Astarte, Manfred may find peace in death.

She refuses to speak at the command of Nemesis or of Arimanes, which Nemesis interprets as a sign of her freedom from their control:

She is not of our order, but belongs
To the other powers.

(II.iv.115–16)

If this is true, Astarte may be aligned with Ormazd and the realm of light. Manfred's impassioned appeal to their love and his torment elicits from her the line we opened with: 'Tomorrow ends thine earthly ills!' But she fails to respond to the three other demands he has addressed to her:

Say that thou loath'st me not – that I do bear
This punishment for both – that thou will be
One of the blessed – and that I shall die.

(II.iv.125–7)

She gives him satisfaction only on the last point: he will die the next day. He has not learned whether the dead continue to feel as they did in life; he has not learned whether she is suffering for what he regards as his crime; he has not learned whether she can attain blessedness. He can take some comfort, however, in her resistance to evil. Perhaps she has escaped an eternity of punishment and will be among the blessed. He cannot draw any such conclusion for his own future.

He masters himself, thanks Nemesis for her 'grace', and returns home, where he discovers Astarte's promise has given him an 'inexplicable stillness' (III.i.5–6). Some of that calm must come from a sense of her independence from Arimanes and his crew.

The Abbot of St Maurice has come to save Manfred from whatever forbidden converse he holds with 'evil and unheavenly spirits' (III.i.37), as the rumours in the village and the abbey claim. This is a second intervention into his world by a mortal representing the Christian faith and offering redemption through 'penitence and pity', emotions not likely to recommend themselves to him. The first intrusion comes with the Chamois Hunter who pulls Manfred back from the brink of the Jungfrau in Act I. Let us return to that episode before we finish.

Rescued by the hunter, Manfred accepts again his 'clankless chain' and submits to the hunter's hospitality. The wine offered by the hunter turns to blood before Manfred's guilty eyes:

I say 'tis blood – my blood! the pure warm stream
Which ran in the veins of my fathers, and in ours
When we were in our youth, and had one heart,
And loved each other as we should not love.

(II.i.24–7)

He addresses himself to Astarte as if she were present, asserts their common bloodline, their consanguinity, and remembers the forbidden love they shared.

Manfred rejects the hunter's advice, his counsel of patience, but recognises the other man's blessings, including 'days of health, and nights of sleep', and prospect of 'a quiet grave' (II.i.67, 69). His own haunted mind and 'scorch'd' soul have no such peaceful future:

I have lived many years,
Many long years, but they are nothing now
To those which I must number: ages – ages –
Space and eternity – and consciousness,
With the fierce thirst of death – and still unslaked!

                                                              (II.i.44–8)

He must endure his unwelcome immortality.

In Act III, the Abbot advocates the same unheroic message of patience
as the Chamois Hunter, enlarging it by counselling submission to and
reconciliation with the church and its vision of heaven. Manfred vehemently rejects any intermediary between himself and his punishment. He
is his own judge. He finds nothing equivalent to his own self-torture:

there is no power in holy men,
Nor charm in prayer – nor purifying form
Of penitence...
Nor agony – can exorcise
From out the unbounded spirit, the quick sense
Of its own sins, wrongs, sufferance, and revenge
Upon itself; there is no future pang
Can deal the justice on the self-condemn'd
He deals on his own soul.

                                                              (III.i.66–78)

He has spent the years since that 'all-nameless hour' of Astarte's death in
his own personal hell, the prison of memory. His suffering has come from

The innate tortures of that deep despair,
Which is remorse without the fear of hell,
But all in all sufficient to itself
Would make a hell of heaven.[8]

                                                              (III.i.70–3)

No retribution imposed by any power in the universe can equal his self-
condemnation. Manfred resists further discussion and excuses himself. He
and the Christian dispensation can only be at cross-purposes. Manfred
does not desire what the simple hunter and the pious priest imagine he
does.

Outside the tower, the old servant Manuel talks to a younger helper
about just 'such / Another evening', when Manfred was there with

The sole companion of his wanderings
And watchings – her, whom of all earthly things

That lived, the only thing he seem'd to love.

(III.iii.43–5)

Manuel is just about to tell us how Astarte and Manfred were related, a problem never resolved by the text, when he is interrupted by the return of the Abbot. The Abbot, perceiving the good present in the Neoplatonic–Manichean mixture of 'light and darkness – / And mind and dust' in Manfred (III.i.164–5), refuses to relinquish him and boldly enters the tower. Manfred warns the Abbot that danger is near, just as the Abbot reports that he sees

> a dusk and awful figure rise
> Like an infernal god from out the earth.

(III.iv.62–3)

Manfred has not summoned this spirit and denies its power over him. He expects death, which he has worked long to achieve. But he recognises no claimant for his soul:

> my past power
> Was purchased by no compact with thy crew.

(III.iv.113–14)

Again he reasons that the punishment he has given himself for his crime exempts him from any other:

> I bear within
> A torture which could nothing gain from thine.

(III.iv.127–8)

Manfred asserts his independence, his absolute freedom from all external judgement:

> The mind which is immortal makes itself
> Requital for its good or evil thoughts –
> Is its own origin of ill and end –
> And its own place and time.

(III.iv.129–32)

Yet the presence of the demons, ready to snatch Manfred at the point of death, seems to confirm that the soul does indeed continue after death – or else they would have no reason to appear. The oblivion and forgetfulness he has sought have escaped him. It seems unlikely that he will find peace, but he can die an independent and human death, owing nothing to anyone outside himself. As Samuel Chew asserts, 'he remains free – free from alliance with evil, free from submission to pain'.[9]

The demons vanish and Manfred's desired death releases him. To the Abbot, he can reveal his readiness: 'Old man! 'tis not so difficult to die' (III.iv.151).

Notes

1 *Byron's Letters and Journals*, ed. by Leslie Marchand, vol. 5 (Cambridge, MA: Harvard University Press, 1976), p. 170.

2 James Twitchell assumes that Byron may be drawing on several Neoplatonic sources including Thomas Taylor's translation of Iamblichus's *On the Mysteries of the Egyptians, Chaldeans, and Assyrians*, which was known to Shelley and therefore a potential source for Byron. (At the very least, Byron knew the legends associated with the pagan philosopher because he introduces Iamblichus as having 'from out their fountain dwellings raised / Eros and Anteros, at Gadara', as Manfred summons the Witch from her rainbow and waterfall.) Olympiodorus, a source given by Iamblichus, places the six demons of Act I in their respective habitats: 'celestial', 'etherial', 'aerial', 'aquatic', 'terrestrial', and 'subterranean'. Marsilio Ficino's *De Daemonibus*, cited by Twitchell as another possible translation available to Byron, would have included a classification of the spirits by yet another source (Michael Psellus): *igneus, aereum, terreneum, aquarium* or *merinum, subterraneaum*, and the *lucifugum*. While it appears to me that these systems have some problems in classifying their imaginary spirits and giving them overlapping spheres of influence, I think Byron's system straightens out some of these ambiguities and makes the distinctions between the demons clearer. James Twitchell, 'The Supernatural Structure of Byron's *Manfred*', *Studies in English Literature* 15:4 (1975), pp. 604, 606.

3 The Seventh Spirit seems to be the sole purposefully malignant influence among these powers; the other six are merely random in their effects, unlike those spirits we meet in the Hall of Arimanes, where malice dominates. Twitchell, 'The Supernatural Structure of Byron's *Manfred*', p. 607.

4 *BLJ*, 5, 170.

5 'The mind is its own place, and in itself / Can make a Heav'n of Hell, a Hell of Heav'n, / What matter where, if I be still the same' (*Paradise Lost*, I, 254–6); 'Myself am Hell' (*Paradise Lost*, IV, 75).

6 'Why, this is hell, nor am I out of it' (*Dr Faustus*, I.ii.80); 'Hell hath no limits, nor is circumscribed / In one self place, for where we are is hell, / And where hell is there must we ever be' (*Dr Faustus*, II.i.121–3).

7 Twitchell places the Witch of the Alps at the level of god in the Neoplatonic cosmos: 'As the ruling principle of material beauty, she controls the purpose of the six daemons' ('The Supernatural Structure of Byron's *Manfred*', p. 609).

8 In this speech Byron again adopts the words and psychology espoused by Milton's Satan.

9 Samuel Claggett Chew, *Dramas of Lord Byron: A Critical Study* (Baltimore, MD: Johns Hopkins University Press, 1970 rpt), p. 83.

The Language of Freedom and the Reality of Power in Byron's *Mazeppa*

GABRIELE POOLE

Byron's 1817 narrative poem *Mazeppa* has a central position in the author's career and a specific bearing on the theme of the present volume: liberty and poetic licence. In this essay I would like to contribute to our discussion by showing how in *Mazeppa* different ideas of freedom interact, ally themselves, and clash also thanks to the dialogism which permeates the poem's narrative structure, characterisation, and imagery.

The Byronic hero, conceived as a variously embodied Weberian type, is traditionally portrayed as an isolated individual at various stages of transition from bitter exile to detached individualist. While this characteristic is constitutive of his psychological stance, it is highly significant that in practice, with the exception of a few interesting borderline cases (Childe Harold, Manfred, Alp), the Byronic hero invariably performs a high-profile social role, as leader of an alternative, anti-institutional if not revolutionary, camp. Notwithstanding the libertarian aura that surrounds him, the Byronic hero invariably exerts absolute control over his men, often coupled with an attitude of emotional detachment and sometimes downright contempt, although his dominion is typically presented as more benign that that of his antagonist, thus ensuring the sympathies of the reader. This tension has been often noted: Bertrand Russell sarcastically observed that the liberty Byron praised 'was that of a German prince or a Cherokee chief, not the inferior type that is presumably allowed to common mortals';[1] and Renée Winegarten wrote that 'while in his poems the outlaws of every creed and race discuss visionary schemes and are distinguished for their fraternity and solidarity among themselves and their enmity to outsiders, the Chief mingles not but to command. He alone has the art of rule that dazzles and chills the vulgar.'[2] Thus, the social role of the hero as leader brings to the fore the tension between the individual freedom of the hero from the constraints of society and convention, and the basic lack of civil or political freedom that characterises the communities he governs.

Another type of freedom that is directly related to the hero's political role is his emotional or psychological freedom. Within the Eastern Tales, the hero's politically domineering attitude is coupled with emotional aloofness. While this is usually presented as a consequence of his individualism, at times Byron describes it as a political tool as well:

> For well had Conrad learned to curb the crowd,
> By arts that veil, and oft preserve the proud.

> > (*The Corsair*, I, 539–54)

Byron's notion of distance as an important element of leadership is well founded.[3] Yet, in Byron's representation, it is not solely a question of the hero not showing his emotions, particularly positive 'social' emotions such as friendship, love, affection. Even *having* these emotions can be a threat to the hero's leadership, as evidenced by the following passage:

> Yet once almost he stopp'd, and nearly gave
> His fate to chance, his projects to the wave;
> But no – it must not be – a worthy chief
> May melt, but not betray to woman's grief.

> > (*The Corsair*, I, 16–19)

In short, the 'distant mien' adopted by Byronic leaders such as Conrad is a mask that can be deliberately used to keep others in a state of psychological subjection, but needs to be internalised in order to allow the hero the possibility of using efficiently and without scruples the power that their subjection gives him. In order to achieve his political objectives, the hero must repress any emotions that might get in the way of those objectives.

This curbing of emotions also affects his sensuality. Disdain for sensual pleasure is a distinctive feature of the Byronic hero:

> But while he shuns the grosser joys of sense,
> His mind seems nourish'd by that abstinence.
> 'Steer to that shore!' – they sail. 'Do this!' – 'tis done!
> 'Now form and follow me!' the spoil is won.

> > (*The Corsair*, I, 75–8)

The passage clearly outlines a link between the repression the 'body' ('joys of sense'), its sublimation ('his mind seems nourish'd), and military success ('the spoil is won').

It is important to note that, while this model might suggest that all emotions are controlled by reason and sublimated towards rational goals, in fact it is only 'social', altruistic emotions that are repressed, while other psychological drives such as ambition, desire for vengeance, and hate are given ample scope. Ultimately it is rationality that is made subservient to these emotions, and used to achieve the goals that these emotions dictate.

Thus, to return to the main point, while the Byronic hero as individual can be described as free in terms of external constraints, in terms of his psychology, he appears to internalise the authoritarian structures of his political world, constraining and repressing certain aspects of his personality in favour of others.

Mazeppa

Elsewhere I have sought to show how, beginning with *Lara*, Byron tried to articulate his reservations about the hero's psychological and political stance by detaching the perspective of the hero from that of the work itself through the adoption of a number of dialogic devices, such as giving more scope to secondary characters, distancing the perspectives of narrator and hero, ironically deflating the heroic rhetoric, making the hero's antagonist a more positive figure, and changing the nature of the hero himself.[4] With regard to this development, works such as *Mazeppa* and *Sardanapalus* are particularly revealing, since they adopt a structure that allows for a dialogic representation of the rhetoric of the Byronic hero, oscillating in complex and sometimes contradictory ways between a critique and an endorsement of the same.

While Byron's ambivalent attitude towards the Byronic hero has been discussed with reference to works such as *The Island*[5] and, especially, *Sardanapalus*,[6] *Mazeppa* has not received the same critical attention. The reading most relevant to the present study is the excellent chapter in Jerome McGann's *Fiery Dust*, in which the author discusses the political and psychological implications of heroism and leadership within the text.

For McGann, Charles XII 'is set off against Mazeppa and his early mentor John Casimir', an opposition used to criticise Charles XII's ambitious militarism and puritanical stance.[7] While I find McGann's overall reading both convincing and insightful, it should be inserted into a larger interpretative framework in order to do justice to the complex and contradictory nature of the poem. More specifically, it is my view that Mazeppa and Casimir cannot simply be set in opposition to Charles XII, since Mazeppa and Casimir themselves differ in significant ways. Also, I want to suggest that the nature of the characters must be considered within a

broader network of discursive tensions, extending beyond characterisation, to the poem's narrative structure, style, and imagery. The result is a
text in which it is impossible in the last analysis to identify a consistent
dominant perspective and to establish a clear hierarchy among the
different attitudes towards the figure of the Byronic hero and the values
that cluster around him. Finally, it is my contention that these tensions
permeate the character of Mazeppa himself, who therefore cannot be
taken to be, as McGann suggests, the bearer of a stable perspective to
which the text as a whole can be anchored.

The Narrative Structure

In *Mazeppa*, Byron adopted the narrative device of the 'story within the
story': the main narrative, recounted by Mazeppa and revolving upon
Mazeppa's youthful affair with a countess and his subsequent punishment,
is set within a larger narrative told by an anonymous narrator, in which
Mazeppa appears as one of the characters, part of the group of officers
who have followed Charles XII in his escape, after the battle of Poltava.

The poem opens with the traditional formula of popular ballads: ''Twas
after dread Pultowa's day' (1), voiced by an anonymous narrator, which
locates the story in time and space. After the defeat suffered at Poltava,
Charles XII, King of Sweden, is on the run, together with a handful of
survivors, all of them noblemen and officers, among whom is his
Ukrainian ally Mazeppa. They takes refuge in a wood where Mazeppa, at
the King's request, takes on the role of narrator, describing an adventure
he had in his youth, when he was a page at the court of King Casimir in
Warsaw. This second story is introduced with another ''twas, when' (128).
Here begins what I term a 'transitional section', in which Mazeppa mediates between the framing narrative and the central one by interrupting his
story with references to the present situation ('I watch'd her like a sentinel
/ May ours this dark night watch as well! [262–3]), as well as direct
addresses to his public and comments on the story itself. This transitional
section coincides, in terms of content, with the description of the love
affair between young Mazeppa and the Countess and their discovery by
the Count. At line 424 ('Away, away, my steed and I') the transitional
section ends, and the central narrative proper begins, describing Mazeppa's
wild ride and his final rescue. Compared to the transitional section, this
part of the story is characterised by a much more discrete narrator,

bordering on the purely diegetic, with the notable exception of one long digression (723–62). At line 841 ('What need of more?') we have another very brief transitional section where the main story is again interlaced with references to the situation in which the story is narrated. Finally, at line 860 ('"Comrades, good night!" the Hetman threw'), we return to the framing narrative and anonymous narrator, with the poem ending shortly thereafter at line 869. The narrative can be schematised as follows:

Frame (Woods) Transition (Affair) Main narrative (Ride) Transition (Revenge) Frame (Woods)

The Framing Narrative

Let us first examine the way the two main characters, Charles XII and Mazeppa, are presented in the framing narrative at the beginning of the poem (lines 1–126).

Charles XII, born in 1682, left Sweden at the age of eighteen to lead his armies in an expansionist policy mostly directed against Denmark, Russia, and Poland. While obtaining a series of impressive results his policy proved strategically unsound and led to the decisive defeat of Poltava in 1709 against the troops of Peter the Great, to the fall of the Swedish empire and eventually to Charles's own death in battle in 1718.

In Byron's source, the *Histoire de Charles XII*, Voltaire, while not unkind to the young King, unfavourably compares him with Peter the Great, who, while fighting off Charles and eventually defeating him, was also able to modernise Russia by importing great numbers of artisans and scientists into his country.

Echoes of Voltaire's criticism are evident in *Mazeppa*: early on, the anonymous narrator distances himself from Charles's militarist policy by referring to his 'ambition' (21) and by comments such as the following:

Are these the laurels and repose
For which the nations strain their strength?

(31–2)

On the other hand, we find nothing like the virulent attack on militarism and military leaders that characterise Cantos 7 and 8 of *Don Juan*. Charles's heroic stature seems to go largely unquestioned, especially on a connotational level. Notwithstanding the havoc and carnage that his largely self-serving ambition has brought about, he remains, like Napoleon, a *mighty* leader. Terms such as 'royal' and 'king' may be viewed as neutral, but this is certainly not the case in 'Kinglike the monarch bore his fall' (40). While the narrator notes that 'thousands fell that flight to aid' (19), he also stresses the ennobling aspects of the event: 'this wreck was true and chival-rous' (47–8). Thus, while Charles's ambition is criticised, it appears to be criticised as tragic hubris, the by-product of the hero's greatness.

To some extent, the framing narrative dramatises the transformation of Charles from a traditional authority figure into one more similar to the Byronic hero (in this resembling the plot of *Lara*), a narrative device that serves to lessen or obscure the hierarchical nature of his relation with his followers. After the defeat of Poltava, Charles appears as the leader of a small band of threatened outcasts:

> A band of chiefs! – alas! how few,
> Since but the fleeting of the day
> Had thinn'd it; but this wreck was true.

> (45–7)

The precariousness of the situation, the fight against overwhelming odds, the natural setting, all these are typical aspects of the Oriental Tales. As in the Tales, the problem of the distribution of power and, therefore, of Charles's responsibility in the disaster, is obscured by the impending presence of an external threat, which creates a strong cause of immediate common concern ('The watch-fires in the distance sparkling – / The beacons of surrounding foes – ' [27–8]). Moreover, the difference in status between leader and follower is diminished by the fact that the group does not include common soldiers but 'a band of chiefs'. This gradual erasure of hierarchical distinctions is also suggested through the representation of horses, through the metonymic chain, horse–men–King:

> Each sate him down, all sad and mute,
> Beside his monarch and his steed,
> For danger levels man and brute,
> And all are fellows in their need.

> (49–52)

Another similarity with the traditional Byronic hero is that he abuses the fact that after the institutional apparatus that supported his dominion has collapsed, Charles's authority appears based purely on hegemony (his Byronic charisma, the admiration and love of his men) and is therefore to some extent *freely* acknowledged by his subjects:

> For thousands fell that flight to aid:
> And not a voice was heard t'upbraid

Ambition in his humbled hour,
When truth had nought to dread from power.

(19–22)

Finally, in terms of his emotional and sensual side, Charles's attitude is marked by the same self-control that characterises Conrad; as in the *The Corsair*, control over the body is associated with political authority:

Kinglike the monarch bore his fall,
And made, in this extreme of ill,
His pangs the vassals of his will;
All silent and subdued were they,
As once the nations round him lay.

(40–4)

On the other hand, one notable difference between Charles and other Byronic heroes lies in the bonhomie that marks Charles's attitude towards his followers, due perhaps also to the fact that they are not common soldiers. Although suffering from his wounds, the King 'smilingly' partakes in his meagre share of food, extols Mazeppa's virtues, and play-fully commands Mazeppa to regale him and the others with the story of Mazeppa's youthful adventure. The agreeableness with which he performs his role of host is in marked contrast to the disdainful gruffness of the heroes of the Tales (although a more forced form of courtesy is occasion-ally attributed to Lara and Conrad).

Notwithstanding this generally positive representation of Charles within the initial section of the poem, some additional criticism is levelled against the King's leadership through an indirect comparison with Mazeppa, con-veyed once again through a metaphorical representation of horses and riders.

For historical as well as intrinsic reasons, the rider/horse relation is an easy analogue for the relation between ruler and subject. In explicit form we find the metaphor in *Don Juan*:

Juan, like a true-born Andalusian
Could back a horse, as despots ride a Russian.

(XIII, 23)

From this perspective, since Charles XII's rule has proved ultimately nefar-ious to his men it is significant that his horses fare no better:

His horse was slain, and Gieta gave
His own – and died the Russian's slave.
This too sinks after many a league
Of well sustain'd, but vain fatigue.

(23–6)

The death of the horses has a specific equivalent in the sacrifice of Gieta, and a more general one in that of the soldiers who die to protect the King's escape. This destructive model of rider/horse relation is in marked contrast to the one exemplified by old Mazeppa and his steed. Mazeppa's equestrian prowess is stressed by Charles himself:

> So fit a pair had never birth,
> Since Alexander's days till now,
> As thy Bucephalus and thou.
>
> (101–4)

More important, however, is the care Mazeppa takes of his horse, which contrasts with the King's inability to protect his men or mounts:

> But first, outspent with this long course,
> The Cossack prince rubb'd down his horse,
> And made for him a leafy bed,
> And smooth'd his fetlocks and his mane,
> And slack'd his girth, and stripp'd his rein,
> And joy'd to see how well he fed;
> For until now he had the dread
> His wearied courser might refuse
> To browse beneath the midnight dews.
>
> (57–65)

The two different images of riding might seem to imply a contrast between an unfeeling (or simply inept) authority and a more benign one, based on respect and care. This seems to be McGann's view, who associates Mazeppa with Casimir, the peaceful and constitutional monarch described in the transitional section of the poem. But the significance of the metaphor is in fact ambiguous. For one thing, old Mazeppa is not a cultivated, peace-loving Casimir but the best warrior of Charles's band (see 97–101), a characterisation confirmed later in the poem, as we shall see. Also, the detailed description of the attentions Mazeppa bestows on his horse is immediately followed by an equally detailed description of the attentions he bestows on his weapons:

> Felt if his arms in order good
> The long day's march had well withstood –
>
> (78–9 and *passim*)

Taken as a whole, the passage clearly suggests that at least one of the reasons Mazeppa takes good care of his horse is that it is an instrument of war whose efficiency needs to be preserved.

Mazeppa's gentleness, too, can also be construed in some ways as a manipulative strategy: his caring attitude brings him love and submission:

> But spirited and docile too;
> Whate'er was to be done, would do.
>
> (68–9)

This submission is what makes the horse an adequate military tool, and again the rider/horse relationship can be read as a metaphor of the leader/soldier relationship. Compare, for example, the anonymous narrator's description of the relation of Mazeppa and his horse, 'That steed from sunset until dawn / His chief would follow like a fawn' (76–7), with Mazeppa's own description of his relation to his soldiers:

> I am – or rather *was* – a prince,
> A chief of thousands, and could lead
> Them on where each would foremost bleed.
>
> (290–2)

The text seems to suggest a positive view of this blind faith in leaders, a view that contrasts the sarcastic attack found in the siege cantos of *Don Juan*:

> But to the tale: – great joy unto the camp!
> To Russian, Tartar, English, French, Cossacque,
> O'er whom Suwarrow shone like a gas lamp,
> Presaging a most luminous attack;
> Or like a wisp along the marsh so damp,
> Which leads beholders on a boggy walk,
> He flitted to and fro a dancing light,
> Which all who saw it follow'd, wrong or right.
>
> (VII, 47)

Thus, while Mazeppa represents an alternative model of leadership to Charles, I would argue that, in this section of the poem, the opposition is not one of militarism versus pacifism. Rather it suggests a contrast between Charles as a young, over-ambitious and possibly inept leader, and Mazeppa as an older, wiser, and more successful one.

To find a more direct attack on militarism and, conversely, an emphasis on political freedom, we have to turn to the following section, where, as we shall see, this attack is associated with the promotion of Mazeppa from character to narrator, with the adoption of a more dialogic narrative structure and ironic tone, and, finally, with a change in the character of Mazeppa himself.

The First Transitional Section

When old Mazeppa starts telling the story of his youthful adventure, he mediates the transition from framing to central narrative with comments on the present situation, as well as direct addresses to his public and other narratorial intrusions. This change in style creates a structural space for the development of an ironic commentary, creating a comic style and atmosphere strongly resembling that of *Don Juan*, which Byron was to begin shortly thereafter.[8]

The very first target of the narrator's irony is heroic militarism. Old Mazeppa's first step is to contrast Charles with an alternative model of leader embodied by Casimir:

> A learned monarch, faith! was he,
> and most unlike your majesty
> He made no wars, and did not gain
> New realms to lose them back again
> And (save debates in Warsaw's diet)
> He reign'd in most unseemly quiet.
>
> (131–6)

Charles XII's expansionistic policy is here downgraded to a frivolous enterprise, a poker game with entire nations as stakes. Casimir's policy is defined as 'unseemly', but the joke is obviously on Charles, suggesting the absurdity of engaging in the horrors of war only to conform to some mistaken sense of decorum. And the more so when such enterprises do not achieve any lasting result. As for political freedom, while there is obviously no celebration of republicanism or democracy, the allusion to debates in the Diet does have the function of contrasting Charles's absolutism with some form of constitutional monarchy, in which the crown's power is balanced by that of the parliament.

Mazeppa's satirical jibes against Charles clearly show his allegiance to Casimir, as McGann notes. Yet, to grasp fully the complexity and ambivalence of the poem, Mazeppa's satirical stance must be contrasted with Mazeppa's own behaviour as represented not only in the framing narrative, as we have already seen, but also later on in the poem. Mazeppa's ambivalent attitude towards leadership seems in many ways related to his narrative function. When promoted to narrator, Mazeppa's personality seems to undergo a sudden change. The hero of the previous section is the reserved, even sullen, general (98), who is reluctant to participate in the conviviality of the troop (111–12), much in the manner of other Byronic heroes. Mazeppa the narrator, on the other hand, is an amiable entertainer, who obviously enjoys his role and artfully lengthens his tale peppering it with digressions, comments, and witticisms. The Mazeppa of the previous section is one of the thousands who did not raise their voice to 'upbraid' the King for his disastrous policy. Here, instead, Mazeppa appears to have made upbraiding his majesty's ambition one of his top priorities.

Mazeppa's comparison between Casimir and Charles continues in the following lines, gradually extending beyond the question of political and civil rights to a form of emotional freedom:

> Not that he had no cares to vex,
> He loved the muses and the sex;
> And sometimes these so froward are,
> They made him wish himself at war;
> But soon his wrath being o'er, he took
> Another mistress, or new book:
> And then he gave prodigious fêtes –

(137–43)

Thus the absence of military ambition is coupled in Casimir with a different psychological attitude, his interest in love and the arts, his preference for Eros over Thanatos. Casimir's relation to time itself seems different. Byronic heroes tend to cherish their resentment, and their mind appears thus absorbed in past wrongs and future vengeance. Casimir prefers to set aside his wrath and focus on the present (a new mistress, a new book). In social terms, Casimir does not exert an absolute authority, imposing discipline and sacrifices, but adopts a more tolerant, though arguably somewhat frivolous, policy, offering his subjects the possibility of partaking to some extent in his hedonistic lifestyle by giving 'prodigious fêtes'.

In his attitude towards 'passion', Mazeppa explicitly aligns himself with Casimir. When speaking of his lost love, he admits his inability to repress this aspect of his personality in contrast with Charles:

> [I] could not o'er myself evince
> the like control.

(293–4)

Mazeppa also stresses once more the link or analogy between a more puritanical stance and hierarchical forms of political power:

> But all men are not born to reign,
> Or o'er their passions, or as you
> Thus o'er themselves and nations too.

(287–9)

In the rest of the transitional section, we find other elements that reinforce the criticism of Charles and that undermine the political and private values of the Byronic hero in general, introducing changes that anticipate *Don Juan*. In terms of character presentation, for example, it is significant that the protagonist of the central narrative, young Mazeppa, is a page, while it is the noble Count who imprisons him who is the villain. This is an inversion of the traditional perspective of the Tales and of the first part of *Mazeppa* itself: the focus shifts from the great leader to one of his subjects, and the sympathies of the readers shift correspondingly. Another significant change, compared to earlier works, is found in the representation of aristocracy. In the Tales, the prerequisite of a noble mind seems always to be noble blood. Here, instead, this questionable equation is brilliantly satirised through the figure of the cuckold Count, who takes deep interest in his ancestors,

> Until by some confusion led,
> Which almost look'd like want of head,
> He thought their merits were his own.
>
> (163–6)

The Main Narrative

The main narrative is largely dedicated to Mazeppa's wild ride and dwells on his altered perceptions as he grows increasingly faint. This part of the poem differs markedly from the preceding transitional section: there are few narratorial intrusions or direct references to political or social issues. However, the contrast between Charles and Mazeppa as leaders can be seen as emerging indirectly, once again through two distinct representations of horses, riders, and riding. While, as we have seen, Charles forces his horses to obey him at the cost of their lives, Mazeppa has no such power over the wild stallion, who is the one who decides the course. Along with underlining the difference in social status between Charles and young Mazeppa, the image also functions as an analogue of the mind/body relation, suggesting the rebellion of the body against the mind. As McGann notes, through this searing experience, Mazeppa learns to accept his emotional side, that which Charles is unable to do: 'Mazeppa struggles to free himself but discovers that every effort only increases the uncontrolled fury of the animal as well as his own agony.'[9]

Conclusion: The Ambivalence of Mazeppa

Up to now, we have seen how the contradictions within Mazeppa the character are juxtaposed with the distinction between framing narrative and
transitional section, and therefore with his transition from character to
narrator. While this is largely true, the picture needs to be further complicated. My main point is that, even within the transitional section,
notwithstanding his satirical debunking of the Byronic hero, old Mazeppa
retains some of the features of this model. This contradiction becomes
evident when Mazeppa deals with his own position in relation to situations
of political or personal conflict. Let us consider again this passage:

> I am – or rather *was* – a prince,
> A chief of thousands, and could lead
> Them on where each would foremost bleed;
> But could not o'er myself evince
> The like control.

> (290–4)

This comment is found in the first transitional section. The first part of the
passage clearly associates Mazeppa with the kind of absolute authority typical
of the Byronic hero, in contrast with Mazeppa's initial association with the
constitutional and peaceful model of leadership, suggested by his earlier
praise of Casimir and critique of Charles. Whereas in his representation of
King Casimir, Mazeppa appeared to equate the acceptance of love and
sensuality with a pacifist and tolerant political stance, in the above passage
he suggests the possibility of disjoining the two aspects ('the like control').
Through this rhetorical move, the previous attack on Charles becomes
largely confined to the private sphere, to his puritanical attitude towards
the body, while, on the public level, the criticism seems largely confined to
his lack of prudence or skill, rather than to his militarism as a whole.[10]

The distance between Mazeppa and the model of pacifist and tolerant
leader embodied by Casimir becomes even more evident towards the close
of the first transitional section, in the passage where Mazeppa describes
the vengeance he reaped against the Count, with the complete destruction
of his castle (and of its inhabitants, one may presume), when he returned
many years later as chief of the Cossacks with

> twice five thousand horse, to thank
> The Count for his uncourteous ride

> (411–12)

Here we are far away from Casimir's short-lived wraths and straight back to the vengeful Byronic hero, with his tendency to treasure wrongs and his egotistic willingness to abuse his public role to achieve his private goals.

The representation of horses performs here, too, a politically symbolic function. While Mazeppa lies on the ground tied to the dying stallion, a band of horses appear. These horses have no riders and are accordingly described in a language that stresses their freedom, their existing in a state of nature which knows no oppression:

> A thousand horse, the wild, the free,
> Like waves that follow o'er the sea.
>
> (677–78)

Yet, significantly, this rhetoric clashes with the military metaphors through which the horses are described: 'a trampling troop' (673), 'one vast squadron' (674), and most notably with the emergence of a leader:

> Headed by one black mighty steed,
> Who seem'd the patriarch of his breed.
>
> (702–3)

The analogy with the Tales is evident. In both representations, we have an emphasis on the freedom of the 'outlaws' living in a state of nature. On the other hand, the alternative community is organised along military and hier- archical lines and subject to the dominion of a charismatic leader, so that the 'freedom' of individuals exists only on a symbolic level, through their identification with their leader and the community as a whole.

In his reading of the poem, McGann argues that it is through his adven- ture that Mazeppa learns the 'wise passivity of the sons of pleasure'.[11] In contrast with this passivity, Charles's control is described as a 'pathetic illu- sion', (179), resulting in destructive ambition.[12] While this interpretation is certainly convincing in many ways, especially in relation to Charles, I think it is important to stress that the moral that Mazeppa draws from his expe- rience is quite different:

> For time at last sets all things even –
> And if we do but watch the hour,
> There never yet was human power
> Which could evade, if unforgiven,
> The patient search and vigil long
> Of him who treasures up a wrong.
>
> (492–7)

Here, Mazeppa seems less interested in the survivors' possibility of escaping a cycle of violence and retaliation than in their chance of getting even with his enemies. 'Do not despair, death goes on' seems to be surprisingly his final moral. In the light of this, even the metaphorical significance of Mazeppa's ride becomes ambivalent. Does Mazeppa really learn to accept his emotional and sensual side, as McGann argues, or does he simply learn to control and manipulate it like he controls and manipulates his men, governing both with the same dexterity with which he rides his 'Bucephalus', that which Charles never learnt to do?

McGann notices the contradiction implicit in Mazeppa's vengeful attitude and makes sense of it by arguing that: 'Byron does not judge him harshly for this, however, for he seems to do it with a calmness and certainty of mind that are quite unlike the fiery converts of revenge in Byron's other stories.'[13] 'Calmness and certainty of mind', however, can also be seen as a traditional feature of the Byronic hero's 'distant mien'. More generally, while it is true that Byron does not judge Mazeppa's attitude 'harshly', this can be interpreted as a sign of the author's ambivalence. In the end the contradiction cannot be explained away, but must be accepted as a distinctive feature of the poem as a whole.

In conclusion, I wish to stress how *Mazeppa* offers us an extraordinary example of Byron's ambivalence towards freedom. At times, Byron seems fascinated with the independence of the exceptional individual from external constraints as a result of the force of his personality: such a hero can charismatically manipulate his followers and his own sensuality and feelings in favour of his goals. At other times, Byron favours different kinds of freedom, including a psychological freedom created by the acceptance of love and sensuality and the rejection of other more destructive drives and a political freedom associated, albeit often in vague terms, with more democratic forms of society.

Once we fully grasp this complexity, it becomes evident that we must renounce the ambition of providing a unitary interpretation of the poem. *Mazeppa* should be seen, instead, as a complex and even contradictory work, where stylistic and structural features intertwine with psychological and political tensions, creating a narrative in which one can easily become side-tracked, distracted by multiple images of the hero riding in opposite directions.

Notes

1   Bertrand Russell, *History of Western Philosophy and its Connections with Political and Social Circumstances from the Earliest Times to the Present Day* (London: Unwin, 1949; 1979): p. 718,

2   Renée Winegarten, *Writers and Revolution: The Fatal Lure of Action* (New York: New Viewpoints, 1974), p. 89.

3   'The discipline of armies and navies … very distinctly recognizes the necessity of those forms which separate superior from inferior, and so help to establish an unscrutinized ascendancy in the former.' Charles Horton Cooley, *Human Nature and Social Order* (New York: Scribner's, 1922), p. 352–3. Compare also the following passage from *Childe Harold*: 'White is the glassy deck, without a stain, / Where on the watch the staid Lieutenant walks: / Look on that part which sacred doth remain / For the lone chieftain, who majestic stalks, / Silent and fear'd by all – not oft he talks / With aught beneath him, if he would preserve / That strict restraint, which broken, ever balks / Conquest and Fame' (2, 19).

4   Gabriele Poole, 'Byron's Heroes and the Byronic Hero', Dissertation, University of Notre Dame, 1998, Ann Arbor: UMI, 1998. 9835541.

5   See James McKusick, 'The Politics of Language in Byron's *The Island*', *English Literary History* 59 (1992), pp. 539–56.

6   See Poole, 'Byron's Heroes and the Byronic Hero', ch. 5.

7   Jerome J. McGann, *Fiery Dust: Byron's Poetic Development* (Chicago, IL: University of Chicago Press, 1968), p. 178.

8   Aside from the counterpoint of diegesis and narratorial intrusion, similarities between *Mazeppa* and the first canto of *Don Juan* can also be found in the content: the description of the affair between young Mazeppa and Therese anticipates the one between Juan and Julia and the *effictio* of Therese, too, closely parallels that of Julia.

9   McGann, *Fiery Dust*, p. 180.

10 This rhetorical strategy closely resembles the one adopted by Byron in his 1818 drama *Sardanapalus*, where Sardanapalus's attack on Salemenes's combination of militarism and puritanical values is gradually deflated as Sardanapalus takes on his role of military commander. As Richard Lansdown notes, 'since Sardanapalus' arousal, there is little to tell between him and his military henchman Salemenes himself'. Richard Lansdown, 'Fantasy Elements in Byron's *Sardanapalus*', *Keats and Shelley Journal* 40 (1991), pp. 47–72, p. 66.

11 McGann, *Fiery Dust*, p. 118.

12 McGann, *Fiery Dust*, p. 179.

13 McGann, *Fiery Dust*, p. 178.

Marino Faliero: Escaping the Aristocratic

ALAN RAWES

My aim in this chapter is twofold. Firstly, I want to throw some light on a largely overlooked thematic concern of *Marino Faliero* and suggest that this is, in fact, a central issue at stake in the play. Secondly, I hope to demonstrate that this issue is one that bubbles under the surface, and informs the progress, of a host of Byron's poems ranging from *Childe Harold* I and II right through to *The Island* and *Don Juan*. It is my contention that *Marino Faliero* throws into sharp relief something that interested Byron throughout his adult life.

What I am focusing on in *Marino Faliero* is its interest in the powerful influence of aristocratic modes of thinking and being. This is not quite what Byron originally claimed was his principal interest in the historical figure of Marino Faliero. When Byron first mentioned Faliero to John Murray in a letter of 1817, he stressed Faliero's pseudo-monarchical position and his unusual occupancy of that position, rather than Faliero's aristocratic background:

> I mean to write a tragedy upon the subject [of Marino Faliero] which appears to me very dramatic – an old man – jealous – and conspiring against the state of which he is the actual reigning Chief – the last circumstance makes it the most remarkable – & only fact of the kind in all history of all nations.[1]

Nevertheless, by the time Byron sat down to write the tragedy his interest in Marino Faliero's history had shifted away from the fact that it shows a 'reigning Chief' 'conspiring against the state' over which he reigns. What became 'the most remarkable … fact' about Faliero's history for Byron – working back from what is most remarked on about Faliero in the play itself – was that he was an aristocrat who turned against his class: Faliero's aristocratic background is insisted upon again and again, as is a sense, on Faliero's part, of being about to betray that background.[2] What the play dramatises, in other words, is not the conspiracy of a monarch against the state so much as the conspiracy of an aristocrat 'whose treason involves betraying his own patrician class'.[3]

Byron's interest in this 'most remarkable ... fact' centres on the possibility that, in betraying the aristocracy to which he belonged, Faliero managed to break free of aristocratic ideals and values. Certainly, many such ideals and values stand in his way:

All these men were my friends: I loved them, they
Requited honourably my regards;
We served and fought; we smiled and wept in concert;
We revell'd or we sorrow'd side by side;
We made alliances of blood and marriage;
We grew in years and honours fairly.

(III, ii, 319–24)

You never broke their bread, nor shared their salt;
You never had their wine-cup at your lips.

(III, ii, 459–60)

In order to do what he is contemplating doing to the patricians, Faliero must not only break free of the bonds of friendship and the obligations imposed by the receipt of hospitality, by the sharing of salt. He must also break free of a value system, an aristocratic social mindset built on honour, fellowship-in-arms and 'alliances of blood and marriage'. He must betray these values and in doing so become 'ignoble'.

To some extent Faliero does break free of aristocratic values and ideals – he is ultimately willing to betray the values he outlines here. And the play speculatively dramatises some of the mental processes Faliero might have gone through in order to achieve that freedom. But it also questions the extent of Faliero's freedom from aristocratic modes of thought and action, and dramatises the continuing hold of other aristocratic ideas, assumptions, and ways of thinking on him.

In the first instance, it shows Faliero making his 'revenge a virtue by reflection' (IV, ii, 103) and reaching for an aristocratic justification for his actions. Byron anachronistically has Faliero project himself as a Whig – a noble acting nobly on behalf of the oppressed population and in the cause of 'Liberty': 'You oppress'd the prince and people; / I would have freed both' (V, i, 246–7) he tells the patricians, articulating an orthodox Whig concern for a tripartite constitutional balance between monarch, aristocracy, and the 'Third Estate', as well as an aristocratic assumption of the right to lead the struggle to maintain such a balance. Byron, in other words, projects the influence of an eighteenth-century English aristocratic mode of thought on to his fourteenth-century hero, and thereby dramatises Faliero remaining enmeshed in aristocratic ways of thinking. Faliero justifies his actions, to himself as well as others, by insisting that his revolt is an aristocratic revolt against corruption and tyranny, led by a patrician and based on patrician values, seeking only to expel corruption and restore the constitution to a state of perfect balance.

In the second instance, the play foregrounds Faliero's inability to drop his own aristocratic assumptions about the lower classes and his own superiority to them:

> DOGE: Am I one of you?
> CALENDARO: Ay, and the first amongst us, as thou hast been
> Of Venice – be our general and our chief.
> DOGE: Chief! – General! – I was general at Zara,
> And chief in Rhodes and Cyprus, prince in Venice;
> I cannot stoop – that is, I am not fit
> To lead a band of – patriots: when I lay
> Aside the dignities which I have borne,
> 'Tis not to put on others, but to be
> Mate to my fellows – but now to the point:
> Israel has stated to me your whole plan –
> 'Tis bold, but feasible if I assist it,
> And must be set in motion instantly.

(III, ii, 215–26)

There is much in Faliero's opening question here that undermines what appears to be a desire to join the rebels on equal terms. His use of 'stoop' and the suggestive dash after 'a band of' are obviously telling: they articulate what M. K. Joseph calls Faliero's 'aristocratic contempt for the mob',[4] his revulsion at what he instinctively sees as their 'ignoble' campaign and his self-loathing at what to him is a damning betrayal of his own 'patriotic' and 'noble' achievements at Zara, Rhodes, and Cyprus. But Faliero's careless and clumsy attempts to cover up these blunders are equally revealing: they show contempt for those he addresses. And though the half-hearted diplomatic gesturing continues – he claims to want to be 'Mate to my fellows' – his sense of superiority immediately overwhelms that diplomacy. With his very next breath he takes charge, inserts himself into their plans as indispensable, and begins handing out orders: their plan 'must be set in motion instantly'.

Marino Faliero, then, dramatises an aristocrat partly breaking free of, but largely remaining trapped in, aristocratic modes of thought and action. There are a number of ways of reading this fact. Byron, we might argue, is moving towards a radicalism that has no place for aristocrats. Less stridently, we might suggest that Faliero offers an exploration of 'the necessity of recognizing and overcoming ideological assumptions and class barriers to bring about social change'.[5]

For Malcolm Kelsall, these possibilities would seem unlikely. Certainly, in *Byron's Politics*, he powerfully argues that Byron's own political assumptions and commitments were fundamentally aristocratic and Whig, and remained so for the duration of his life.[6] But Byron came to maturity at the end of the Whig tradition – at the end of that period of the eighteenth century when the aristocratic ideals of the Whigs held sway over the British political system, and at a time when the final demise of those ideals seemed increasingly inevitable. The aristocratic assumptions and values of the Whig tradition were giving ground to radicalism on the one hand, and losing ground to a resurgent but increasingly bourgeois conservatism on the other.[7]

Byron, as an aristocrat and a Whig, was interested in the obsolescence of these aristocratic values. Indeed, he was interested in the aristocratic and its influence more generally, and this interest most often manifests itself in his poetry in one of two ways: in individuals who find themselves caught up in, or in danger of being caught up in, a usually decadent, often moribund, aristocratic way of life; in noble heroes driven, usually by noble motives or ideals, towards a tragic end. And a key question informs Byron's development of these figures: how strong is the influence of aristocratic modes of thinking and being, and is it possible to escape that influence altogether?

Let me offer some examples of the ways in which Byron returns to this question again and again. Let's begin with an early poem, *Childe Harold* I and II. Harold is a very different kind of aristocrat from Faliero, but, in a different way and for different reasons, he too is driven to try and shake off his aristocratic conditioning. However, in the 'Addition to the Preface' to these two cantos, Byron tells us that the moral of the first instalment of *Childe Harold* is 'that early perversion of mind and morals leads to satiety of past pleasures and disappointment in new ones, and that even the beauties of nature, and the stimulus of travel ... are lost on a soul so constituted, or rather misdirected' (*Childe Harold's Pilgrimage* [henceforward *CHP*] I and II, Addition to the Preface, 88–92). Clearly, *Childe Harold* I and II are not concerned with escaping aristocratic ideals and values. But they are concerned with the equally tenacious influence of another form of aristocratic conditioning: they depict an aristocrat's attempt to escape the 'fulness' of his 'satiety' (*CHP* I, 4) with the debauchery of his decadent aristocratic existence. And they insist that the influence of such a conditioning is absolute and that escape is thus impossible. A 'soul', once 'misdirected' by that mode of being, is trapped in that misdirection: 'the early perversion of mind and morals' is permanent, and the satiety generated by the aristocratic world inhabited and once enjoyed by Harold is inescapable. As a result, *Childe Harold* II tells us, Harold simply 'saw' (*CHP* II, 55), 'pass'd' (*CHP* II, 56), 'saw' (*CHP* II, 66), 'did address / Himself to quit' (*CHP* II, 69), 'was ... a welcome guest' (*CHP* II, 70), 'stood / And view'd' (*CHP* II, 72). Indeed, after stanza 29 of Canto I, Harold shows very little interest in anything. He remains locked in his aristocratic satiety.

The more we focus on Byron's interest in the power of the aristocratic, the more frequently we encounter figures that seem to insist on the all-consuming influence of aristocratic modes of thinking and being. Take, for example, Christian Fletcher in *The Island*, on whom aristocratic ideals exert a fatal influence. In Christian we see a figure, 'of an higher order' (*The Island* III, 139) than his fellow mutineers, for whom the influence of notions of 'noble conduct' results in death:

> 'Yes,' he exclaimed, 'we are taken in the toil,
> But not a coward or a common spoil;
> Dearly they have bought us – dearly still may buy, –
> And I must fall; but have *you* strength to fly?
> 'Twould be a comfort still, could you survive;
> Our dwindling band is now too few to strive.
> Oh! for a sole canoe! though but a shell,
> To bear you hence to where a hope may dwell!
> For me, my lot is what I sought; to be,
> In life or death, the fearless and the free.'

(III, 155–64)

Christian assumes the role of patriarchal leader and the responsibilities that go with it: he, as leader, is responsible for his followers and honour-bound to suffer whatever punishment they incur under his leadership. Noble to the end, he stands rigidly by these obligations. Not only 'must' he 'fall', he must also continue to worry about the welfare of those in his care, and, accordingly, we see him still hoping for a chance for at least one of his followers to escape the fate of the rest.

His sense of superiority, akin to that of Marino Faliero – a sense of his own 'uncommon' nobility – is most pointedly heard in the assumption that his own values are not shared by the likes of Torquil. 'Have *you* strength to fly?', he asks, but takes it for granted that Torquil is prepared to do so. He, of course, is not, and his death is thus to a large extent self-imposed, or, rather, imposed by the values he insists upon – honour, courage, obligation, and self-sacrifice. The prisoner of a 'noble' code, his nobility proves to be his tragic flaw. The last Byronic hero, is, it would seem, doomed to death by his own ideology.

But, for Byron, the absolute power of aristocratic influences is by no means universal. Escape from them is certainly possible, for some. *The Island* offers an example of this in the figure of Torquil. 'Unlike the aristocratic heroes of … other tales', Torquil 'is a low-born Hebridean', but 'nevertheless has all the *potential* to fill a conventional heroic' and, I would suggest, an aristocratic 'role'.[8] He certainly seems influenced by a code of conduct that is very similar to Christian's:

> We'll make no running fight, for that were base;
> We will die at our quarters, like true men.
> …
> But whatsoe'er betide, ah, Neuha! now
> Unman me not.
>
> (II, 517–29)

Like Christian, Torquil is determined to act 'honourably' – is willing to sacrifice his life rather than act in a 'base' way. Indeed, here we may well be seeing the direct influence of Christian, and we might say that Torquil is here inspired by, and aspiring to, the heroic nobility he sees in his leader. But such aspirations could prove fatal: 'We will die at our quarters' he insists, pushing to one side, for now, the single influence able to save him – Neuha. Torquil is not Christian, however, and does not cleave to his principles to the bitter end:

> There was no time to pause – the foes were near –
> Chains in his eye and menace in his ear;
> With vigour they pulled on, and as they came,
> Hailed him to yield, and by his forfeit name.
> Headlong he leapt – .
>
> (*The Island* IV, 61–5)

Torquil achieves what Christian cannot – his 'headlong' leap is a leap out of one set of ideological commitments and into another. Suddenly, Torquil is prepared to make a 'running fight', to act in what he previously called a 'base' way. No longer concerned with being a 'true man', he can now put his faith entirely in the feminine, and abandon rather than die at his quarter.

This shift, from an insistence on one kind of masculinity to an absolute faith in, and total capitulation to, a female is a complete shift – the impulsiveness of his leap demonstrates Torquil's absolute severance from the ideals that pushed Neuha to one side as a dangerous distraction, and his complete commitment, now, to Neuha as his only possible salvation. Indeed, we might say that it is not simply Neuha that saves Torquil, but his own final willingness – and ability – to break free from a dangerous code of conduct.

So, alongside Christian, doom'd to death by the unshakeable influence of a code of 'noble conduct', we have Torquil, drawn to the kind of heroic nobility displayed by Christian, but saved from death precisely by his ability to break free from the influence of this kind of idealism. In *The Island*, in other words, Byron does not insist on the inescapable power of aristocratic modes of thought. Rather, he seems equally interested in the idea that freedom from that power is possible. Thus, he offers a hero who, though brought into contact with aristocratic modes of thought and action in the figure of Christian, can detach himself entirely from the example Christian offers.

Other poems also demonstrate Byron's interest in figures that win complete freedom from aristocratic influences. Take, for example, *Beppo*. Beppo, like Torquil, is not an aristocrat. He is a 'merchant' who 'sailed upon the Adriatic, / And made some voyages, too, in other seas' (*Beppo*, 25). But he has been brought into direct contact with the aristocratic – indeed, he clearly has one foot in the aristocratic Venetian world inhabited by his wife, Laura, and her subsequent lover, 'the Count' (*Beppo*, 98). But Beppo is another, non-aristocratic character that, though touched by the aristocratic, can escape its influence. We see this in the narrator's brief account of Beppo's latest adventures:

> was cast away
> About where Troy stood once, and nothing stands;
>   Became a slave of course, and for his pay
> Had bread and bastinadoes, till some bands
>   Of pirates landing in a neighbouring bay,
> He joined the rogues and prospered, and became
> A renegado of indifferent fame.
>
> But he grew rich, and with his riches grew so
>   Keen the desire to see his home again,
> He thought himself in duty bound to do so.

(*Beppo*, 94–5)

Beppo is forcibly detached from the aristocratic Venetian world. But his response to this 'change of scene' (*Childe Harold* I, 6) is very different from Harold's response to his. There is no sense here that Beppo responds with anything like Harold's weary resignation born of boredom and satiety: he extends his adventures and prospers. Indeed, there is no suggestion that Beppo shows any aristocratic characteristics at all. He not only seems free of the aristocratic satiety that hounds Harold, but also, for example, free of the pleasure-seeking triviality that marks Laura and the Count: he does not seem in the least bit interested in seeking out the kind of pleasures and entertainments they do – what he seems to want is adventure. And he shows no notions of, or aspirations to, superiority in any of the adventures he finds: we do not, for instance, see him assuming, or aspiring to, the kind of leadership role naturally assumed by Faliero or Christian; as a 'pirate' his fame is 'indifferent' and he is no Byronic corsair, leader, or pioneer. Nothing marks him out as different from any other 'renegado', then, and it seems that, free entirely from the influence of the aristocratic world of Venice, he has settled into being simply another 'rogue' among 'rogues'.

Of course, Beppo eventually returns to Venice, and we might suggest that the aristocratic world he seems to have left behind does, in the end, exert an influence on him – though Beppo returns home for a number of reasons: 'to reclaim / His wife, religion, house, and Christian name' (*Beppo*, 97), for example. Whatever his motives for returning, however, they only produce the desire to do after 'several years' (*Beppo*, 27). In the meantime, Beppo displays no evidence of the influence of aristocratic Venice and seems to have escaped that influence entirely.

For Byron, however, other aristocratic worlds were able to exert a much more powerful influence than the aristocratic world of Venice. *Don Juan* makes this very clear. For the influence of the aristocratic English Whig world is, initially, a great deal stronger on Juan than the influence of aristocratic Venice is on Beppo. Indeed, the final cantos of *Don Juan* are clearly interested in the powerful influence of the aristocratic English Whig tradition on the world around it generally. And, according to Kelsall, these cantos, in which Juan is subjected to the charms of the English Whig world, are an attempt to celebrate that world, its continued existence and value and the continuing force for good its influence might be.

Juan's adventures in Europe, Kelsall argues, demonstrate that 'Lord Henry and Norman Abbey represent the best that is on offer' to him, politically and socially.[9] Thus, despite Byron's recognition of Lord Henry's many shortcomings, this figure – who represents 'the Whig revolution in practice' – is nevertheless offered as '"the very model" of an officer of state'.[10] In 'Lord Henry and Norman Abbey', Kelsall insists, 'if anywhere in *Don Juan*, one perceives a social ideal implied beneath the comic surface of the satire'.[11] And, for Kelsall, Byron's aim in these cantos is to celebrate the survival of this ideal; to celebrate the still valuable existence of the Whig world, which had 'survived', at the time of Juan's visit, 'twenty-five years of tumult unreformed'.[12]

Kelsall offers a strong reading of these cantos. But he does not give Lady Adeline the centrality the poem does and it is difficult to align her with Kelsall's reading. She suffers a 'model ... but cold' marriage to Lord Henry (*Don Juan* XIV, 86), and, as a result, has become emotionally 'vacant' (XIV, 85). She is further detached from her own impulses – 'She knew not her own heart' (XIV, 91) – by long habituation to her 'grand role' (XVI, 96) as Lady Amundeville, and is so good at that role – indeed, at acting 'all and every part' required by that role 'By turns' (XVI, 97) – that Juan begins to wonder 'how much of Adeline' is '*real*' (XVI, 96). And in her public role she presides over, and holds together, an aristocratic world of 'sameness', 'dull and family likeness', 'varnish', the 'common-place', 'wit without much salt', 'smooth monotony / Of character', and '*Ennui*' (XIV, 15–17). If, as Kelsall suggests, Lord Henry represents the Whig political ideal in action, Lady Adeline highlights, in her own person and as a hostess, a world of vacuous, tedious, spirit-numbing activity surrounding and supporting that ideal. Taken together, then, Lord and Lady Amundeville do not offer a very rosy picture of the aristocratic Whig world they represent.

However, they do suggest that this world is capable of appearing extremely attractive and, therefore, of exerting various kinds of powerful influence. Certainly, Lady Adeline, 'beauteous', 'the glass of all that's fair' (XIII, 2, 13), virtuous (XIII, 14), 'chaste' (XIV, 97), and the model hostess, is able to make the moribund world she presides over appear attractive enough to draw others in. This is why she is the 'fair most fatal Juan ever met' (XIII, 12).

Cantos XIII and XIV even hint at the possibility of a liaison between Juan and Adeline.[13] Juan is clearly in some danger here. But the Amundevilles do not form the only centre around which the final cantos of *Don Juan* are built: 'Juan himself appears to acknowledge a different centre' in the figure of Aurora Raby.[14] And Aurora, too, serves a representative function. Like most of the other party guests, she is a 'noble' (XV, 44), but, in the case of this particular 'noble' world, she

> gazed upon a world she scarcely knew
> As seeking not to know it.
>
> (XV, 47)

She is, and remains, an outsider, detached and belonging elsewhere.

This elsewhere is not some other aristocratic world. She is of 'the best class' (XV, 43), but I can't agree with Caroline Franklin that her 'significance is social'.[15] She is also 'better than her class' (XV, 43) and her superiority is clearly and directly related to her Catholicism and her 'sincere, austere' adherence to this 'old faith' (XV, 46). Indeed, she represents one kind of spiritual retreat from the social: her

> spirit seem'd as seated on a throne
> Apart from the surrounding world, and strong
> In its own strength.

(XV, 47)

Clearly, this kind of spirituality is completely immune to the influence of the aristocratic world that surrounds Aurora at Norman Abbey. And by stressing her immunity to it, Byron uses Aurora to point to one of the limits of that world and its influence. For she points to the survival, in England, of an older mode of thinking and being that the Whig tradition may well have obscured but which it has never entirely overwhelmed. Equally, we might tentatively suggest, she is one of the ways in which the poem dramatises the declining power of the world represented by the Amundevilles at the end of the eighteenth century:[16] she helps to dramatise the declining vitality and influence of the Whig tradition by showing another, older, mode of thinking and being re-emerging and once again beginning to exert its own influence.

'The reader is certainly asked to compare Adeline and Aurora',[17] to compare the power they exert over Juan as a visitor to one of the strongholds of Whiggism, and thereby to draw conclusions about England – and particularly about the state of Whiggism there – at the end of the eighteenth century. And both women exert considerable power over Juan: while Cantos XIII and XIV hint at a likely liaison between Juan and Adeline, Canto XV shows Aurora drawing Juan's attention: he sees her as a possible bride because she is, like him, a Catholic (XV, 50); she is 'radiant' (XV, 45) and he is drawn into paying her 'some attentions' (XV, 80) by her 'indifference' (XV, 77) to him. We watch, in other words, as Juan moves between these two women, drawn to both, and between the very different worlds they embody – between, in the very broadest terms, a moribund, but potentially dangerous, aristocratic world and a 'strong', 'serene' (XV, 47) religious one.

And there is a progression in that movement. The dangerous, indeed potentially 'fatal', attractions of Adeline are suggested first, but then this suggestion is overwhelmed by Juan's increasing attraction to Aurora. The beginning of this progression is neatly dramatised at the dinner table, when Juan is by 'some odd chance … placed between / Aurora and Lady Adeline' (XV, 75) but pays considerably more attention to Aurora while Adeline seems simply to watch the relationship develop. The pull of Adeline and the world she represents is clearly waning here, while the pull of Aurora is increasing. Juan 'hovers', we might say, 'Between two worlds' (XV, 99), a hazardous aristocratic one and a potentially redeeming religious one, but is clearly being drawn progressively closer to the latter in the figure of Aurora.[18]

All this clearly suggests that, despite the strong initial influence that the aristocratic Whig world of late eighteenth-century England exerts over Juan, he was going to escape that influence under the even stronger one of the Catholic Aurora. It also suggests that the final cantos of *Don Juan* are not concerned with celebrating the survival of a political and social 'ideal' so much as dramatising the declining vitality and decreasing influence of that ideal and the world to which it has given birth. But we need to be cautious here because *Don Juan* is, of course, unfinished. We do not see how the relationship between Juan and Aurora was going to develop. Indeed, if Aurora was going to pull Juan away from the influence of the aristocratic world of Lady Adeline, she has not done so by the end of what we have of Canto XVII. Instead, at the beginning of Canto XVII, we see Juan and Lady Fitz-Fulke coming down to breakfast manifesting all the signs of a night of passion, and it seems that the pull of Aurora and what she represents is brief and finally overwhelmed by the seductive charms of a second female representative of the aristocratic world of Norman Abbey. If something other than the aristocratic is glimpsed in Aurora, able to over-whelm its influence, it would seem that the glimpse is brief and chimerical. But Aurora's presence is not so easy to dismiss from the poem. As 'an orphan' (XV, 44) she is brought back into view in the discussions of orphans that opens Canto XVII, and her evocation here, at the opening of a new canto, strongly suggests that she was to play some central part in forthcoming events. Of course, any guess as to that role is only a guess, but her continuing presence, and the implicit hint at her immanent centrality at the beginning of Canto XVII, do not, on the face of it, suggest that Byron intended to go on to dramatise the tenacious influence of the aristocratic English world on Juan. They suggest, rather, a continuing interest in the idea that, in the case of Juan, this other, very different, mode of thinking and being would prove strong enough to fight off the still powerful, but waning, influence of that aristocratic world.

The final cantos of *Don Juan* are concerned with a particular moment in British history, and with the influence of a particular aristocratic ideology and the lifestyle it has generated. But it is not the first of Byron's poems to show an interest in the idea that a religious mindset might prove strong enough to overwhelm powerful aristocratic influences. Indeed, Byron opens this possibility up to Marino Faliero when, even after the patricians have Faliero totally in their power, we see him suddenly articulate a way of thinking strikingly different from that of his fellow aristocrats:

DOGE: I speak to Time and to Eternity,
Of which I grow a portion, not to man.
Ye elements! in which to be resolved
I hasten, let my voice be as a spirit
Upon you! Ye blue waves! which bore my banner,
Ye winds! which flutter'd o'er as if you loved it,
And fill'd my swelling sails as they were wafted
To many a triumph! Thou, my native earth,
Which I have bled for, and thou foreign earth,
Which drank this willing blood from many a wound!
Ye stones, in which my gore will not sink, but
Reek up to Heaven! Ye skies, which will receive it!
Thou sun! which shinest on these things, and Thou!
Who kindlest and who quenchest suns! Attest!
I am not innocent – but are these guiltless?
I perish, but not unavenged; far ages
Float up from the abyss of time to be,
And show these eyes, before they close, the doom
Of this proud city, and I leave my curse
On her and hers for ever!

(V, iii, 26–45)

For A. B. England, this speech 'seems clearly to represent a further and vigorous attempt by Faliero's mind to find ways of transcending the imme-diate actualities of political defeat and death'.[19] I suggest that it also shows Faliero trying to take refuge from the aristocratic values that damn him – in his own eyes as well as in those of his fellow patricians. And the only refuge available to him is another set of values, another mindset, that damns the aristocrats for the very values they hold dear. I am not sure that we can go so far as to say that Faliero finds this set of values, but he does go some way towards doing so: he is at least able to believe that such a set of values exists, that there are cosmic forces that stand for them, and that these cosmic forces are able to sit in judgement on aristocratic values and impose their judgement.

We might want to dismiss this as little more than a delusion, but, as England points out, 'it does seem clear that Byron is not seeking to reduce' Faliero's speech 'to an absurd gesture. For example, he underpins the prophecy [of future ills that follows the extract above] with a series of foot-notes that draw attention to the accuracy of even the most outlandish of his [Faliero's] forecasts'.[20] In other words, Byron encourages us to take seriously Faliero's new-found, pseudo-pagan beliefs – and particularly his belief in an ultimate authority, and a moral law, beyond the aristocratic laws that destroy him. We should, of course, be wary of suggesting that this leap of faith frees him completely from the influence of aristocratic modes of thought: the desire for vengeance certainly suggests some remnant of an aristocratic mindset. And, of course, he is not free from aristocratic power since the patricians kill him. But before he dies, he achieves a leap of faith that goes a long way towards mentally freeing him from the ideological absolutes that underpin his execution.

Such a reading of Faliero's final speech suggests that it is not enough simply to say that '*Marino Faliero* both represents and enacts Byron's ambivalence about his own social status'.[21] The speech articulates much more than ambivalence. In the first instance, it dramatises the enormous difficulties, for someone of that status, of escaping the influence of those modes of thinking and being that, for Byron, go along with it – while refusing, nevertheless, simply to give in to those difficulties. In the second instance, the speech links Byron's interest in the possibility of escaping the powerful influence of the aristocratic with what a number of commenta-tors have seen as a profoundly religious impulse in Byron's work – especially in his late work.[22] Faliero may lose his life, but he achieves considerable mental freedom from the aristocratic values that damn him in a new and consoling belief in powers belonging to 'Time' and 'Eternity'. In a parallel way, Don Juan is offered, and begins to move towards, an alter-native to Lady Adeline's aristocratic world in Aurora's Catholicism. In both poems, in other words, we see one of the key ways in which Byron's poetry looks to win some degree of freedom from the influence of aristo-cratic modes of thinking and being: not by inhabiting some form of political radicalism, or by occupying a cynically ironic perspective, but by achieving 'a narrow escape into faith'.[23]

Notes

1   Letter to John Murray of 25 February 1817, in *BLJ*, 5, 174.

2   See, for example: I, ii, 424; I, ii, 579–86; II, i, 83; II, i, 98–102; III, i, 22–47; III, ii, 200–2; III, ii, 319–24; III, ii, 458–71; IV, ii, 4–7; IV, ii, 20–9.

3   Nigel Leask, *British Romanticism and the East: Anxieties of Empire* (Cambridge: Cambridge University Press, 1992), p. 56.

4   M. K. Joseph, *Byron the Poet* (London: Gollancz, 1964), p. 113.

5   Daniel P. Watkins, 'The Dramas of Lord Byron: *Manfred* and *Marino Faliero*', in *Byron*, ed. by Jane Stabler (London and New York: Longman, 1998), pp. 52–65, p. 63.

6   Byron, argues Kelsall, not only 'found temporary home within the party of the Glorious Revolution' in 1812, but also 'until his death … maintained his loyalty to its traditions'. Malcolm Kelsall, *Byron's Politics* (Sussex: Harvester Press, 1987), p. 7.

7   The decline of the Whigs can be traced back to the end of Tory exclusion in 1760. Their progressive loss of cohesion, authority, and credibility is marked out by such events as: the party's ineffective opposition to the Tories after the Gordon Riots of 1780; the defeat of the Fox–North alliance in 1783 and the rise to power of Pitt; the failure of the India Bills in 1783–1784; the party's fragmentation in the face of the French Revolution and the Portland–Fox split of 1794; the secession of the Foxites from both houses of Parliament in 1797; Fox's death in 1806; the failure of the 'Ministry of All the Talents' in 1807; the Prince Regent's abandonment of the Whigs in 1812. For useful discussions of this period in British political history see: Kelsall, *Byron's Politics*, pp. 1–33; Linda Colley, *Britons: Forging the Nation* (New Haven, CT, and London: Yale University Press, 1992), pp. 237–364; J. Steven Watson, *The Reign of George III: 1760–1815* (Oxford: Clarendon Press, 1960); L. G. Mitchell, *Charles James Fox and the Disintegration of the Whig Party 1782–1794* (Oxford: Oxford University Press, 1971); F. O'Gorman, *The Whig Party and the French Revolution* (London: Macmillan, 1967).

8   Leask, *British Romanticism and the East*, p. 66.

9   Kelsall, *Byron's Politics*, p. 179. Kelsall argues that 'on his Odyssean Grand Tour of Europe he has seen nothing abroad but the arbitrary powers of Courts, the slavery they induce, and the crowning carnage of Ismail. In England the social element in which he moves is manifestly different and, with all its faults, better … If there is a chosen station for freedom, where else except at Norman Abbey can he find it, somewhere between "tyranny" and "anarchy"?' (p. 177).

10 Kelsall, *Byron's Politics*, pp. 184, 189, quoting *Don Juan* XIV, 70.

11 Kelsall, *Byron's Politics*, pp. 179–80.

12 Kelsall, *Byron's Politics*, p. 179.

13 See: XIII, 12; XIV, 91–2; XIV, 97.

14 Bernard Beatty, *Byron's Don Juan* (London: Croom Helm, 1985), p. 140.

15 Caroline Franklin, *Byron's Heroines* (Oxford: Clarendon Press, 1992), p. 157.

16 I am assuming here, with Kelsall, that 'Juan visits England [in] about 1790', that is, in 'the age of Fox and Pitt, Sheridan and Burke' (*Byron's Politics*, p. 153).

17 Drummond Bone, *Byron* (Tavistock: Northcote House, 2000), p. 62.

18 For Beatty, Juan moves much closer to Aurora, and in more complex and subtle ways, than my necessarily brief reading of their relationship suggests. Specifically, Beatty argues, Juan moves towards the 'holiness' that Aurora 'represents' (p. 152) and, according to Beatty, the 'ghost and the old house together work this change in him' (p. 149). For Beatty's persuasive argument in full see *Byron's Don Juan*, pp. 137–211.

19 A. B. England, 'Byron's *Marino Faliero* and the Force of Individual Agency', in *The Plays of Lord Byron: Critical Essays*, ed. by Robert Gleckner and Bernard Beatty (Liverpool: Liverpool University Press, 1997), pp. 87–115, p. 112.

20 England, 'Byron's *Marino Faliero* and the Force of Individual Agency', p. 112.

21 Jerome Christensen, *Lord Byron's Strength: Romantic Writing and Commercial Society* (Baltimore, MD, and London: Johns Hopkins University Press, 1993), p. 264.

22 See, for example, G. Wilson Knight, *Lord Byron: Christian Virtues* (London: Routledge and Kegan Paul, 1952); the work of Wolf Z. Hirst; M. K. Joseph's discussion of 'Byron's fundamental seriousness about religion' (p. 305) in *Byron the Poet*, pp. 305–12; Beatty's *Byron's Don Juan*, especially ch. 4.

23 Christopher Fry, 'Comedy', in *The Tulane Drama Review* 4:3 (1960), p. 77.

Byron, 'Inkle and Yarico', and the Chains of Love

ANDREW M. STAUFFER

The hero of Byron's *Don Juan* stands in a complex relation to freedom. Plainly associated with a kind of errant liberty (if not libertinism), Juan is also a notoriously passive protagonist, less often acting than acted upon, especially by the women who caress and control him. By the time he is manacled and sold in Cantos IV–V of *Don Juan*, Juan's enslavement has come to feel somehow inevitable, a logical conclusion to the fragile paradise of Haidée's love. Part of this depends on a familiar Byronic assertion that to be in love is to be a slave; his lyrics attest amply to a conception of romantic passion as a chain. Thus the progress of Juan, the quintessential lover, from Haidée's arms to slavery's fetters, enacts as literal consequence what the poet elsewhere presents as coeval metaphorical events. This trajectory in the Juan–Haidée relationship owes nothing to the traditional Don Juan story but a great deal to one that has had an immense influence on British and American portrayals of love and slavery. Like so many authors of the eighteenth and nineteenth centuries, Byron here revises the tale of Inkle and Yarico, in which a marooned white merchant falls in love with, impregnates, and then betrays and sells a native (Indian or black) woman into slavery.[1] In tracing Byron's use of this story in the *Don Juan* narrative (and, to a lesser extent, in *The Island*), we learn more about the complex relation of love to slavery in his imagination.[2] Ultimately, we find that in altering the issues of race and class in 'Inkle and Yarico', in reversing the gender of the enslaved lover, and in eliminating the theme of betrayal, Byron transforms this ethical fable into an amoral meditation on the fate of love in the world.

The story of 'Inkle and Yarico' as such dates from Richard Steele's 1711 presentation of it in the pages of the *Spectator*,[3] although Steele was himself reworking a scene from Richard Ligon's 1657 history of the 'Barbadoes'.[4] The basics of the tale can be briefly narrated: a young Englishman travels to an exotic island and is separated from his companions, all of whom are slain or lost. He is found by a native female, who is enamoured at the sight of him, and particularly at the differences in their appearances. She protects his life and devotes herself to him, conveying him to a cave, feeding him with fruits, offering him various gifts, and soon becoming his lover. The lovers learn to communicate and the man expresses a desire that she see his country. Eventually a ship comes to the island and carries the couple away. Upon re-entering English territory, the man decides to make up for the financial losses of his journey by selling the native woman into slavery. She pleads for him to spare her this, as she is pregnant with his child. But, as Steele puts it, 'he only made use of that Information, to rise in his Demands upon the Purchaser' (p. 124).

Richard Price, Werner Sollors, and Frank Felsensen have shown that this anecdote had a significant influence on eighteenth- and nineteenth-century writings on race, and became a kind of ur-text for the abolitionists, both in England and in the United States. In a preface to his anthology of adaptations, sequels, and appropriations of the story, Felsensen writes: '"Inkle and Yarico" has begun to be recognized once again as one of the great folk epics of its age ... Its opaque but seamless fusion of fact and fiction may be invoked to account for its potency as a defining myth of the Enlightenment'.[5] He finds 'well over sixty discrete versions' of the story published between 1711 and 1810, and admits that there were surely many more.[6] The story's status as a myth or fable – that is, a 'fusion of fact and fiction' – makes it especially susceptible to ideologically-motivated rewritings that transform its political content. In tracing the political implications of various versions of 'Inkle and Yarico' – from Stedman's *Narrative* to John William De Forest's 'A Gentleman of an Old School' – Sollors demonstrates that later texts consciously measured themselves in relation to Steele's narrative, which he calls 'the representative liberal story on the theme of enslavement';[7] for example, Stedman claims he 'acted a part the reverse of Inkle to Yarico', assuring his readers of his fidelity to the mulatto Joanna.[8] In other words, a wide range of politicised literature in the wake of Steele worries at the case of Inkle and Yarico, and obsessively revisits their story in order to subvert or confirm its patterns.[9] That the tale got under the skin of its many readers is clear from its legacy: a series of rewritings and revisions visited upon it.

Steele's text anticipates this feature of its own reception in two ways: Steele presents the story of Inkle and Yarico as itself a revision of Ligon (who is mentioned), and also as a moral fable told in order to subvert another, previous tale. As Felsensen points out, it is presented as part of 'a larger debate on sexuality'.[10] In the *Spectator*, Arietta has been impatiently listening to a male 'Common-Place Talker' rehearse Petronius's 'celebrated Story of the Ephesian matron' (p. 49), in which a supposedly disconsolate widow is seduced on the tomb of her husband. This is meant as a parable illustrating the inconstancy of female affections, to which Arietta takes umbrage and responds by offering the Inkle–Yarico story as illustrative of the opposite point, in terms of gender. Thus, from its beginnings, the story comes as a moral and political engagement with a previous, similar narrative; Steele himself thinks it 'should be always a Counterpart to the *Ephesian Matron*' (p. 51).

The two anecdotes have much in common – enough to establish this initial revisionary exchange as paradigmatic for the reception of 'Inkle and Yarico'. Both involve the rescue of one lover by another, particularly by the provision of food, and the retirement to a cave-like retreat from the outside world, in which their love is consummated. In Petronius, the widow has followed her husband's body to an underground vault where she has remained for almost a week without food, weeping night and day for her loss.[11] But a soldier takes pity on her, brings food and wine, and persuades the widow not only to break her fast, but also to become his lover, in the very tomb of her husband; they spend not just one night together, 'but the next and a third, of course shutting the door of the vault'. We learn that 'the soldier was delighted with the woman's beauty, and his stolen pleasure; he brought up all the fine things his means permitted, and carried them to the tomb the moment darkness fell'.[12] Later, when the solider fears punishment for neglecting his duties in guarding the body of a crucified robber, the widow encourages him to replace the missing corpse with that of her husband, thus completing her betrayal. In both 'Inkle and Yarico' and 'The Ephesian Matron', the tale turns upon the expedient objectification of someone formerly held dear: Yarico is sold, and the husband's body is outraged. These parallels suggest that, as imagined by Steele and appropriated by his numerous successors, the Inkle and Yarico story has always been involved with the process of revision.

Herein lies a paradox, involving the powerful but vexed cultural influence of the tale. Given its radical malleability, what precisely does this 'defining myth' define? Its own antecedents and heirs offer many different answers to this question: male infidelity, the triumph of money over love, the inhumanity of slavery, the encounter between the 'civilised' and the 'savage', the perils of miscegenation, the origins of the tragic mulatto, the subjugation of women, the vicissitudes of human love. Like all mythic narratives, the political and moral content of Inkle–Yarico versions depends on which features of the tale are retained or excised, emphasised, or downplayed. Thus, in the long view of literary history, the Inkle and Yarico fable has no definitive political content, but rather deploys a recognisable series of props, settings, and characters in the service of certain ideological needs. To recognise that a given narrative – by John Stedman, Lydia Maria Child (*Clotel*), William Wells Brown (*The Octoroon*), or Lord Byron – revises 'Inkle and Yarico' is to perceive a critical mass of analogues, rather than any particular arrangement, progression, or purpose.[13] Byron's *Don Juan* is a good example of this because the Juan–Haidée story abjures nearly all of the moral content and plot of Steele's 'Inkle and Yarico', and yet is still plainly indebted to that work. In measuring the distance between the two narratives, we thus gain a perspective on Byron's purpose in this section of what might be called his own 'great folk epic of its age'.

Before proceeding to such a comparison, we might well ask what evidence exists that Byron knew of the Inkle and Yarico narrative. The immense cultural influence of the story is perhaps the strongest argument. He does mention the *Spectator* in a familiar way in his writings, but does not directly refer to any of its essays.[14] Furthermore, he knew the dramatist George Colman the Younger, who wrote a famous and successful adaptation of the story for the Drury Lane Theatre, but again does not mention the relevant title.[15] However, in both cases it is fair to assume Byron's exposure to both the Steele and Colman versions. Furthermore, we may find circumstantial evidence in one of Byron's less well known works, which itself raises issues pertinent to the 'Inkle and Yarico' story. In 1821, Byron wrote *The Blues*, a satire on bluestocking women. The work has not been well received,[16] but it cannot be overlooked in the present discussion for one important reason: its hero is named 'Inkel'.

McGann follows Beatty in finding the source of this name to be Anstey's *Election Ball, in Practical Letters from Mr. Inkle ... to his Wife* (1776).[17] Certainly, Anstey was one of the immediate inspirations for Byron's poem, particularly as the *Election Ball* and *New Bath Guide* (1766) both satirise fashionable society using the anapestic couplets that characterise *The Blues*. Yet Steele's Inkle also haunts the poem in significant ways. In the *Spectator*, the tale of Inkle and Yarico is told by Arietta, a learned society lady who is 'Visited by all Persons of both Sexes, who have any Pretence to Wit and Gallantry', and whom Steele praises for her 'Taste and Understanding' (p. 49) and 'good Sense' (p. 51). In other words, Arietta is a proto-bluestocking and thus connects to Byron's satire. Moreover, throughout Byron's poem, intellectual women are labelled and mocked as 'Blues', and the chromatic metaphor produces dialogue reminiscent of the racial (and sexual) concerns of 'Inkle and Yarico'. Miscegenation with 'women of colour' is at issue in Byron's satire, and is particularly focused through a character named 'Inkel'.

In the First Eclogue of *The Blues*, Inkel remonstrates with his friend Tracy, after being told of the latter's attraction to Miss Lilac:

> *Ink:* The Blue!
> The heiress!
> *Tra:* The angel!
> *Ink:* The devil! why man,
> Pray get out of this hobble as fast as you can.
> *You* wed with Miss Lilac! 'twould be your perdition:
> She's a poet, a chymist, a mathematician.
>
> (I, 62–6)

A few lines later in their discussion, Inkel asserts: 'I say she's a Blue, man, as blue as the ether', to which Tracy responds; 'And is that any cause for not coming together?' (I, 69–70). Byron casts this argument over Miss Lilac's eligibility as a wife in terms of her colour which is a double synecdoche for her intellectual interests (signified by figurative blue stockings) rather than a metonymy for her racial background (signified by approximate skin colour); Miss Lilac's name repeats this identification. Here Tracy questions Inkel's assumption that her 'colour' places any obstacles in the way of a happy marriage, but the satire as a whole depicts Blueness as shading into the diabolic, at least as far as male–female relations are concerned.

Because of Inkel's association with Steele's Inkle who seduced then betrayed Yarico (rather than wedding her), we see his advice as part of a larger narrative of male self-interest and opposition to mixed marriages. Byron makes a point of depicting unions with 'Blue' women as a mistake: Inkel warns Tracy against it, and, in the second Eclogue, Sir Richard laments his marriage to Lady Bluebottle as a foolish error that has ruined his life. Note also how Inkel refers here to Tracy's incipient passion for Miss Lilac as a 'hobble', a figure for enslavement which is in keeping with Byron's conceptions of romantic love. Associated with the marriage-yoke, the 'hobble' also represents the limits that marriage to a 'Blue' will place on a man: 'No pleasure! no leisure!' laments Sir Richard Bluebottle of his post-nuptial existence (II, 19). If we hear Yarico's Inkle speaking in the

Byronic Inkel's language of 'hobbles', we become aware of a masculinist logic of choice: enslave the 'coloured' woman or become enslaved to her in wedlock.

Once the story of Inkle and Yarico is brought to bear on Byron's work, then new configurations of meaning begin to appear, both in 'The Blues' and in *Don Juan*, where we will be alerted to special resonances in the allusions to slavery and the absolute avoidance of any suggestion of betrayal. Readers of the latter poem will recognise the first half of the Inkle–Yarico story as similar to that of Juan and Haidée. After a shipwreck and its consequences have claimed the lives of every one of his fellow travellers, Juan 'at last, with swimming, wading, scrambling ... Roll'd on the beach, half senseless, from the sea' (*Don Juan*, II, 107). Haidée, 'walking out upon the beach' finds him

> almost famish'd, and half drown'd;
> But being naked, she was shock'd, you know,
> Yet deem'd herself in common pity bound,
> As far as in her lay, 'to take him in,
> A stranger' dying, with so white a skin.

> (II, 129)

Byron's hero is treading (and wading and scrambling upon) epic ground here; this scene recalls Odysseus's encounter with Nausikaa on the beach of Phaiakia, after a shipwreck and a marathon swim in the 'winedark sea'. Yet given its sequel, Haidée's rescue of Juan seems to conform more closely to the Inkle–Yarico narrative, which itself glances at the Homeric tradition (Inkle's ship is named the *Achilles*) and particularly recalls the *Odyssey* in which groups of men landing on strange islands find death or love or some combination thereof at the hands of the natives. As Steele describes it, Inkle flees from marauding Indians and, 'coming into a remote and pathless Part of the Wood, he threw himself, tired and breathless, on a little Hillock, when an *Indian* Maid rushed from a Thicket behind him: After the first Surprize, they appeared mutually agreeable to each other' (p. 50). Similarly, Juan's first sight of Haidée is that of 'A lovely female face of seventeen', that

> watch'd with eagerness each throb that drew
> A sigh from his heaved bosom – and hers, too

> (II, 112, 114)

Steele continues: 'The *Indian* grew immediately enamoured of him, and consequently sollicitous for his Preservation: She therefore conveyed him to a Cave, where she gave him a Delicious Repast of Fruits' (p. 50). Haidée behaves in precisely this manner with regard to Juan: 'she thought it best … To place him in the cave for present rest' (II, 131) and feeds him (a bit more elaborately) with 'eggs, fruit, coffee, bread, fish, honey', and 'Scio wine' (II, 145).

Haidée's recognition that Juan has 'so white a skin' initially recalls the pleasure Yarico and Inkle take in their racial and cultural differences (although in *Don Juan* it is the European who is naked): 'If the *European* was highly Charmed with the Limbs, Features, and wild Graces of the Naked *American*; the *American* was no less taken with the Dress, Complexion and Shape of an *European*, covered from Head to Foot' (p. 50). Byron spends six stanzas describing Haidée's Grecian beauty and attire, and seven more in Canto III on the same theme, in order to emphasise her exotic appeal (II, 116–21; III, 70–6). However, despite the fact that 'Her mother was a Moorish maid, from Fez' (IV, 54), she too is 'white' (II, 118, 194). The narrator describes her gold bracelet as

> The purest ore inclosed the whitest skin
> That e'er by precious metal was held in.

(III, 71)

Byron's couple is less interracial than multicultural, their only recognisable differences being those of language (which gives place to the unspoken language of love), food (Juan misses 'beefsteak' but is too hungry to care), and clothing (which matters little to these lovers who are at least 'half-naked'). Haidée is even a Christian, 'devout as well as fair' (II, 1541).

Issues of race are thus forced underground in Byron's narrative, and questions of class fare similarly. In both 'Inkle and Yarico' and *Don Juan*, the exotic female native is no mere peasant, but a lady, thus following the common pattern of European romances of encounter. Mary Louise Pratt has identified in sentimental travel-writing 'the beneficent female figure of the "nurturing native", who tends to the suffering European out of pity, spontaneous kindness, or erotic passion'; these women 'are rarely "pure" non-whites or "real" slaves. Like Joanna, they are typically mulattoes or mestizos who already have European affiliations or, renewing an older motif, are "really" princes or princesses'.[18] That is, the racial and cultural exoticism of the heroine is leavened with 'whiteness' (Haidée plainly owes more to her Greek father than her African mother) and nobility, in order to make her more romantically palatable to a European audience. In Byron's poem, Haidée's racially other and middle-class bloodlines are covered over by ostentatiously white skin and aristocratic wealth.

In the narratives that concern us here, material wealth marks the heroine as part of a non-European aristocracy, in a translation of noble blood to forms more negotiable in the colonial marriage market. As Steele says of Yarico: 'she was, it seems, a Person of Distinction, for she every Day came to him in a different Dress, of the most beautiful Shells, Bugles, and Bredes' (p. 50). Similarly, Haidée is the daughter of a Greek slaver-pirate and a 'Moorish maid', and yet she is 'the greatest heiress of the Eastern Isles' (II, 128); 'Her brow was overhung with coins of gold', and

> in her air
> There was a something which bespoke command,
> As one who was a lady in the land.
>
> (II, 116)

Both women thus come to their European lovers bearing evidence of rich dowries on their bodies, as signs that they are of distinction. They also both display an attitude of command over their own sexuality, putting off native lovers in favour of their European visitors. Like Yarico, who brings Inkle 'many Spoils, which her other Lovers had presented to her' (p. 50), Haidée has

> Rejected several suitors, just to learn
> How to accept a better in his turn.
>
> (II, 128)

Nevertheless, Inkle and Juan themselves occupy very different class positions – Thomas Inkle being a trader and merchant (despite being the 'third son of an eminent Citizen') and Juan being a Don, his father 'A true Hidalgo, free from every stain / Of Moor or Hebrew blood', who 'traced his source / Through the most Gothic gentlemen of Spain' (I, 9). Steele's tale mocks the 'prudent and frugal' monetary concerns of members of the merchant class (such as Inkle), who would sell their own wives and children to make a profit. The natural gentleness of Yarico stands in sharp relief to Inkle's base behaviour; her nobility makes her enslavement at the hands of this middle-class trader all the more galling. But Byron's revision eliminates, or at least sublimates, this class differential between the two lovers. Juan is well born, but penniless and rather uncultivated; Haidée is a pirate's daughter but 'the greatest heiress of the Eastern Isles' who carries herself with the grace of a lady. Thus their union exposes no ideological disjunction; they follow equally the gospel of pleasure and passion, with a cavalier disregard for finances or moral prohibitions.

Given these basic differences regarding issues of race and class, one might begin to suspect *Don Juan*'s debt to Steele's narrative.[19] Further evidence comes from the following description of Yarico:

> She would carry him in the Dusk of the Evening, or by the favour of Moonlight, to unfrequented Groves and Solitudes, and shew him where to lye down in Safety, and sleep amidst the Falls of Waters, and the Melody of Nightingales. Her Part was to watch and hold him awake in her Arms ... In this manner did the Lovers pass away their Time, till they had learn'd a language of their own.
>
> (p. 51)

Byron's poem presents long meditations upon each of the items in this passage: learning a common language (stanzas 161–7), watching over one's sleeping lover (stanzas 195–8), and romancing by the water at twilight (stanzas 183–94). Yarico learns English from her male counterpart, but Byron tells us that Juan, 'by dint of fingers and of eyes, / And words repeated after her ... took / A lesson in her tongue', learning the Greek 'alpha beta' from Haidée (II, 163). Thus Byron's revision begins its reversal of the Inkle–Yarico gender roles that will culminate in the enslavement of Juan. Furthermore, Haidée's watching over Juan, both immediately after she rescues him ('she bent o'er him, and he lay beneath, / Hush'd as the babe upon its mother's breast' [II, 148]) and after the consummation of their love, 'Amidst the barren sands and rocks so rude' (II, 198); 'She slept not, but all tenderly, though fast, / Sustain'd his head upon her bosom's charms' (II, 195). Just as he follows the presentation of Juan's language acquisition with a digression on the pleasures of being taught by women, Byron follows this description with a hymn to the joys of 'they who watch o'er what they love while sleeping' (II, 196). Finally, the consummation scene by the ocean at dusk (in which 'the sea-bird's cry' [II, 181] replaces Steele's 'Nightingales') recalls the evening, moonlight, waterfalls, and solitude of the Inkle–Yarico story – standard furniture of romantic bowers of bliss.

These correspondences – and there are others, such as the delight of both Yarico and Haidée in playing with the hair of their lovers[20] – suggest we are justified in evaluating the significance of the variant trajectories of both relationships. In both stories, the arrival of a sailing ship puts an end to the island paradise of the couple, bringing with it the spectre of slavery: both relationships soon terminate with the enslavement of one of the lovers, which separates the now-pregnant woman from her mate. Of the genre of sentimental travel-writing that includes 'Inkle and Yarico', Pratt writes: 'Whether love turns out to be requited or not, whether the colonised lover is female or male, outcomes seem to be roughly the same: the lovers are separated, the European is reabsorbed by Europe, and the non-European dies an early death.'[21] More specifically, she reminds us that 'Joanna and Yarico end up husbandless and enslaved in the colonies while Inkle and Stedman end up back in England'.[22] At one level, *Don Juan* conforms to this pattern, in that Haidée 'dies an early death' while Juan is 'reabsorbed by Europe' in the end. But Juan's return is accomplished by means of his own enslavement, in a curious reversal of the Inkle–Yarico ending. In Steele's tale, the pregnant Yarico is sold by her false lover, whereas Juan is sold and the pregnant Haidée dies, both victims of her father Lambro, who terminates their idyllic relationship. Yet the narrator suggests that it is not Lambro, but love itself, that is to blame for this conclusion; he writes of his heroine's death:

> If she loved rashly, her life paid for wrong –
> A heavy price must all pay who thus err,
> In some shape; let none think to fly the danger,
> For soon or late Love is his own avenger.

(IV, 73)

As Franklin notes, this sounds a bit like a conventional condemnation, 'reserved for fallen women ... But the narrator gives an alternative explanation' for Haidée's death: 'Were their story to continue, they would inevitably lose their love, which would be even more tragic.'[23] In other words, Byron transforms his source from a moral parable on male inconstancy to a philosophical romance displaying the fate of human love despite all best efforts. No betrayal marks the conclusion of the Juan–Haidée union, except the existential one Byron saw as entailed upon all men and women: 'Time', the 'foe to love' (IV, 8), forces one to witness

> The death of friends, and that which slays even more –
> The death of friendship, love, youth, all that is,
> Except mere breath.

(IV, 12)

The awareness of such losses depends upon memory, the register of time in human consciousness. Thus the idyllic love affairs between European men and exotic, 'native', women are typically portrayed as dependent upon a species of forgetfulness; the hero gets away from it all, and the reader does too. As Byron writes of Juan and Haidée:

> theirs was a love in which the mind delights
> To lose itself, when the old world grows dull,
> And we are sick of its hack sounds and sights.
>
> (IV, 17)

Both escapes and escapist, the romantic relationships found by Inkle and Juan fairly constitute the genre of travel romance. Their tragic conclusions signal a return of memories of the outside world and one's own past: Inkle remembers that he is a trader and 'began seriously to reflect upon his loss of Time' (i.e. money), and Haidée confronts her father's 'dark eye' (IV, 34) in a moment metaphorically representative of the return of memory, as he reprimands her,

> I must do my duty – how thou hast
> Done thine, the present vouches for the past.
>
> (IV, 46)

Lambro's return thus brings to bear heretofore unknown pressures and concerns upon the relationship of the lovers, who 'were not made in the real world to fill / A busy character in the dull scene', and who, as a couple, were meant never to 'know the weight of human hours' (IV, 15). We are told that

> They should have lived together deep in woods,
> Unseen as sings the nightingale; they were
> Unfit to mix in these thick solitudes
> Call'd social, haunts of Hate, and Vice, and Care.
>
> (IV, 28)

The end of their sovereign solitude marks the conclusion of their idyllic relationship which, like that of the English sailor Torquil and the Polynesian princess Neuha in Byron's *The Island*, depends upon islands and caves as protective retreats. Inkle and Yarico are happy until 'a Vessel from the Main arrives in that Island' (p. 51) to take the couple 'into *English* Territories', just as Juan and Haidée feel themselves to be in 'another Eden' (IV, 10), until the slave-merchant Lambro

> shaped his course to where his daughter fair
> Continued still in her hospitable cares.
>
> (III, 19)

As Max F. Schulz observes, 'Byron looked on islands as tentative havens at best'.[24] The threat of enslavement or death always hovers close: Yarico and Juan are sold into slavery, and Torquil is threatened with imprisonment and execution.

Written after the Haidée episode of *Don Juan*, *The Island* also invokes the Inkle–Yarico romance in its portrayal of interracial love enacted as the rescue and preservation of a stranded Englishman, a 'blue-eyed northern child ... the fair-haired offspring of the Hebrides' (II, 163–5), by a 'daughter of the Southern Seas' (II, 141), 'Dusky like Night' (II, 129), and

> Highborn ...
> Of a long race, the valiant and the free,
> The naked knights of savage chivalry.

(II, 214–17).[25]

Furthermore, like both Yarico and Haidée, Neuha preserves the life of her lover – Torquil, the 'truant mutineer' (II, 209) – when the Royal Navy arrives, spiriting him away to a hidden cave filled with 'golden fruits' (III, 184) and other now-familiar accoutrements of native luxury, while his companions are killed or captured and 'Chain'd on the deck' of the ship (IV, 359). As Franklin puts it: 'as with Haidée, Neuha's love for the stranger is an inextricable blend of the sexual and charitable'.[26] The key difference with this later pair is that their union manages to survive the threat of chains, unlike the Inkle–Yarico and Juan–Haidée relationships, because, as McGann has argued, Torquil chooses love above all else, including life itself.[27] Giving up memory and all past allegiances, Torquil is reborn as a child in the paradise of a 'yet infant world' (IV, 20) with Neuha at his side. Uniquely of Byron's heroes, he escapes the corollaries of 'passion's desolating joy' (II, 112), which we see in the Juan–Haidée relationship, among so many others in Byron's work: loss, enslavement, and death.[28]

If *The Island* thus offers a reprise of the Juan–Haidée relationship, it functions like the *Don Juan* narrative in relation to 'Inkle and Yarico'. There is apparently something in the basic story of a European traveller romancing an exotic female in a lush natural setting that demands rewritings, as is amply evidenced in the work of Price, Sollors, Felsensen, and Pratt. The myth of Eden clearly stands behind much of the work in this tradition, and that explains part of its enduring popularity through the eighteenth and nineteenth centuries. However, these many versions – by Steele, Colman, Stedman, Byron, and scores of others – speak to a set of anxieties particular to the circumstances of England during this period of its colonial history. 'Inkle and Yarico' versions inevitably figure the often perilous and guilty consequences of encounters with imperial others, who are nevertheless surrounded by hopeful auras of eroticism, material wealth, natural beauty, protective kindness, and even – unsteadily – love.

Byron, then, I have argued, clearly knew and used the 'Inkle and Yarico' story as a way of addressing the connections between love and enslavement. But while he draws many details from his source, Byron redirects its themes of the tragic relations among lovers, lost innocence, and the chains that bind us to others, to worldly concerns, and to our own pasts.

Notes

1   For the best introduction to the Inkle–Yarico story, see *English Trader, Indian Maid: Representing Gender, Race, and Slavery in the New World: An Inkle and Yarico Reader*, ed. by Frank Felsenstein (Baltimore, MD: Johns Hopkins University Press, 1999). Also, see Lawrence Marsden Price, *Inkle and Yarico Album* (Berkeley, CA: University of California Press, 1937). I would like to thank John Cleman for his generous help with this essay.

2   On Byron's attitudes towards slavery and abolition per se, see Eva B. Dykes, *The Negro in English Romantic Thought* (Washington, DC: Associated Publishers, 1942), pp. 85–7; Joan Baum, *Mind-Forg'd Manacles: Slavery and the English Romantic Poets* (North Haven, CT: Archon Books, 1994), pp. 96–9; and Debbie Lee, *Slavery and the Romantic Imagination* (Philadelphia, PA: University of Pennsylvania Press, 2002).

3   *The Spectator*, ed. by Donald F. Bond, 3 vols (Oxford: Clarendon Press, 1965), I, pp. 47–51. This is issue number 11, dated 13 March 1711. Subsequently referred to in the text.

4   *A True and Exact History of the Island of Barbadoes* (London, 1657). On the role of 'Retellings' in the history of the Inkle–Yarico legend, see Werner Sollors, *Neither Black nor White yet Both: Thematic Explorations of Interracial Literature* (Oxford: Oxford University Press, 1997), pp. 188–219.

5   *An Inkle and Yarico Reader*, p. xi.

6   *An Inkle and Yarico Reader*, pp. 1–2.

7   Sollors, *Neither Black nor White yet Both*, p. 199.

8   *Narrative of a Five Years' Expedition against the Revolted Negroes of Surinam*, ed. by Richard and Sally Price (Baltimore, MD: Johns Hopkins University Press, 1988), p. 100.

9   See Mary Louise Pratt, *Imperial Eyes: Travel Writing and Transculturation* (London: Routledge, 1992), esp. ch. 5, for more on this issue.

10 *An Inkle and Yarico Reader*, p. 21.

11 This and the following accounts are paraphrased from the 'Satyricon' in *Petronius*, trans. by Michael Heseltine, Loeb Classical Library (Cambridge, MA: Harvard University Press, 1969), pp. 269–77.

12 Petronius, 'Satyricon', p. 275.

13 Also see Catherine Moore, 'Robinson and Xury and Inkle and Yarico', *English Language Notes* 19:1 (1981), pp. 24–9.

14 *BLJ*, 2, 56; see also Byron's 1807 'Reading List' in *CMP*, p. 6.

15 See the index entries for Colman (*BLJ*, 12, 77). 'In Byron's opinion, only one man in Regency London was a better drinking-companion than Sheridan. That was George Colman the younger.' Leslie Marchand, *Byron: A Biography*, 3 vols (New

York: Knopf, 1957), ii, p. 402.

16 In *Byron's Poetry: A Critical Introduction* (Cambridge, MA: Harvard University Press,
    1968), Marchand calls it 'a disappointment from the beginning', one in which 'the
    satiric thrusts … rarely run into cleverness' (p. 35). Claude Fuess thinks the work
    'little deserving of attention' aside from its form; see his *Lord Byron as a Satirist in
    Verse* (New York: Columbia University Press, 1912), p. 207. Frederick Beaty in
    Byron the Satirist (Dekalb, IL: Northern Illinois University Press, 1985) finds that it
    'lacks both the original wit and substance of his better satires' (p. 180).

17 *CPW*, 6, 665; Beaty, *Byron the Satirist*, p. 214n.

18 Pratt, *Imperial Eyes*, pp. 96, 100. On the theme of 'The Noble Negro', especially
    with regard to 'Inkle and Yarico', see ch. 3 of Wylie Sypher's *Guinea's Captive Kings:
    British Anti-Slavery Literature of the XVIIIth Century* (Chapel Hill, NC: University of
    North Carolina Press, 1942).

19 A number of critics think that Byron may have been drawing on a Cretan pastoral
    romance, 'The Fair Shepherdess', in creating the Haidée episode in *Don Juan*. See
    Panos Morphopoulos, 'Byron's Translation and Use of Modern Greek Writings',
    Modern Language Notes 54 (1939), pp. 317–26, esp. 324; and Kiriakoula Solomou,
    'The Influence of Greek Poetry on Byron', *Byron Journal* 10 (1982), pp. 4–19, esp.
    pp. 15–16. Elizabeth Boyd, in *Byron's Don Juan* (New Brunswick, NJ: Rutgers
    University Press, 1945), seems to accept this (p. 121), as does Caroline Franklin in
    Byron's Heroines (Oxford: Clarendon Press, 1992), p. 136.

20 Byron tells us that Haidée 'would softly stir his locks so curly' each morning (II,
    161), and we find that Yarico also 'would sometimes play with his Hair, and delight
    in the Opposition of its Colour to that of her Fingers' (p. 50).

21 Pratt, *Imperial Eyes*, p. 97.

22 Pratt, *Imperial Eyes*, p. 100.

23 Franklin, *Byron's Heroines*, pp. 12, 142–3.

24 Max F. Schulz, *Paradise Preserved: Recreations of Eden in Eighteenth- and Nineteenth-
    Century England* (Cambridge: Cambridge University Press, 1985), p. 101.

25 Compare Paul D. Fleck, 'Romance in 'The Island', *Byron Journal* 3 (1975), pp. 4–
    23; Bernard Blackstone, *The Lost Travellers: A Romantic Theme with Variations*
    (London: Longmans, 1962), pp. 181–219; James McKusick, 'The Politics of
    Language in Byron's *The Island*', *ELH* 59 (1992), pp. 839–56, p. 849.

26 Franklin, *Byron's Heroines*, p. 97.

27 See Jerome McGann, *Fiery Dust: Byron's Poetic Development* (Chicago, IL: University
    of Chicago Press, 1968), pp. 196–8.

28 See Schulz, *Paradise Preserved*, p. 103.

'I Have a Means of Freedom Still': Aesthetic Dialectic in *Sardanapalus*

JONATHON SHEARS

If the freedom of imaginative play that we associate with Romanticism exists within the text of *Sardanapalus*, then where is it to be found? The question, I think, has dominated criticism of the Tragedy for many years without any satisfactory conclusions having been drawn.[1] The reason for this is fairly straightforward. Much criticism, in keeping with wider scholarly trends, has tended to focus on the autobiographical nature of the drama. Leslie Marchand, for example, described the play 'as a self-revelatory romantic poem'.[2] What he meant by this was that Byron projects into the text the dilemma he was facing in Ravenna at the time of composition, a point which becomes quite obvious when Byron's journals and correspondence are read in conjunction with his work. Yet, if freedom exists in *Sardanapalus*, it is not political freedom, or at least not a satisfactory resolution to Byron's actual political quandary in his support of the patriot Carbonari in Ravenna.[3] Myrrha realises as early as the end of Act I that the only freedom available to her and to Sardanapalus is the questionable triumph of death:

> If not, I have a means of freedom still,
> And if I cannot teach him how to reign,
> May show him how alone a king can leave
> His throne.

> (I.ii.663–6)

The real freedom of *Sardanapalus* is less political than aesthetic. The present essay will attempt to explain what is meant by this, and why thinking in this way changes our understanding of the drama.

It has often been commented that Byron removes any idly drawn equivalence between the events of his biography and those of the play simply through the use of the exotic setting of Assyria. The desire to immerse himself so fully in the aesthetics of effeminacy, androgyny, and infidelity in *Sardanapalus* also suggests a deliberate attempt to investigate the power of art to objectify the artist's lived experience. Eric Auerbach comments that textual freedom emerges from a lack of 'historical, social, economic, and regional determinants'.[4] This is true of Sardanapalus himself, a mythical figure free from the constraints of time and place. Yet, this freedom does not magically occur merely through Byron's use of source material. It is equally won through the poet's art, and as such there is no reason why we should not be able to describe it more precisely.[5]

In his correspondence during the months leading up to composition, Byron makes a plea for what we could describe as liberty from the restrictions of his own public persona. In response to a review in *Blackwood's* of the initial cantos of *Don Juan*, which contained personal criticism of the poet, Byron complained that 'my case as an author, is peculiarly hard, in being everlastingly taken or mistaken for my own protagonist'.[6] Byron's language is ambiguous. He wishes to be neither entirely removed from association with his characters, nor thought to be synonymous with them. David Erdman has observed, in recounting Byron's supposed 'stage fright', that the poet's fickle attitude to drama was conditioned largely by public and political praise or indifference.[7] Here, too, it appears that Byron desires neither of these exclusively, but this is not necessarily the result of indecision or of a fragile self-belief. In this instance the ambiguity is by design. He ridicules the paradox in which those would-be critics, who are able to think only in absolutes, find themselves: 'Childe Harold, Byron, and the Count in *Beppo*, were one and the same person; thereby making me turn out to be, as Mrs Malaprop says, "*like Cerberus, three gentlemen at once*".'[8]

What Byron objects to is a lack of aesthetic independence. His overt intention is that he would rather sacrifice all artistic claim to *Don Juan* than have each line reduced to the details of his own life. He demonstrates an intuitive understanding of the reading process, inviting the reader to follow a subtext which purports to reveal that his verse *is*, in fact, overtly biographical.[9] But this would be to overdetermine the drama as a projection of the personality of the dramatist, which is precisely what Byron is complaining about. Byron did not believe, as say Eliot did, that poetry is primarily 'objectified' emotion. Neither did he believe that poetry was entirely a reproduction of his own political opinions. He redirects onto the reader the question which concerns me: How is aesthetic freedom to be achieved through verse?

The question is partly answered in a letter to Shelley of 26 April 1821, during the composition of *Sardanapalus*. Byron praises Shelley for the distance *The Cenci* maintains from contemporary English drama, a distance which Byron cannot find in the work of Keats:

> You know my high opinion of *that second-hand* school of poetry. You also know my opinion of your own poetry, – because it is of *no* school. I read *Cenci* – but, besides that I think the *subject* essentially *un*dramatic, I am not an admirer of our old dramatists as *models*. I deny that the English have hitherto had a drama at all. Your *Cenci*, however, was a work of power, and poetry.[10]

This praise implicitly contains a statement of intent. What at first seems to be couched in contradiction (a conflation of the terms 'drama' and 'poetry'), actually directs us for the first time towards what we could describe as a clear theory of creative emancipation. The interaction of poetry and drama (and by drama I mean specifically dramatic 'action') absent from the contemporary English stage, *is* present in Shelley's 'closet' drama.

The distinction between drama-in-action and (lyrical) verse is made clearer in the Preface to *Sardanapalus*. Although Byron's opinions can again appear contradictory, his reason for adhering to the neo-classical 'unities' is as set out above. He opens in claiming that 'In publishing the following Tragedies I have only to repeat, that they were not composed with the most remote view to the stage'[11] suggesting that Byron would rather appeal to the literary than the visual eye. Yet, the concerns of Byron the poet stand side by side with those of Byron the dramatist: 'The author has in one instance attempted to preserve, and in the other to approach, the "unities"; conceiving that with any very distant departure from them, there may be poetry, but can be no drama.' As Richard Lansdown points out, the 'unities' were 'not only a set of instructions to the artist, but also a group of ideas, which sought to describe and explore dramatic form'. They were, in Lansdown's phrase, a 'dialectic of constraint and opportunity'.[12] In the case of *Sardanapalus* the two sides of this dialectic are drama, or more specifically dramatic 'action', and 'poetry', particularly lyrical verse.

Both terms require further definition, especially with reference to the neo-classical tradition that Byron declares to be his immediate dramatic context. Aristotle wrote that Tragedy is 'the art of imitation in the form of *action*'. He identifies dramatic 'action' as the major contributory factor to the tragic experience. While Tragedy can function without *ethos* and *dianoia*, it cannot produce *katharsis*, the desired end of Tragedy, without 'action'. For Aristotle, dramatic 'action' would appear to be synonymous with plot. Its function is to propel the Tragedy to the closure of the formal narrative:

'the incidents of the action, and the structural ordering of these incidents, constitute the end and purpose of the tragedy. Here, as elsewhere, the final purpose is the main thing'.[13] Aristotle describes happiness and misery not as states of being but as forms of activity. Accordingly action is the most important element of Tragedy. The unity of action is very much the 'art' of dramatic poetry as, in theory, *katharsis* could occur without character – character is revealed through action rather than access to poetic interiority.

Yet the problem with the *Poetics*, at least as far as it aids a consideration of Byron's drama, is that Aristotle makes no distinction between the function of dramatic 'action' and the function of 'poetry'. His taxonomy of Tragedy suggests that action and poetry combine to propel the narrative to its cathartic end. This may be true of Sophocles and even the French neo-classical school of Racine and Corneille, but not of *Sardanapalus*. There are several reasons for this. Firstly, Byron's influences were more disparate than neo-classicism. Romanticism is, in some ways, characterised by an attempt to verbalise the ineffable, including essences such as the 'self' or 'nature', while the 'neo-classical' privileges representations of general reality. *Sardanapalus* contains enough of the Romantic sublime, and the Preface enough contradictory uses of the terms 'poetic' and 'dramatic', to suggest that Byron was revisiting neo-classicism to innovate rather than imitate. Secondly, these moments of 'poetic' ineffability characteristic of Romanticism have the effect of retarding the narrative and are therefore essentially undramatic. Geoffrey Ward comments that language has a tendency to 'proliferate', a factor which must, on some level, delay narrative momentum. In discussing stanza 97 of *Childe Harold* III Ward argues that Byron's 'actual communicating medium depends upon proliferation, in itself a barrier to the conclusive singularity he craves'.[14] This is probably truer of lyrical language use than of any other. The implication for drama is the effect of an impediment to the action. Ward's 'conclusive singularity' is suggestive of Aristotle's own belief that 'the final purpose is the main thing'. When language is the active medium of conveyance, narrative is eviscerated from within by the capacity to 'proliferate' or in dramatic terms delay.

Sardanapalus is a text unlike *Mazeppa*, which Gabriele Poole rightly describes, elsewhere in this volume, as schizophrenic. What I mean is that *Sardanapalus* has less of a dialogic structure in Bakhtin's sense, which he described as 'a plurality of independent and unmerged voices and consciousnesses'.[15] I am not arguing that each character is not distinctive. On the contrary, most characters in the drama have an instantly recognisable political voice, without ever becoming caricatures. This is particularly true of Sardanapalus and Salemenes, between whom the larger ideological debate of the play is dramatised. Nevertheless, despite the clear plurality of perspectives on political tyranny, none of the 'voices' convince the reader that they will supply a route to freedom. Perhaps the only exception is Myrrha, who recommends that Sardanapalus rule by 'awe and law'. But, significantly, even this political ideology is subsumed into the tragic action. In fact, it is this most workable of opinions which directly causes the Tragedy: Beleses and Arbaces mistake Sardanapalus's benevolent intentions, his attempt to rule by 'awe and law', for an act of despotism that propels the tragic conclusion to the action.[16]

Political freedom, or lack of it, results in Sardanapalus's Tragedy, but aesthetic freedom, through the interaction of drama and poetry inherent in the 'unities', does not. By setting the Tragedy over a period of twenty-four hours, Byron makes the reader acutely aware of the passing of time. This is most vividly realised with the introduction of the conspirators at the beginning of Act II. While Salemenes is undoubtedly Sardanapalus's political antonym, Beleses is his artistic counter. Sardanapalus is a character who variously desires to be immortal and human, although he craves, more than anything, to be suspended in a state of Keatsian 'negative capability' claiming 'there's something sweet in my uncertainty'. He is an enigma – as Altada puts it, 'The man's inscrutable' (III.i.319) – whose wishes correspond to those of Byron when faced with his critics. Beleses, on the other hand, is the critic, the interpreter of signs and portents who searches for certainties in the stars, as those literary hacks searched Byron's work for details of his life. In his opening speech the dialectic of poetry and dramatic action reveals his lack of certainty long before he admits to his co-conspirator, Arbaces, that 'I do not doubt of victory – but the victor' (II.i.44):

> The sun goes down: methinks he sets more slowly,
> Taking his last look of Assyria's empire.
> How red he glares amongst those deepening clouds,
> Like the blood he predicts! If not in vain,
> Thou sun that sinkest, and ye stars which rise,
> I have outwatch'd ye, reading ray by ray
> The edicts of your orbs, which make Time tremble
> For what he brings the nations, 'tis the furthest
> Hour of Assyria's years.
>
> (II.i.1–9)

In this striking description, Byron perfectly captures Beleses's subjectivity, as the reader witnesses the dialectic of poetry and action at work. The two heavy syllables, 'last look', follow and precede two unstressed pairs which creates the feeling that the verse is attempting to slow the momentum of the sun down, and hence delay the action of the drama. Yet the content of the speech pulls in the opposite direction, providing constant reminders to the reader of the unerring progression of dramatic action which will eventually consume the protagonists: 'Thou sun that *sinkest*, and ye stars which *rise*', 'make *Time* tremble' and 'the furthest *Hour* of Assyria's *years*'. The verse exudes a lyric aesthetic, which creates the impression that rather than waiting for the sun to set, Beleses is controlling its movement. It is only when he attempts to interpret the sun's significance to the temporal action that the momentary spatial beauty of the image is lost. His sudden certainty that the sun predicts violence is mimicked in the collocation of the hard consonantal 'Like the blood he predicts!' The conclusion seems to speed the sun's fall leaving the reader with the feeling that it is at this moment that it should have dropped from sight. Yet, the sun resists Beleses's attempts to 'read' its portents and speed its action. It remains resolutely spatial and aesthetic, as does the verse. When it finally sets twenty-five lines later the reader is not struck by the blood-red connotations of revolution or the significance of the sun's setting upon the temporal action of the drama. Instead, the lyrical impression of the recently set sun which 'leaves his beauty, not his knowledge' (II.i.31) plays briefly upon the eye of Beleses but also the imaginative retina of the reader.[17]

As a result, the opening of the Act II expresses an aesthetic liberty beyond signification, but the consequent reassertion of the action is a pattern reproduced throughout the play. In this case it is Arbaces's chiding:

> Dost thou stand
> Gazing to trace thy disappearing god
> Into some realm of undiscover'd day?

> (II.i.37–9)

His intention to mock Beleses's superstitions, however, only reinforces Byron's artistic point. He encourages the reader to experience the aesthetic freedom of his verse without needing to reach, as Beleses does, into 'undiscover'd' and undiscoverable historical details.

Of course, a Keatsian suspension of choice is the standard to which Sardanapalus consistently appeals. Yet he is caught between two impulses; to be immortal and to be mutable, recalling Marc Antony in Dryden's *All for Love*. Ventidius, Dryden's lieutenant (anticipating Byron's Salemenes), argues for action:

> I can die with you too, when time shall serve;
> But Fortune calls upon us now to live.
>
> (I.323–4)

Ventidius represents the necessity of Time; Antony the opposite force of Death. The two are dramatic, as well as political, antagonists. Dryden explicitly states the political neo-classical dialectic; by implication the aesthetic dialectic is also acknowledged, 'thou and I [are], like Time and Death' (I.449–50). What I mean by this is that dramatic action (Time) attempts to hurry the narrative to its conclusion, whilst poetry (a version of ideal Keatsian or lyrical Death) attempts to delay it. Byron knows what his character does not, that the indulgences of Sardanapalus, and the indolence of the Keatsian Ode, do not equate to freedom. Aesthetic freedom in poetry only emerges through its juxtaposition with dramatic action, because such a poetic independence must have something to work free from. Despite his advocacy of neo-classical methods Byron runs contrary to Aristotle's *Poetics* here. Poetry and dramatic action form a dialectic because they produce something more vividly creative than either could alone. Sardanapalus can only conceive of an abstract aesthetic freedom that becomes reduced to the tired political escapism of his protracted adolescence, manifested in the text as the pursuit of luxury. The reader, on the other hand, has been made aware of a timeless aesthetic freedom than can exist in narrative and dramatic verse.

Political freedom does not exist, and cannot exist, within the text, a fact that is evident in the toast Sardanapalus drinks to Bacchus, ironically anticipating the toast he demands from his subjects at the feast. In the former he chides Salemenes for his worship of Bacchus as a barbarian and urges him to exhibit human, rather than godly, qualities:

> Here's that which deified him – let it now
> Humanize thee.
>
> (I.ii.182–3)

Yet, at the feast of Act III, he arrogantly proclaims himself immortal:

> Down on your knees, and drink a measure to
> The safety of the king – the monarch, say I?
> The god Sardanapalus!
>
> (III.i.25–7)

While his political intentions are admirable his execution of them is flawed, but deliberately so. More than this, the action is symbolically morbid in the context of the blood-filled goblets of both *Manfred* and *The Cenci*. Sardanapalus's crude attempts to emancipate himself from political life inevitably lead to a self-indulgence which is artistically cloying; not a release but escapism:

> Fill full! Why this is as it should be: here
> Is my true realm, amidst bright eyes and faces
> Happy as fair! Here sorrow cannot reach.

(III.i.1–3)

Sardanapalus's protestations of joyfulness are unconvincing. Despite claiming a state without sorrow Sardanapalus is immediately reminded of the legacy of his ancestors. Just like Manfred, Sardanapalus desires to forget, but is constantly besieged by reminders, feeling the pressure to keep history at bay:

> Is not this better now than Nimrod's huntings,
> Or my wild grandam's chase in search of kingdoms
> She could not keep when conquer'd?

(III.i.5–7)

The questioning tone reveals an uncertainty and suspicion that revelry fails to provide the desired freedom. Instead the reader is reminded of the tragic imposition of history on Sardanapalus, and, more importantly for our discussion, the necessary progression of dramatic action. The dialectic previously described becomes momentarily lost as one side, dramatic action, asserts itself at the expense of the other, poetry.

It is only when Sardanapalus neglects his vices that he loses self-consciousness and gains freedom, simultaneously allowing poetry to assert its power and create an equivalent aesthetic freedom in the reader's imagination. Standing alone he muses on the nature of royalty and his soft clay seems momentarily to harden into the speaking statue he visualises:

> ... I
> Am softer clay, impregnated with flowers:
> But as our mould is, must the produce be.
> If I have err'd this time, 'tis on the side
> Where error sits most lightly on that sense,
> I know not what to call it; but it reckons
> With me ofttimes check for pain, and sometimes pleasure;
> A spirit which seems placed about my heart
> To count its throbs, not quicken them, and ask
> Questions which mortal never dared to ask me,
> Nor Baal, though an oraclar deity –
> Albeit his marble face majestical

Frowns as the shadows of the evening dim
His brows to changed expression, till at times
I think the statue looks in act to speak.

(II.i.521–35)

G. Wilson Knight wrote that *Sardanapalus* 'might be said to dramatize eternity into action and hence it has a stillness, a plastic quality',[18] and this could well be an example of what he meant. There is something in the interaction of verse and content which is concrete and permanent. As Sardanapalus identifies elsewhere, his freedom does indeed lie in uncertainty, but not the self-consciously constructed variety of the banquet. This is an indulgent uncertainty, again a type of Keatsian 'negative capability'. Alone, Sardanapalus experiences something more akin to Blake's visionary poetics; 'a sense, I know not what to call it' suggesting a momentary glimpse of an eternal aesthetic permanence which exists beyond the pleasure and pain he can describe. This is an analogy for the play itself. An aesthetic freedom emerges which is beyond poetry and drama, yet is a product of their dialectic. The ineffable 'sense' described here applies as much to the reader as to Sardanapalus. It is a spirit which, momentarily, seems to slow the heart's beatings, 'not quicken them', just as the rhythm of the verse itself, because of the central spondee which is enclosed by stressed syllables and a natural pause through the punctuation, slows almost to a halt. An aesthetic freedom is created despite the subtle reintroduction of the action. Sardanapalus is not Don Giovanni witnessing the waking of the dead. It is the altering light of evening, in other words the progression of the action, which seems to animate the statue of Baal, reminding the reader of the progression of drama and causing Sardanapalus to quit his 'vain thoughts' (II.i.536).

What I have returned to then, is my original question: how is aesthetic freedom to be achieved? The answer which Byron has proposed, and the reader has come to appreciate, is the use of the neo-classical 'unities'. They offer a dialectic of lyrical poetry (X) and dramatic action (Y). While X attempts to move the narrative forward, Y attempts to delay it. It is curiously at the moments when the action is most significant to the temporal progression of the drama that poetry is thrust to the foreground. The result is a collection of tableaux or operatic arias that have the timeless quality of the characters on Keats's urn. Myrrha bemoans that

no kind hand will gather
The dust of both into one urn.

(V.i.475–6)

But this is not entirely true as the Tragedy functions as an urn for images which can exist beyond political signification, requiring only an aesthetic order.

This is an explanation which would be fine as it stands, were it not for the fact that in practice Byron does not in fact adhere to the 'unities' quite as conveniently as I have suggested. True, the first two acts are largely expository, as are the last two. Act III complicates our discussion. The majority of the action takes place on stage, while previously all significant action was mediated through the verse, allowing our dialectic of poetry and action to function. Why has Byron done this? Martyn Corbett suggests that Byron had received information from England that *Marino Faliero*, which he had written in strict accordance with the 'unities', had been a dramatic failure: 'for at least part of the time he spent writing the third act of *Sardana-palus*, Byron was writing *not* under "the stimulation of success" but under the misconception of failure'.[19] Corbett argues that Byron responded to this by making Act III more of a theatrical spectacle, and hence directed it towards contemporary taste. By the time he came to Act IV he had learnt that the truth was somewhat different; *Marino Faliero* had run for seven nights and been well received. This news encouraged him to return to his original formula.

While this may be partly true, Act III is not written in a different *spirit* to the rest of the drama. If any part 'stands out', it is the introduction of Zarina in Act IV. As such, I would argue that the third act is not only an extension of the dialectic of poetry and drama, but an amplification of it. Byron intentionally juxtaposes stage spectacle with poetry, a dialectical method, which has been touched upon by Richard Lansdown, without, I think, having been fully articulated. In his second definition of fantasy, Lansdown describes 'a story made up of whimsical or random elements which the author is entirely at liberty to summon or dismiss at will'.[20] He denies that this definition applies to *Sardanapalus*, and he is right to do so. All drama needs a temporal narrative structure in order to make sense – this is the difference between poetry and the plastic arts. The former must be understood in a definite linear progression of parts, while the latter can be understood immediately in any part. However, while the author cannot summon or dismiss narrative elements at will, this is not the case with the reader. The reading process has an imaginative freedom beyond the order of the poetic drama itself which allows verse to be simultaneously temporal and spatial. In Act III Byron activates this freedom, opposing dramatic action and poetry more explicitly than before.

The difference between the action on stage and the action reported is striking. Whilst on stage it is deliberately clumsy. Sardanapalus feels the discomfort of his cumbersome armour which is reflected in the fragmented verse:

Give me the cuirass – so: my baldric; now
My sword: I had forgot the helm – where is it?
That's well – no, 'tis too heavy: you mistake, too –
It was not this I meant, but that which bears
A diadem around it.

(III.i.127–31)

Byron again recalls Dryden's Antony who struggles with a bracelet, transforming him into the emasculated Sardanapalus, at ease with effeminate jewellery, but not as a soldier.[21] Sardanapalus is 'awkward', but not in the same sense as Antony to whom soldiering comes first, amatory liaisons second. The bold stage direction, '[arming himself]' deliberately undercuts his actions. His reflection in the mirror, as Camille Paglia argues, acts as his spouse, creating a solipsistic feminine unity.[22]

However, the description of Sardanapalus fighting off stage exercises an imaginative poetic space for which action has no equivalent:

Baal himself
Ne'er fought more fiercely to win empire, than
His silken son to save it: he defies
All augury of foes or friends; and like
The close and sultry summer's day, which bodes
A twilight tempest, bursts forth in such thunder
As sweeps the air and deluges the earth.
The man's inscrutable.

(III.i.312–19)

The passage describes the most active spectacle of the Tragedy: 'Ne'er fought more fiercely' and 'defies / All augury of foes and friends'. The reader is besieged by reminders of the progression of the action and the imposition of history and politics upon Sardanapalus. Baal, who represents history to Sardanapalus as much as Semiramis or Nimrod do, is mentioned again. Words such as 'augury' and 'bodes' reach forward towards a dramatic conclusion, yet also look back to the speech of Beleses and his need to interpret natural phenomena as portents. The subject of the whole passage is the significance of action on Sardanapalus's character. It is therefore of crucial significance to understanding the curious mixture of liberal, anti-authoritarian, yet aristocratic political ideology which he represents. This is of course the same ideology Byron held throughout his life which means it reverberates with biographical significance.

Yet, despite all this, there is more to this image. It remains possibly the most vivid with which the reader leaves the work; Sardanapalus, out of his humour and roused to the action of battle, paradoxically creates an image which has a stillness, almost a quality of stasis, set apart from the temporal momentum of the narrative. Byron uses assonance, 'close and sultry summer' in juxtaposition with clusters of heavily stressed syllables, 'bursts forth' to alternate the pace of the verse. The pace of the action described is consequently increased before being held back in a moment which seems to capture the action in a lyrical stop. The momentum of action must be present for the indolent poetry to work itself free. The dialectic sustains an image, and the reader, in a moment of imaginative release. The vigour of the poetry allows Sardanapalus to metamorphose into the expected tempest, a point which is of course meant figuratively, but the power of the verse makes it all but literal. Sardanapalus becomes like Keats's nightingale, made eternal through his song. In this case the song is his poetic incarnation as the immortal thunderstorm which will resound to all ages.

Three caveats naturally occur, although space will not permit me to pursue them further here. Firstly, have I pushed aesthetic freedom too far? I am aware I have given what might be described as a Keatsian reading of *Sardanapalus*. Perhaps I have not foregrounded, as I might have done, the unfolding of political characters in the text and their significance in understanding Byron's own political views. Secondly, I am aware that the formulation of a dialectic of poetry and dramatic action which attempts to either delay or hurry the narrative, touches on issues central to feminist criticism. The ideas of a feminine open-endedness and a masculine closure correspond to the dialectic I have described. It seems to me that the two may be linked, but that the dialectic I have described is possibly less of a struggle or antagonism.[23] Thirdly, and finally, unlike a text such as *Don Juan*, the reader does not leave *Sardanapalus* experiencing the same complicity of guilt at the unerring progression of the narrative. Instead, the reading experience is a wholly more stirring and positive one.[24] I would suggest that this is also due to the freedom allowed by the Sardanapalian aesthetic I have described.

Notes

1 See Richard Lansdown, *Byron's Historical Dramas* (Oxford: Clarendon Press, 1992), pp. 140–70. G. Wilson Knight, '"Simple" and "Bright": *Sardanapalus*', in *The Plays of Lord Byron*, ed. by Robert Gleckner and Bernard Beatty (Liverpool: Liverpool University Press, 1997), pp. 181–99. Also Samuel Chew, *The Dramas of Lord Byron* (New York: Russell and Russell, 1964).

2 Leslie Marchand, *Byron's Poetry: A Critical Introduction* (London: John Murray, 1965), p. 105.

3 The spring and summer of 1821 saw a military clampdown on the manoeuvres of the Carbonari and Byron declaring Ravenna 'the seat of war'. On 25 July Teresa Guiccioli actually left Byron for Florence under threat from the state authorities that she would be sequestered in a convent. See Fiona MacCarthy, *Byron: Life and Legend* (London: John Murray, 2002), pp. 393–7.

4 Quoted in Lansdown, *Byron's Historical Dramas*, p. 154.

5 It seems that Byron's search for aesthetic freedom had become closely linked to a religious or moral programme in his own thoughts. While his source was Diodorus Siculus, it is significant that he was also reading Seneca at the time. He was keen to liberate his drama morally from the corrupt English stage through well-defined aesthetic models. Martyn Corbett argues a similar case concerning Byron's advocacy of Pope at this point, 'He is the moral poet of all civilization, and, as such, let us hope that he will one day be the national poet of mankind' (*BLJ*, 5, 560). Corbett rightly argues that Byron's choice of neo-classical form 'though never used by Pope, would, in Byron's analysis anyway, have recommended itself to the moral poet of all civilization'. Martyn Corbett, *Byron and Tragedy* (Hong Kong: Macmillan, 1988), p. 3.

6 *BLJ*, 11, 229. Byron's attitude to his public was fickle. Philip Martin argues that this was because their applause 'was alluring and simultaneously the subject of his contempt'. Martin also correctly suggests, however, that other factors than Byron's relationship with his audience must be taken into consideration in the case of *Sardanapalus*. Byron's artistic concerns, particularly his desire to employ neo-classical dramatic devices, were motivated by a sincere desire to create 'great' art, 'the critique of the contemporary stage implicit in the dramas [*Marino Faliero, Sardanapalus, The Two Foscari*] and the remarks that accompany them are apparently sincerely felt'. Philip W. Martin, *Byron: A Poet before His Public* (Cambridge: Cambridge University Press, 1982), p. 137. Martyn Corbett similarly points out that Byron's serious aesthetic message is made to sound like a 'peevish whim' (p. 4).

7 David Erdman, 'Byron's Stage Fright', in *The Plays of Lord Byron*, ed. by Gleckner and Beatty, p. 5.

8 *BLJ*, 11, 229.

9 Byron challenges his audience's capacity here actively to collaborate with an author in the creation of meaning. In *Semiotics of Poetry* (Bloomington, IN, and London: Indiana University Press, 1978), Michael Riffaterre describes a 'Super-reader' as one who attempts to analyse texts beyond the (often) contrary meanings of subtext and supertext. I would suggest that Byron's desire for aesthetic freedom

in *Sardanapalus* equates to this 'Superreader'; a reader who appreciates that a text can contain a variety of meanings – political, aesthetic, biographical – which can co-exist despite being contradictory.

10 *BLJ*, 8, 103. See also Dryden's Preface to *All for Love*. Byron chooses the 'unities' because he is hostile to English drama. Dryden, on the other hand, is an Anglophile, commenting 'I desire to be tried by the laws of my own country, for it seems unjust to me that the French should prescribe here till they have conquered'. *Restoration Plays*, ed. by Robert G. Lawrence (London: Everyman, 1994), p. 220. Paradoxically, considering the implacable precepts of classical drama, both poets turn to neo-classicism for freedom.

11 Frederick Page, *Poetical Works of Byron* (Oxford: Oxford University Press, 1970), p. 453. All subsequent references to the Preface are taken from this edition.

12 Lansdown, *Byron's Historical Dramas*, pp. 171, 173.

13 *Aristotle on the Art of Poetry*, trans. by Lane Cooper (New York: Harcourt Brace, 1913), p. 24.

14 Geoffrey Ward, 'Byron's Artistry in Deep and Layered Space', in *Byron and the Limits of Fiction*, ed. by Bernard Beatty and Vincent Newey (Liverpool: Liverpool University Press, 1988), p. 209.

15 Mikhail Bakhtin, *Problems of Dostoevsky's Poetics*, ed. and trans. by Caryl Emerson (Manchester: Manchester University Press, 1984). Bakhtin makes a contrast between a 'monologic' text in which the author has final control over all character's 'voices', and a 'dialogic' text in which characters are allowed to speak in their own voices free from authoritative control. This does not mean that characters are distinguished by idiosyncratic styles of speech. In *Sardanapalus* I would argue that characters are idiosyncratic in speech and behaviour, yet the text is not dialogic. The first fact is perhaps the cause of the second.

16 See also Corneille, *Le Cid*, trans. by Ranjit Bolt (London: Oberon, 1999), p. 180. Don Fernando represents the ideal neo-classical model of kingship when he adapts natural energy (in this case love) to human law (the two sides of the usual neo-classical dialectic); 'That custom, here established far too long, / Ostensibly designed for righting wrongs, / Robs nations of their bravest and their best. / No. I exempt Rodrigo from the test' (IV.v). Interestingly this example of rule by 'awe and law' results in a 'tragi-comedy' and not a tragedy.

17 Compare this with the final stanzas of *Childe Harold* I. Byron prolongs the death of the bull. In stanza 93 the narrator comments, "'tis past', yet it is not until the next stanza that the bull actually dies. Byron revels in the aesthetic tragedy as his poetic medium prolongs the bull's fate. Paul Elledge notes that Byron has trouble in valedictory stanzas in *Childe Harold*. However, his inability to provide 'closure' in Beleses' speech owes as much to poetry or Romanticism clashing with action or neo-classicism as it does to declining poetic responsibility as Elledge argues of *Childe Harold* in 'Chasms and Connections: Byron Ending (in) *Childe Harold's Pilgrimage* 1 and 2', in *Byron*, ed. Jane Stabler (London: Longman, 1998), pp. 123–37.

18 Wilson Knight, '"Simple" and "Bright": *Sardanapalus*', p. 199. Note how his stillness is achieved through the integration of 'action' and poetic subject, i.e. 'eternity'. This captures action in stasis.

19 Corbett, *Byron and Tragedy*, p. 82. See also *CPW*, 6, 606.
20 Lansdown, *Byron's Historical Dramas*, p. 152.
21 Dryden, *All for Love*, II, 219–21.
22 Camille Paglia, *Sexual Personae: From Nefertiti to Emily Dickinson* (London: Penguin, 1991), p. 351.
23 See also Paglia, *Sexual Personae*, pp. 347–64. Paglia applies a feminist reading of this phenomenon in *Sardanapalus* and elsewhere in Byron's work.
24 I would be loath to label *Sardanapalus* a 'Tragedy' at all, although it is hardly a tragi-comedy in the manner of *Le Cid*, because there is no positive resolution to the story. All positive feeling is instead created in the aesthetic releases of the reading process.

Byron, Milton, and Doctrines of Christian Liberty: *Cain* and *Paradise Regained*

JOAN BLYTHE

At the beginning of *Paradise Regained* Milton says that his subject, the temptations of the Son of God in the wilderness (recounted in Matthew 4 and Luke 4), is 'worthy t'have not remain'd so long unsung'.[1] This paper examines a subject I think worthy not to have remained so long unexplored: the relationship between *Paradise Regained* and Byron's *Cain*. I will compare these two works with particular, but not exclusive, emphasis on the concepts of intellectual freedom and Christian liberty. To understand Milton's view in these matters I cite his posthumously published *De Doctrina Christiana*. First, I offer a general introduction to the subject. Second, I discuss Miltonic influence on *Cain* via Salomon Gessner's *The Death of Abel*. Third, I point out parallels between *Paradise Regained* and *Cain* in terms of characterisation, structure, Biblical reference, and the kingdom within. Last, I speculate on unorthodox Socinian perspectives in the two works.

I

Milton proclaims in the autobiographical section of his 1654 *Defensio Secunda* (*Second Defense of the English People*) that there are 'three species of liberty which are essential to the happiness of social life – religious domestic, and civil' (830–1). More so than any of the younger English Romantics, Byron may be said to have embodied in word and action Milton's passion for such liberties. In *Don Juan*, Byron calls Milton an 'independent being in his day' (III, 91), celebrates him for 'clos[ing] the tyrant-hater he begun', and implicitly condemns that dichotomy which holds Milton '*sublime*' yet 'execrates his wrongs' ('Dedication', p. 10), that is to say, his suspect political and religious views.

William Hayley, for example, whose biography of Milton became, according to Joseph Wittreich, '*The Milton* of Blake, Wordsworth,

Coleridge, and Shelley' – but not of Byron[2] – regards Milton's activities on behalf of the Good Old Cause and Cromwell as a regrettable aberration. Following the earlier biography of John Toland, Hayley presents Milton as a bulwark of English Christianity; his genius resided in 'sublime religious enthusiasm' which operated purely and orthodoxically after he withdrew from politics in 1660.

This perspective is not supported by the historical record nor was it Byron's view. Bernard Beatty writes that Byron 'is always in some sense a religious poet'.[3] As that 'religious poet' Byron has affinity with Milton in more and different ways than have been recognised. In his conversations with Dr Kennedy, Kennedy reported that poetically Byron 'places himself on a level with Shakespeare and Milton'.[4] Byron also expressed at that time religious views in accord with Milton's. One example is Byron's attraction to Socinianism, an interest he declared he shared with Lady Byron and a subject he discussed at length with Dr Kennedy.[5] Byron could not have known, but surely would have been interested to know that Milton, as official licenser for Cromwell, acted as an 'independent being in his day' when he approved for publication in 1650 an English translation of the heretical Socinian *Racovian Catechism*. This decision may have cost the poet his job.[6]

While Byron was conversing with Dr Kennedy in Cephalonia the Latin manuscript of Milton's controversial Socinian-tending theological tract *De Doctrina Christiana* was found among State Papers at Whitehall. Public notice of the discovery of what Milton termed his 'dearest and best possession'[7] was published 17 January 1824; an English translation by Charles Sumner appeared in 1825.

Byron would have found Milton's unorthodox views riveting. They have appalled readers from the time of *De Doctrina*'s publication up to the present day, so much so that orthodox Christians especially have been in the vanguard of those who dispute Milton's authorship of the tract. For example, during the last decade William Hunter led a vigorous campaign among Miltonists against Miltonic authorship of *De Doctrina*. Though he has received support from computer analyses of Milton's prose style by Thomas Corns and others, the main impetus for Hunter's challenge is the treatise's lack of orthodoxy.[8] Most disturbing to orthodox Christians is Milton's apparent anti-trinitarianism: Milton does not accord the Son of God equal status or essence with the Father. He is rather the means (Latin *per*) through which the Father works on earth. Milton also opined that there was no Biblical warrant necessitating regular attendance at orthodox worship services. He felt one could worship God appropriately at any time anywhere (there is no evidence Milton ever attended church regularly after leaving Cambridge). He still supported divorce in *De Doctrina Christiana* as he had in his five divorce pamphlets of the mid-1640s. *De Doctrina Christiana* also entertains tolerant views on polygamy (based on the examples of the Old Testament Patriarchs) and incest.

But more than for any particular opinion, Byron would have responded to Milton's general mindset throughout *De Doctrina Christiana*, one which continues to ask questions, even in the face of (to borrow Angus Fletcher's words) 'an infinitely receding galaxy of answers'.[9] Milton believed it was necessary for Christians to

> be free not only to sift and winnow any doctrine, but also openly to give their opinions of it and even to write about it according to which each believes ... Without this freedom to which I refer there is no religion and no gospel ... without this freedom we are still enslaved.

> (6:122–3)

Miltonists have found evidence of the unorthodox views expressed in *De Doctrina Christiana* in many of his works from 'Upon the Circumcision' of 1629–1633 to *Paradise Lost* (1667; 1674) and *Paradise Regained* (1671), as well as in Milton's late prose treatises such as *Of Toleration* (1673).[10] Here I consider such views in *Paradise Regained* in relation to Byron's *Cain*, a work which certainly demonstrates a Miltonic freedom to sift through doctrine.

Barbara Lewalski identifies the mission of the Son in *Paradise Regained* as 'the restoration of man's inner freedom'.[11] Though he does not connect *Paradise Regained* and *Cain*, Jerome McGann has found the restoration of freedom a theme in Byron's Biblical drama. McGann calls attention to Byron's view of Milton's mind 'as searching and unsettled as his own', a mind which 'is not only not made up, [but] positively avoids "argument" on a system or "proof" for a set of fixed ideas. He too provokes one to wonder about the issues ... by his nondogmatic handling of certain very dogmatically conditioned materials'.[12] Responding to charges of obscurity in his poetry, Byron reportedly observed to Medwin, 'But as to obscurity, is not Milton obscure?'[13]

Unlike William Hunter, several Milton scholars, especially John Rogers and William Kolbrener, have focused on Milton's 'resistance to embrace uncomplicated perspectives' and his exploration of 'multiple truths' in *De Doctrina Christiana*.[14] In a 1999 paper, Rogers argued that *Paradise Regained* is a poetic exploration of the non-dogmatic and Socinian-tending aspects of Milton's *De Doctrina Christiana*.[15]

According to Medwin, Byron declared, 'I am too happy in being coupled in any way with Milton, and shall be glad if they find any points of comparison between him and me'.[16] Medwin also repeats Shelley's pronouncement that *Cain* was the 'finest poetry that has appeared in England since the publication of *Paradise Regained*'.[17] Shelley seems to have been one of the few readers to associate two works that are bound together by more than poetic merit. I argue that it is the Satanic drama of Milton's brief epic (with its infusion of non-dogmatic aspects of *De Doctrina Christiana*) rather than that of *Paradise Lost* which more interestingly informs *Cain*.[18] Prior to analysing some general and specific similarities between Byron's *Cain* and *Paradise Regained* and how both may be said to reflect what might be termed 'Christian liberty' in their Socinian views, I shall offer as background for Milton's influence on *Cain* a brief digression on the epic poem *Der Tod Abels* by the Swiss Salomon Gessner.

II

Although studies were made of Byron, Milton, and Gessner long ago,[19] recent Byron scholarship has tended to adopt a disdainful attitude towards the subject. The notes to McGann's Oxford Authors *Byron* puts down *The Death of Abel* as 'a sentimental drama with only superficial resemblances to *Cain*'.[20] Byron himself in his Preface to *Cain* dismissed the influence of Salomon Gessner's *The Death of Abel* as a work he hadn't read since he was eight; yet Hazlitt was not the only contemporary to point out that Byron was being disingenuous here, as he often was about his influences. What current scholars and readers of Byron perhaps do not realise is just how popular Gessner was in Byron's time and how extensive his influence was upon the international reading public. Wordsworth's ranking of Gessner along with Shakespeare and Milton in Book VII of *The Prelude* is not an isolated example of Gessner's eminence in the first half of the nineteenth century.[21] Gessner's *The Death of Abel* would inspire William Blake's tempera painting *The Body of Abel Found by Adam and Eve* (1826) as well as a popular sculpture by Thorwaldsen.[22]

Gessner's *The Death of Abel* had been published first in German in 1758. By 1821, when Byron was working on *Cain*, *The Death of Abel* had had twenty printings in German, fifty-one in French, one in Greek, fifty-nine in English (in England and America), one in Polish, six in Swedish, seven in Danish and Norwegian, five in Dutch, two in Czech, four in Portuguese, one in Spanish, one in Latin, and four in Italian.[23] This does not include its appearance in the numerous collected editions of Gessner's works. It is tempting to speculate whether Teresa Guiccioli read and was particularly fond of *The Death of Abel* since it exalts Thirza, a beautiful devoted woman who sticks by her exiled lover. The positive aspects of Adah, Byron's version of Thirza, are discussed in section III.

To understand Miltonic influence on Byron's *Cain*, we also have to take into consideration Miltonic influence on *The Death of Abel*. Bodmer's and Huber's translations of Milton had inspired Gessner's narrative. The influence of *Paradise Lost* predominates in *The Death of Abel*, but Gessner, especially in depicting Cain's tormenting dreams, also drew upon *Paradise Regained*. In spite of Byron's claim to Medwin that he read Gessner as a child in German,[24] he probably knew the poem primarily through English translations, which stylistically often consciously imitated Milton. Mary Collyer, who invoked Milton as her muse as she translated Gessner into prose, created the most popular English version of *The Death of Abel*. By 1821 it had gone through more than forty printings. Collyer's language often borrows directly from both of Milton's epics or strongly alludes to them. Though not nearly as popular as Collyer's, Thomas Newcombe's English translation of 1761 also deserves mention. On the title page he proclaims (as Collyer does not) that his version is 'In the stile of Milton'. Newcombe's blank-verse text likewise borrows extensively from Milton. Thus added to the passages in Gessner which originally were indebted to Milton we have the Miltonic overlay of Gessner's English translators.

Blumenthal's important study of Milton, Gessner, and *Cain* does not enter into issues of how Milton influenced English translations, but addresses parallels in content. Like most Byron scholars who discuss Milton and *Cain*, Blumenthal draws on *Paradise Lost* exclusively. Blumenthal's critique of the lack of drama in *Cain*, however, sounds not unlike how some scholars respond to *Paradise Regained* in relation to *Paradise Lost*.[25] 'the conversation is so much intermixed with philosophical remarks and metaphysical reflections that question and answer follow each other very slowly and do not sufficiently raise and hold our attention and expectations'.[26] Yet it is just this Socratic questioning, calling all into doubt which typifies the dialogue in both *Paradise Regained* and *Cain*. In the former, Louis Martz says, 'The meditative mind is exploring its own problems, as well as those of mankind, through the speeches of the "characters".'[27] The same might be said of *Cain*.

I now turn to a closer examination of Byron's drama and Milton's brief epic.

III

The Son in *Paradise Regained* and Cain seek through inner dialogues and
dialogues with their tempters to understand their identities.[28] Both protagonists are described as much given to thought and as isolated from the rest
of humanity. The Son is prone to 'contemplation and profound dispute'
and recollects to himself, 'I thought alone' (1.178). He has had 'a multitude
of thoughts at once / Awak'n'd in me' and 'growing thoughts' which his
mother encourages: 'High are thy thoughts / O Son, but nourish them and
let them soar' (1.196–7; 227–30). Similarly Cain speaks of 'Thoughts which
rise within me, as if they / Could master all things: – but I thought alone'
(1.1.177–8) and says he has a 'mind which overwhelms me' (1.189). It is
significant that the principal setting *Paradise Regained* and all of *Cain* is not
Eden, as in most of *Paradise Lost*, but 'savage Wilderness' (3.23).

Unlike Satan in *Paradise Lost*, Satan in *Paradise Regained* appears as a man,
not as a toad or an elegant serpent. First he comes to the Son of God as
an 'aged man clad in rural weeds' (1.314). For the next two temptations he
appears as an urbane fashionable courtier. In *Cain* Lucifer's exact looks are
not delineated. One assumes his impressive 'majestic mien and bearing' is
manlike, as well as angelic in some sort. Lucifer is at pains to distinguish
himself from the serpent that tempted Eve. Eve, astonished to hear a
serpent discourse so intelligently, says very little as she is seduced by a
barrage of eloquence. Unlike this model, the temptations in *Paradise
Regained* and in *Cain* unfold as rational, philosophical exchanges, often cast
in catechetical language. What Eve wants is an easy elevation of her status.
What Cain and the Son in *Paradise Regained* want is understanding and clar-
ification of their beings.

Both Satan in *Paradise Regained* and Lucifer in *Cain* treat their prey as
those who have never been anywhere, don't know enough, and need help
to attain their desires. In the first day's temptation in *Paradise Regained* Satan
chides the Son:

> all thy heart is set on high designs,
> … but wherewith to be achiev'd?
> Thou art unknown, unfriended, low of birth.
>
> (2.410–13)

At the beginning of the second temptation he mocks the Son for being
'over-ripe' in years without having achieved anything (3.21–42). In a similar
vein Byron's Lucifer derisively twits Cain:

> But I speak to thee of what thou know'st not,
> With all thy tree of knowledge.

$$(1.1.246)$$

At the start of Act II Lucifer promises to show Cain 'worlds beyond thy little world … beyond thy little life' (2.1.13–15). Both Satan and Lucifer assume that they will be able to intimidate and co-opt, respectively, the Son and Cain through sophisticated and intellectually specious repartee along with fantastic glimpses of other realms.

Both the Son and Cain are borne up and away for the most significant part of their temptations. For the temptations of the kingdoms Satan takes the Son off on an 'aery flight' to one side of a mountain, then to the other where the Son sees past and present things through an 'aery microscope'. For the last temptation Satan wafts the Son up to the summit of the temple's pinnacle. At the beginning of Act II of *Cain* Lucifer tells Cain 'thou shalt be / Borne on the air' and

> Fly with me … and I will show … the history
> Of past, and present, and of future worlds.

$$(2.1.2–3;\ 22–5)$$

A point of character comparison less obvious than the examples given above is the broadly analogous roles of Mary in *Paradise Regained* and Adah in *Cain*. As I have argued elsewhere regarding Medora, Adah needs rehabilitation, not condescension, as a Byronic heroine.[29] Adah's anxiety when Cain goes off with Lucifer is comparable to Mary's concern in *Paradise Regained* when the Son is away in the wilderness. Neither knows where her loved one is. Both women are involved in establishing the identity of the protagonist. The last lines of *Paradise Regained* read 'he unobserved / Home to his mother's house private returned'. At the end Cain goes off in the context of the home environment anchored by Adah.

Structurally, *Cain* is divided in three acts. *Paradise Regained*, though physically partitioned into four books, has a stronger tripartite division that accords with the three temptations of Jesus in the wilderness recounted in Matthew 4 and Luke 4: to turn stones into bread, the temptation to accept from the devil worldly goods and power (known as the 'temptation of the kingdoms'), and the temptation to cast Himself down from the top of the temple pinnacle in Jerusalem. That in *Paradise Regained* the temptations of the kingdoms occupy centre stage may be compared to Lucifer's attention-commanding temptation of the mental kingdoms which occupies the middle portion, indeed all of Act II, of *Cain*.

One of the most striking links between *Paradise Regained* and *Cain* is the dramatic use of Matthew 4:9: 'All these things will I give thee, if thou wilt fall down and worship me.' The passage is central to the Biblical temptation of Jesus by the devil in the wilderness. In *Paradise Regained* Satan offers the Son all the kingdoms of the world

> if thou wilt fall down
> And worship me as thy superior Lord.
>
> (4.166–7)

This deal the Son vehemently refuses. Lucifer suggests a comparable exchange: he will show Cain 'what is true knowledge' and teach him 'all' on one condition:

> That
> Thou dost fall down and worship me – thy Lord.
>
> (1.1 301–4)

Though for different reasons, Cain, like the Son, rejects the proposition.

Both *Paradise Regained* and *Cain* deal with the idea of freedom, particularly inner freedom. In discussing this aspect of *Cain* in relation to Milton, McGann cites the archangel Michael's 'final exhortation to Adam and Eve in *Paradise Lost*' to achieve 'a paradise within thee, happier far' (12.587).[30] But a more powerful parallel exists in *Paradise Regained*. In this work one of the major temptations of the kingdoms is for the Son to free men from tyranny. First Satan proposes that the Son free his Israelites from the Roman yoke. Later he urges the Son to free the Romans from the tyranny of the cruel and monomaniacal Tiberius. When the Son rejects the role of liberator, Satan in rapturous lyricism, offers the Son all the aesthetic intellectual glories of the Greek Platonists, Stoics, Peripatetics, and Epicureans whereby one can become a kingdom in oneself:

> These rules will render thee a king complete
> Within thyself.
>
> (4.282–3)

Critics have often thought the ravishing collation of humanistic learning that Satan offers the Son vastly more appealing than what the Son offers in its place: Biblical instruction. To this critical stance we might compare McGann's enthusiastic praise of 'Lucifer's final two speeches in *Cain*' which he terms 'a commitment to intellectual freedom that has never been surpassed in English verse'.[31] What Lucifer shows Cain is based on the scientific discoveries which divided intellectuals of Byron's day. The caveat of human response to the immensities of possible knowledge is similar to what the Son says regarding the fascination of humanistic studies in Milton's time:

> who reads
> Incessantly, and to his reading brings not
> A spirit and judgment equal or superior ...
> Uncertain and unsettl'd still remains,
> Deep verst in books and shallow in himself.

(4.322–7)

For both Milton and Byron 'freedom' – whether religious, political, or intellectual – has no value as an abstract concept, but depends upon the historically responsible and self-aware social engagement of the individual with the world.

IV

Even more pertinent to the theme of Byron, freedom, and liberty, is the correspondence between *Cain* and *Paradise Regained* in terms of the Socinian ideas that Milton discussed in *De Doctrina Christiana* and elsewhere. For the English of Milton's time Socinianism from abroad served as a corrective to the 'harsh Calvinism' of the era with, in H. John McLachlan's words, 'its rigorous views of Justification and Atonement, a corrective to irrational and intolerant dogmatism, a standing criticism of the ... dogma of the Trinity'. These ideas joined 'English protests against the prevailing orthodoxy and at length' were to 'bear fruit in the rational Christianity of a John Locke and an Isaac Newton and in the Unitarianism of a Joseph Priestley'.[32] Priestley is known now primarily for his discovery of oxygen, but his most controversial role in the eighteenth century was as a Socinian dissenting minister and theologian. In writing to Douglas Kinnaird in February 1822 about the outcry against *Cain*, Byron as he rallies authorities to his defence, significantly uses Priestley's name first: 'The same outcry was raised against Priestley – Hume – Gibbon – Voltaire – and all men who ever dared put tithes to the question' (*BLJ*, 9, 100).[33]

The progenitor of Socinianism was Fausto Sozzini (born in Siena in 1539). By 1580 he had emigrated to Krakow where he enjoyed (as was possible in no other city in Europe) immunity from persecution for his radical ideas. These were most popularly promulgated in *The Racovian Catechism* begun in 1603 and brought to completion after his death by his followers. The main tenets held by Socinians of the seventeenth and early eighteenth century and their heirs, the Unitarians, include: 'scrupulous and rigorous biblicism', strong adherence to 'the rights of reason in religion' (right reason and divine truth must agree), rejection of the doctrine of original sin and the 'atoning sacrifice of Christ', denial of the divinity of Christ on a par with God (anti-trinitarianism) and the importance of merit in achieving salvation.[34]

According to Dr Kennedy, Byron claimed he began every day by reading the Bible. So, we know, did Milton. In his preface to *Cain* Byron insists on his close adherence to the Bible: the language of his characters he says is 'taken from actual *Scripture*'. He claims he has made 'little alteration … I must take words as I find them, and reply with Bishop Watson, upon similar occasions when the Fathers were quoted to him, as Moderator in the Schools of Cambridge, "Behold the Book!" – holding up the Scripture' (*CPW*, 6, 228). This assertion of scriptural authority parallels the position of Milton in *De Doctrina Christiana* when he writes in the preface that there 'was more than I realised which still needed to be measured with greater strictness against the yardstick of the Bible' (6:120). The only authority Milton accepted was the Holy Scriptures themselves. This position is in keeping with that of the Son in *Paradise Regained* who after rejecting Satan's offer of the classical humanistic learning proclaims fervently that any virtues the Greek arts may have had are 'ill imitated' from the Bible and but 'varnish on a Harlot's cheek'. Biblical prophets better teach

> the solid rules of Civil Government
> In their majestic unaffected style
> Than all the oratory of *Greece* and *Rome*.
>
> (4.330–60)

Like the Socinians, neither Milton nor Byron had orthodox views about the Trinity. Milton's anti-trinitarianism surfaces clearly in *De Doctrina Christiana*, but also comes to play in *Paradise Regained* with its emphasis on the manhood (rather than the godhood) of the Son: God tells Gabriel,

> I can produce a man
> Of female seed.
>
> (1.150–1)[35]

Byron told Dr Kennedy that he thought 'the doctrine of the Trinity … is alone quite appalling'.[36] Dr Kennedy was so alarmed by Byron's 'peculiar' thoughts about the Son of God that he gave him a book on the Trinity.[37] In *Cain* Lucifer insists upon the manhood of Jesus,

A man shall say to a man, 'Believe in me
And walk the waters' and the man shall walk the billows and be safe

(2.1.18–20)

Also like the Socinians, neither Milton nor Byron seemed to favour the Christian doctrine of atonement. It is clear in *Cain* that Byron (like Gessner in his treatment of Abel's sacrifice in *The Death of Abel*) abhors the theology of original sin and the concept of blood sacrifice as a means of atonement. In his dialogue with Lucifer Cain repeatedly complains that he does not deserve what is in store for him on account of his parents' sin, and he rejects Adam's justification of the lamb's sufferings:

from evil
Springs good.

(2.2.298–9)

Lucifer's allusion to the atoning death of Christ is part of his negative characterisation of God the Father: 'Perhaps he'll make one day a son onto himself ... that son will be a sacrifice' (1.1.163–6). His rage that Enoch should suffer for sins he did not commit almost causes Cain (so it would seem) to murder his own son. Cain here ironically participates in a kind of typology of God the Father as well as of Abraham. And when making his offering to God, Cain's 'shrine without a victim, / And altar without gore' seems vastly preferable to Abel's atoning sacrificial lamb's

whose limbs now reek
in sanguinary incense to thy skies.

(3.1.257–8)

Milton critics have often remarked that Milton avoids the subject of Christ's passion. He seems uncomfortable with a Father/God who seems to demand human suffering beyond the dictates of merit.[38] Importantly for *Cain*, God at the beginning of *Paradise Regained* and the angelic chorus at the end say that the Son by virtue of his *merit* in 'vanquishing / Temptation' – not by his death – has redeemed mankind and 'regain'd lost Paradise' (1.166–7; 4.606–9). In accord with Socinian views, the Son's role in *Paradise Regained* comes across as a revealer, a means through which God's plans are made known, rather than the sacrificial reconciler to God's anger.[39]

Broadly speaking, Cain's responses to the allurements of Lucifer also demonstrate his merit and a rational self-sufficiency which is comparable to the Son's in *Paradise Regained*.[40] The death of Abel is an accident of passion provoked by the self-righteously nagging Abel.[41] Byron himself

said the 'Catastrophe' came from 'mere *internal* irritation – *not* premedita-
tion or envy – of Abel' (*BLJ*, 9, 53–4). In my opinion, Cain's 'individuation'
does not depend on this tragic violence,[42] but on his sustained questioning
of his received belief system, a questioning Milton deemed essential for
Christian liberty and freedom. Cain's triumph in countering Lucifer lies, in
large part, in his insistence on the immediate beauties of the world before
him, especially of Adah. He, like the Son in *Paradise Regained*, refuses to
become consumed by a world of abstractions, the realm of Milton's Satan
and of Lucifer in *Cain* who loves only

> some vast and general purpose,
> To which particular things must melt like snows.
>
> (2.2.314–15)

At the end of *Paradise Regained* Milton invokes the story of Antaeus striving
with Jove's Alcides. Antaeus was finally killed when he was separated from
Earth. Lucifer in his airy transport attempts to separate Cain from healthful
earth. He does not succeed. Cain asserts that link in his celebratory
speeches (as in 2.2.255–68) and in his acceptance of Adah and his family
as he goes into the wilderness where (it is implied) his pangs of conscience
might lead to a purified inner space. In Milton's view, this would entitle
him to salvation.[43]

Traditional Christian theologians for centuries have interpreted Abel as
a prototype of Jesus. Reading *Cain* in light of *Paradise Regained* invites a
radical rethinking of that view. Through his allusions to *Paradise Regained*
in *Cain* Byron implies that there is a relationship between the Son of God
who is elevated by virtue of his merit – not his death – and Cain, the exile
and wanderer, the seeker after intellectual and personal liberty, the man
who much more than Abel, is, or might be like us. This interpretation
opens up redemptive possibilities for ourselves as well as for Byron's hero.

Notes

1   John Milton, *Complete Poems and Major Prose*, ed. by Merritt Hughes (New York:
    Macmillan, 1957), *Paradise Regained*, 1.16. Unless otherwise indicated, all reference
    to Milton's works is to this edition.
2   Joseph Wittreich, Jr, 'Introduction' to William Hayley's 1796 *The Life of Milton*
    (Gainesville, FL: Scholars' Facsimiles & Reprints, 1970), p. xiii.
3   Bernard Beatty, 'Fiction's Limit and Eden's Door', *Byron and the Limits of Fiction*,
    ed. by Bernard Beatty and Vincent Newey (Totowa, NJ: Barnes & Noble, 1988),
    p. 33.

4   James Kennedy, *Conversations on Religion with Lord Byron and Others* (London: John Murray, 1830), p. 331.

5   Kennedy, *Conversations on Religion*, 194–7.

6   For an analysis of Milton vis-à-vis *The Racovian Catechism*, see Stephen B. Dobranski, 'Licensing Milton's Heresy', in *Milton and Heresy*, ed. by Stephen B. Dobranski and John P. Rumrich (Cambridge, Cambridge University Press, 1988), pp. 139–58.

7   *Complete Prose Works of John Milton*, ed. by Don M. Wolfe *et al.*, 8 vols (New Haven, CT: Yale University Press, 1953–1982), 6:121. All references to Milton's *De Doctrina Christiana* are to this edition.

8   For an intelligent, short overview of the subject see Anthony Cinquemani's review, 'Milton and the Authorship of "De Doctrina Christiana"', *ANQ* 13, no. 4 (2000), pp. 56–60. The most comprehensive treatment of the subject to date is by Michael Lieb: '*De Doctrina Christiana* and the Question of Authorship', *Milton Studies* 41 (2002), pp. 172–230.

9   Angus Fletcher, *Colors of the Mind: Conjectures on Thinking in Literature* (Cambridge, MA: Harvard University Press, 1991), p. 89.

10 For the most comprehensive overview of Milton and Socinianism see Michael Lieb, 'Milton and the Socinian Heresy', in *Milton and the Grounds of Contention*, ed. by Mark Kelley, Michael Lieb, and John T. Shawcross (Pittsburgh, PA: Duquesne University Press, 2003), pp. 234–83, 318–33. According to Lieb, 'It little matters whether we can prove that Milton accepted "this aspect," as opposed to "that aspect," of Socinianism. What does matter is that the Socinian heresy was a crucial movement in his own time and that he responded to it at various points in his career. What also matters is that those who did express their allegiance to the movement were inclined to draw upon certain elements in Milton's work to proclaim him as one of their own. They must have seen *something* in his delineation of doctrinal matters (either implicit in the poetry or explicit in the prose) to justify their readings' (p. 283).

11 Barbara Lewalski, *Milton's Brief Epic: The Genre, Meaning, & Art of 'Paradise Regained'* (Providence, RI: Brown University Press, 1966), p. 277.

12 Jerome McGann, *Don Juan in Context* (London: John Murray, 1976), pp. 30–1.

13 *Medwin's Conversations of Lord Byron*, ed. by Ernest J. Lovell, Jr (Princeton, NJ: Princeton University Press, 1966), p. 162.

14 William Kolbrener, *Milton's Warring Angels* (Cambridge: Cambridge University Press, 1997), pp. 76 and 66.

15 'Family Heresies in *Paradise Regained*', paper delivered at MLA, December 1999. See also Rogers, 'Milton and the Heretical Priesthood of Christ', in *Heresy, Literature and Politics in Early Modern English Culture*, ed. by David Lowenstein (Cambridge: Cambridge University Press, 2006), pp. 203–20.

16 *Medwin's Conversations of Lord Byron*, p. 122.

17 *Medwin's Conversations of Lord Byron*, p. 126.

18 The only apparent reference to *Paradise Regained* in Truman Guy Steffan's magisterial *Lord Byron's 'Cain'* (Austin, Texas: University of Texas Press, 1968) is the mention of Counsellor Lancelot Shadwell's defence of *Cain* by saying that the seemingly 'blasphemous and impious' passages in Byron's drama are no more so

that 'what Milton has done also both in his Paradise Lost and Regained' (p. 14).

19 The most notable is Friedrich Blumenthal's 'Lord Byron's Mystery "Cain" and its Relation to Milton's "Paradise Lost" and Gessner's "Death of Abel"', *Beilage zum 48. Jahresbericht der Städtischen Ober-Realschule zu Oldenburg* (Oldenburg, 1891), pp. 1–12.

20 *Byron: A Critical Edition of the Major Works*, ed. by Jerome J. McGann (Oxford: Oxford University Press, 1986), p. 1072. McGann here seems to follow Peter Thorslev who condemns *The Death of Abel* as 'cloyingly sentimental', a defect 'accentuated in its abominable English translations'. Thorslev, *The Byronic Hero: Types and Prototypes* (Minneapolis, MN: University of Minnesota Press, 1962), p. 95.

21 See Bertha Reed, 'The Influence of Salomon Gessner on English Literature', *Germanica Americana* 4 (1904), pp. 380–8.

22 See William Vaughan, *German Romanticism and English Art* (New Haven, CT: Yale University Press, 1979), pp. 107–9, 257, 264.

23 For a comprehensive listing of the editions of Gessner's works see P. Leemann-Van Elck, *Salomon Gessner. Dichter, Maler und Radierer 1730–1788* (Zurich: Orell Füssli Verlag, 1930). Byron appears to allude to the international dissemination of Gessner in his Preface to *Cain*: 'The author has by no means taken the same liberties with his subject which were common formerly as may be seen by any reader curious enough to refer to those profane productions whether in English, French, Italian or Spanish.'

24 *Medwin's Conversations of Lord Byron*, p. 125.

25 For a review of critics who have found *Paradise Regained* lacking in drama and passion in comparison to *Paradise Lost* see John T. Shawcross, *Paradise Regain'd: Worthy T'Have Not Remain'd So Long Unsung* (Pittsburgh, PA: Duquesne University Press, 1988), ch. 10, 'Afterword.'

26 Blumenthal, 'Lord Byron's Mystery "Cain"', p. 11.

27 Louis Martz, '*Paradise Regained*: the Meditative Combat', *ELH* 27 (1960), p. 239, cited in *A Variorum Commentary on the Poems of John Milton* 4 (London: Routledge & Kegan Paul, 1975), pp. 340–1.

28 For the Son's search for identity see Shawcross, especially ch. 5, 'The Mythic Substruct'; and Joan Heiges Blythe, 'The Cloistered Virtue: Rhetorical Posture in *Paradise Regained*', *Neuphilologische Mitteilungen* 89 (1988), pp. 324–32.

29 Joan Blythe, 'Beacon Fire: The Corsair and Milton's Hero-Poet', *Lord Byron: A Multidisciplinary Open Forum*, ed. by Thérèse Tessier (Versailles: French Byron Society, 1999), pp. 73–9.

30 McGann, *Don Juan in Context*, p. 32.

31 McGann, *Byron* (1986), p. 1072. Unfortunately for students using this text, McGann leaves his superlative claim here unqualified by the excellent discussion of the limitations of Lucifer's offer in his earlier *Don Juan in Context*.

32 H. John McLachlan, *Socinianism in Seventeenth-Century England* (Oxford: Oxford University Press, 1951), p. 144.

33 Compare a letter to Thomas Moore of 28 February 1822, which again gives primacy to Priestley: 'All this is curious enough, I think, – after allowing Priestley, Hume, and Gibbon, Bolingbroke and Voltaire to be published, without depriving the booksellers of their rights' (*BLJ*, 9, 116).

34 McLachlan, *Socinianism in Seventeenth-Century England*, pp. 11–13.

35 Rogers gave a detailed discussion of this aspect of *Paradise Regained* in his MLA paper, 'Family Heresies'.

36 Kennedy, *Conversations on Religion*, p. 176.

37 Kennedy, *Conversations on Religion*, pp. 261 and 259.

38 For this aspect of Milton's thought see John Rogers, 'Milton's Circumcision', in *Milton and the Grounds of Contention*, pp. 188–213; 311–16.

39 In speaking about the Son's role in *De Doctrina Christiana* Milton repeatedly uses the Latin *per* as a preposition of agency, thus, 'through, by, by means of'.

40 For the Son's 'rational self sufficiency' see Rogers, 'Milton's Circumcision'.

41 Byron's Abel at this point reminds me of Shakespeare's Desdemona who, totally absorbed in her virtuous position and oblivious to the psychological torment her husband Othello is suffering, nags him with self-righteous relentless zeal about restoring Cassio to his good graces.

42 Ricardo J. Quinones says of Biblical Cain, 'The violence of Cain against his brother comes to represent necessary physical and psychological facts of individuation.' *The Changes of Cain* (Princeton, NJ: Princeton University Press, 1991), p. 19.

43 There is a long-standing tradition in Hebrew and Christian writings supporting the eventual redemption of Biblical Cain. See Ruth Mellinkoff, *The Mark of Cain* (Berkeley, CA: University of California Press, 1981) and Quinones, *The Changes of Cain*.

Byron's Afterlife and the
Emancipation of Geology[1]

RALPH O'CONNOR

Byron's interest in geology is rarely treated as more than a minor footnote to his work.[2] It has recently been shown that early nineteenth-century geology significantly informs and illuminates Byron's later work, such as *Cain* and *Don Juan*.[3] But I hope here to demonstrate something more unexpected: that Byron's poetry both prompted and helped geologists in England to promote their science, and to free it from Biblical literalism in the public eye. During this 'heroic' age of geology, the science won a large following in Britain, partly because its pioneers were also men of letters. Treatises such as Charles Lyell's *Principles of Geology* were literary masterpieces, whose poetic imagery and rhetoric were crucial in advocating this strange new science.[4] These literary factors, in which Byron looms large, complicate the simple Moses-to-Darwin narratives typical of scientific secular positivism.

In the intensely conservative political climate of post-Napoleonic England, geology was a young science with much to prove. As the science of the Earth's distant past, it found itself jostling uncomfortably against the Book of Genesis: extinction and pre-human aeons were ideas with the potential to alarm a public widely used to taking Moses literally. Geology was perceived by some as 'infidel'. However, it gained a foothold in English universities, thanks largely to the charisma and cunning of William Buckland. His celebrated, eccentric Oxford lectures were described by the young John Henry Newman in 1821 as 'most entertaining, and open[ing] an amazing field to imagination and to poetry'.[5] This imaginative geology spawned an intriguing corpus of geological occasional verses, circulated among gentlemen of science and their genteel students.[6]

The literary affiliations of English geology underpinned its academic survival. Buckland presented geology as Francis Bacon's 'book of God's works', read historically. At first this 'text' served to prove Moses correct.[7] Buckland was a follower of Georges Cuvier, whose celebrated 'catastrophe

geology' had been ingeniously popularised in Britain as an adjunct to
Biblical commentary.[8] Buckland happily went along with this ruse – not
because of any lack of integrity,[9] but because geology did not yet wield
enough authority to confront Moses (so to speak) on his own ground. The
testimony of the rocks entered the curriculum like a Trojan horse.

But Buckland's strategies were soon upset. From 1822 onwards, radicals such as Richard Carlile suddenly began using Cuvier's historical
geology as a weapon against the Church. They were undoubtedly encouraged by the example of Byron's *Cain* (December 1821), whose importance
to geological popularisation has never been properly acknowledged.
Byron's Lucifer proclaims mankind's cosmic irrelevance by showing Cain
the vast reaches of space and the myriads of former worlds beneath the
earth's surface. Lucifer wields Cuvier's 'Catastrophism' directly against
natural theology, to convince Cain of God's injustice. *Cain* is a magnificently complex drama, but to Byron's annoyance, its hijacking by the
radicals fixed its meaning at once.[10] Carlile's 1822 review claimed that the
Church's end was nigh. A torrent of radical geology-writing followed in
Cain's wake, to the horror of Buckland and his colleagues, whose vulnerable new science now faced a serious threat.[11]

Cain was particularly dangerous for four reasons. Firstly, it contained
superb poetry. Secondly, it possessed a coherent scientific agenda. Thirdly,
in its 'Preface' it blasphemously pretended to Biblical orthodoxy. Finally,
it was read extremely widely.[12] The effect was devastating, even among
those who disapproved: Countess Harriet Granville thought it 'most
wicked', but when her husband read it aloud to her in 1822, the effect was
so 'magnificent ... [that] I roared till I could neither hear nor see'.[13] Even
more than *Don Juan*, *Cain* was seen as 'propagating' a deadly moral
'plague',[14] calculated to 'spread desolation' by virtue of its aesthetic
appeal.[15] An antidote was required: *Cain* must be neutralised on its own
terms. Many hostile reviews, therefore, were either written in satirical verse
or reprinted the play with lengthy, sarcastic commentaries. The satirical
strategy usually attacked Byron's personal life, representing him as Cain or
Lucifer;[16] the reprint-plus-commentary tended to focus more on his philosophical bad faith.[17] Still others wrote their own Cain drama or epic.[18]

Cain's most dedicated opponent, Henry Wilkinson, combined these
three strategies.[19] After attacking Byron's metre (pp. 7–17), he reprints
Cain's 'Preface' (pp. 19–20), and launches into his own Cain epic. After
twenty-six pages, he 'introduce[s] the Antidote' (p. 48). This directly attacks
Cain's heterodoxy, especially its geology (by 1824 'the favourite topic of

Atheists and Deists', p. 65). He drags down Byron's impressive epithets to rhyme with his own cumbersome fulminations. He also reprints the relevant sections of the drama, which occupy the lower half of each page. The visual effect is striking, but to an unsympathetic eye Wilkinson's verse comes off rather badly from the comparison he invites. Then come critical notes (pp. 75–97) mocking Byron's scientific ignorance and lack of imagination, solemnly calculating that Lucifer and Cain could not possibly have flown through space because it is a vacuum, and asking with lumbering sarcasm what sort of hinges the gates of Hades turned on. This level of engagement may seem trivial – one wonders what Wilkinson made of *Paradise Lost* – but many reviewers used similar pseudo-scientific ammunition to undermine Byron's philosophical credibility.

In this light it is interesting to see how a practising gentlemanly geologist responded to *Cain*. Before examining Buckland's twofold 'antidote', I shall outline the very specific challenge posed by *Cain* to the new historical geology.

Just as *Cain* appeared, Buckland made a discovery which allowed him to transform, decisively, geology's self-image and public profile. A complex assemblage of fossil hyænas and other bones in Kirkdale Cave (Yorkshire) gave him the opportunity to do more than just describe the shapes and species of fossil animals found. Applying contemporary evidence of hyænas' feeding habits and behaviour (including, later, that of his own hyæna Billy), Buckland brought a whole pre-human 'world', or ecosystem, into sharp focus.[20] It takes some mental effort today to appreciate how startling this imaginative leap was. At the time it was often compared to recent advances in astronomy, after which Byron himself viewed 'the Moon and Stars through Herschell's telescope – and saw that they were worlds'.[21] The first-ever published illustration of a 'scene from deep time' was a contemporary cartoon of the Kirkdale hyænas by William Conybeare (Fig. 1), with Buckland himself magically watching, bridging the chronological chasm between human and pre-human.[22] Geology could now appeal to the public imagination as never before.

But *Cain* challenged this new-found visual power. Lucifer, too, *shows* Cain the wonders of geology, again as an extension of astronomy. This play apparently demonised the new geology, flaunting its contradictions with Christianity. Buckland and his colleagues now needed to purge the Satanic/radical connotations from their exciting new science. Among friends, Buckland circulated a satire on *Cain* called 'The Professor's

Fig. 1. Lithographed caricature designed or commissioned by William Conybeare in 1822, representing the geologist William Buckland entering
Kirkdale Cave and finding himself in an antediluvian hyænas' den. Reproduced by permission of Professor Martin Rudwick.

Descent'. Telescoping *Cain* with Thomas Gray's 'The Descent of Odin',
this ingenious production equates the fratricidal but extinct Kirkdale
hyænas with today's bloodthirsty, Cain-like radicals Byron, Shelley, and
Carlile. Buckland's professorial hero ignores the hyænas' 'fruitless yell',
being a 'man of Geologic Spell'. He fearlessly recapitulates Cain's voyage
into 'Lord Byron's Hell & Chaos', i.e. Kirkdale Cave, where he summons
up Lucifer to answer geological questions. Outwitted, Lucifer goes grum-
bling back to bed.[23] Pointed references to Byron and *Don Juan* also
appeared in verses accompanying Conybeare's hyæna cartoon, and in
several other items of hyæna doggerel.[24] The fact that these verses were
intended for circulation only among elite geologists suggests that Buckland
was here defending the science's *self*-image. Once *Cain* had been dealt with
on this level, Buckland could reassure his public that whatever Byron might
have told them, geology was both imaginatively exciting and theologically
orthodox.

These two requirements were apparently satisfied by Buckland's luxurious cave-fossil treatise *Reliquiæ Diluvianæ*, published in 1823 by John Murray – to whom, still smarting from the embarrassment of having published *Cain*, Buckland's brand of geological 'poetry' appealed far more than Byron's. Disguised as a proof of Noah's Flood, this book distracted the reader's attention from theological controversy with its picturesque descriptions of caves containing hyæna bones. All admitted that it 'render[ed] the science of geology popular …. The general reader has been charmed with the novel scenes which it discloses, while the Christian has hailed it with joy.'[25] But its concealed rejection of traditional ideas about Noah's Flood angered literalists.[26] So the real fighting began – not a 'war between science and religion' (many of the most progressive geologists, like Buckland, were clergymen), but a clash of cosmologies between two competing elites, between genteel geologists and Biblical literalists, over who had the authority to tell the story of Creation.[27]

During the 1820s, genteel geologists developed a tongue-in-cheek self-image as latter-day (possibly Coleridgean) apostles, complete with itinerant 'disciples', melodramatic 'conversions', and even miracles.[28] Their burgeoning traffic of occasional verses had allowed them to explore the science's imaginative potential privately. Now that popular literalist accounts of geological phenomena were threatening to flood their market, the geological elite had to publicise their new paradigm, translating their accumulated 'text' of physical data into a far grander narrative than the six-day Creation. Reaching deep into the remote past, they evoked an awesome succession of former worlds, designed by an infinitely creative (if rather distant) God. It was a new creation-myth for the industrial, imperial age. And it was kept safe from controversy within the broad-church framework of natural theology, which pointed from 'Nature up to Nature's God' – some writers tacitly accepting this framework, and others explicitly championing it. The common keynote was wonder. If the public could be induced to feel awe rather than suspicion at the sublime diorama unfolded before them, the literalists' bare creation-narrative would lose its hold on them. The successful populariser must overwhelm the audience's imagination.

The result might be called 'poetical geology' – not a genre, but a literary mode into which writing of the period often swerves, characterised by sudden and self-conscious flights of fancy, and the use of poetical conceits alongside self-styled 'objective' geological exposition to invest the latter with further meanings. These passages were deployed to kindle the reader's imagination, clothing fact in the seductive garments of fantasy – yet without fantasy's immoral tendencies towards fiction.

What, then, are the distinctive features of this mode? Here we return to the 'geological poetry' of Byron. By the 1830s, Byron's personal notoriety dominated his reputation, obscuring his later poetry and political engagement. Less controversial works did remain relatively unscathed (the supreme example being *Childe Harold*), and 'Byromaniacs' there were aplenty, in Britain no less than in continental Europe;[29] but for some of the more original young writers – those who have since become canonical – a creative 'rejection of Byronism' seems to have been necessary.[30] In the 1830s, even radicals began to find him less politically useful.[31] *Cain*'s fortunes bifurcated: Byron addicts recast it to suit conservative tastes in distended verse dramas and epics, taking care to dissociate themselves from the original drama's gloomy cosmology;[32] but most simply dismissed it as the vehicle of Byron's atheistic malice.[33] It may, therefore, seem curious that most of the 'poetical' *topoi* with which geologists wooed their public are identical to those with which Lucifer wrecks Cain's soul. Notwithstanding the common influence of Cuvier and others, these similarities are telling.

These *topoi* are numerous. The most obvious is the insistence that man is but a small and recent tenant of the earth. Byron's Lucifer recalls the

> Mighty Pre-Adamites who walk'd the earth
> Of which ours is the wreck.

> (*Cain* II.ii.359–60)

This 'former world' was designed for grander beings, and Cain feels his 'littleness' keenly. Similarly, Gideon Mantell in 1831 proclaimed the existence of an 'Age of Reptiles', comparing 'the colossal *Megalosaurus* and *Iguanodon* of the ancient world' to the 'pigmy' animals of today, and exclaiming with none-too-subtle Biblical anthropomorphism that 'reptiles were the *Lords of the Creation*, before the existence of the human race!'[34] Mantell knew his Byron better than any other geologist:[35] in his case, allusions to *Cain* were probably intentional. But he cautiously waited until 1844 before making the link explicit in print, now calling the same reptiles 'Pre-Adamites' and quoting the above passage from *Cain* directly.[36] More intriguingly, the 1836 review in the *Quarterly* of Buckland's treatise *Geology and Mineralogy* quoted the same passage – doubtless emboldened by anonymity – in order to extol Buckland's persuasive powers:

an eloquence which ... absolutely calls up before his audience –

> 'The monstrous shapes that one time walk'd the earth,
> Of which ours is the wreck'.[37]

This review was written by two elite geologists to 'puff' Buckland's book, months before it appeared. To whip up excitement, they effectively equated Buckland with Byron's Lucifer, reversing the strategy of Buckland's own 'Professor's Descent'. The misquotation illustrates how *Cain*'s portrayals had penetrated the geological imagination: the author wrote from memory here, subconsciously ironing out Byron's metrical ruggedness into smooth iambs.

Byron's 'former worlds' are presented as phantoms of the past, among which Lucifer leads Cain. Mantell's geologist, too, descends into the 'abyss' of time, and 'the shades of other creations teem around him', shifting in successive panoramas just like Cain's visions.[38] The link with Hades was taken to an extreme by the eccentric Thomas Hawkins, who thought ichthyosaurs had been created by Satan, 'a teeming Spawn fitted for the lowest Abysm of Chaos'.[39] Like Byron, geologists engaged in a charged dialogue with Milton's *Paradise Lost*, a favourite source for poetic quotation in their writings ('deep time' being figured as Hell or Chaos).[40] But Byron's Lucifer also expresses nostalgia for that 'world' as if it were Paradise:

> *Their* earth is gone for ever –
> So changed by its convulsion, they would not
> Be conscious to a single present spot ...
> Oh, what a beautiful world it *was!*
>
> (*Cain* II.ii.120–4)

Buckland's reviewers used the first line of this passage to illustrate his rhetorical brilliance;[41] in 1847, no longer anonymously, William Broderip used the first three lines to head a chapter on pterodactyles.[42] And the same nostalgia seems to inform Mantell's reverie about 'a country which is now swept from the face of the earth ... more marvellous than any that even romance or poetry has ventured to pourtray.'[43] Deliberately or accidentally, these writers all seem to invoke or echo Byron's Lucifer when their own powers of imaginative evocation, in calling up the mysteries of the 'Age of Reptiles', are most sorely taxed.

If they resemble Lucifer in their spectacular showmanship, then what of their heroic literary personae? Here, too, they seem to join the devil's party. Lucifer is a Promethean figure, a daringly transgressive hero with supernatural power over time and space – a descendant of Milton's Satan. Lucifer tells Cain,

> With us acts are exempt from time, and we
> Can crowd eternity into an hour ...
> We breathe not by a mortal measurement.

(Cain I.i.535–8)

The geologist-persona is formed in the same mould, 'penetrat[ing] the secret recesses of the globe',[44] 'spurn[ing] the bounds of space and time'.[45] Hawkins, as ever, goes further: 'by these extinct Dragons we ... look over the Edge of Matter into Chaos, ... metamorphosed as gods.'[46] The paradox of the Romantic Prometheus, chained to a rock but intellectually almost omnipotent, is encapsulated in Lucifer's parting shot to Cain, rather like Milton's Satan:

> Think and endure, – and form an inner world
> In your own bosom – where the outward fails.

(Cain II.ii.463–6)

So Lyell (another jewel in John Murray's crown) eulogises the godlike geological mind: 'chained to a mere point in space, ... the human mind is ... enabled ... to trace the events of indefinite ages before the creation of our race ...; free, like the spirit ... animating the universe'.[47] Milton's Satan lurks here, too. William Whewell praised Lyell's ambitious attempt to follow in Satan's footsteps 'through the realms of Night and Chaos', building a bridge from hell to earth, from deep time to the present.[48]

The most transgressive element of the geologists' sorcery was their ability to resurrect the dead, in a secular Apocalypse.[49] Their occult authority over their resurrected fossils inspired poems and caricatures of servile mammoths and puppy-like Iguanodons (Fig. 2). The hubris latent within this self-deification erupts in comparisons with that 'New Prometheus', Victor Frankenstein, another descendant of Milton's Satan. Like composite beasts, the geologists' monsters were stitched together and recalled from death.[50] Reconstructing Iguanodon, Mantell, 'like Franken-stein, ... was actually appalled at the being which rose beneath his meditations'.[51] Poems and caricatures echoed this fear of retribution by portraying the creatures turning voraciously upon their 'creator'.[52] The exaggerated awe with which Hawkins viewed them is borne out by this purely random selection of characteristics, memorably illustrated by John Martin (Fig. 3): 'frightful', 'fiendish', 'lusty', 'leathery', 'spotted and mottled', 'livid, or green', 'impy', 'eerie', 'execrable and dreary', 'egregious',

Fig. 2. 'Dr. M[antell] in extasies at the approach of his pet Saurian': drawing by Henry De la Beche to commemorate Gideon Mantell's identification of the 'Maidstone Iguanodon' in 1834. Ink on paper, 229 x 184 mm. Reproduced by permission of the Alexander Turnbull Library, Wellington, New Zealand (shelfmark E-295-q-003).

'venomous', 'gluttonous', 'grim', 'uncouth', 'unclean', 'ungainly', 'ugly', 'unquenchable in gore', 'gaunt – unutterable', 'dire', 'deathy', 'quadrupedal and deadly', 'crunching the gristles of his dying prey'.[53] Such were the images by which geologists replaced the serene authority of Moses with a lurid narrative of their own devising.

In this act of narrative displacement we can locate the underlying similarities between *Cain* and 'poetical geology'. Byron was no atheist: like the geologists, he wanted to broaden his public's imagination. His warning seems to be this: if your idea of God comes straight from the Old Testament, modern science will wreck your faith. The scepticism of Byron's

Fig. 3. 'The Sea-Dragons as They Lived' (1840): John Martin's mezzotint frontispiece for Thomas Hawkins's *Book of the Great Sea-Dragons*. Reproduced by permission of the Syndics of Cambridge University Library.

geological vision is consistently directed against narrow conceptions of man's relation to God – not only in *Cain,* but in his dramas generally, as well as *Don Juan* and *Childe Harold* IV. Accordingly, Lyell and Mantell both used the still-respectable *Childe Harold* to advocate geology's emancipation from old paradigms. Lyell concludes the climactic chapter of the first volume of *Principles of Geology* by pitting Byron's 'Ocean' stanzas against an outdated poetical conceit ultimately responsible for scientific prejudices:

the rock as the emblem of firmness – the sea as the image of inconstancy. Our modern poet, in a more philosophical spirit, saw in the latter "The image of Eternity," ...

———————————————— Their decay
Has dried up realms to deserts: – not so thou,
Unchangeable, save to thy wild waves' play:
Time writes no wrinkle on thy azure brow;
Such as creation's dawn beheld, thou rollest now.

CHILDE HAROLD, Canto iv.[54]

Lyell aimed at an imaginative revolution in geology: to push this point home, he here harnesses Byron's imaginative and philosophical potency. The rhetorical capstone of the entire volume derives from the 'philosophical' poet Byron rather than from a man of science. His ally Mantell went further, quoting the entire stanza (clxxxii) to the same effect at the end of introductory lectures in two works from 1836 and 1838,[55] and in 1849 he added two more stanzas, with additional exclamation marks and italics.[56]

Lyell's own paradigm was itself derided (in certain particulars) as hopelessly 'visionary', for instance by Henry de la Beche, a skilled caricaturist as well as geologist. Here too Byron's verse offered handy ammunition. The most 'poetical' passage in Lyell's *Principles* lyrically evoked a future world when ichthyosaurs might return to the seas, vividly illustrating Lyell's belief that the progress of life was not unidirectional.[57] Those who disagreed had ample scope for mockery here. De la Beche's 1830 caricature *Awful Changes* (Fig. 4) depicts a future world in which man is 'found only in a fossil state',

Fig. 4. 'Awful Changes' (1830): lithographed engraving by Henry De la Beche satirising Charles Lyell's cyclical vision of earth history. Reproduced by permission of the Department of Geology, National Museum of Wales.

his remains being lectured on by 'Professor Ichthyosaurus' – who cannot believe how this degenerate species ever survived with such pathetic jaws.[58] The cartoon's epigraph quotes the refrain of Byron's 1816 poem 'The Dream': 'A change came o'er the spirit of my dream'. With this quotation De la Beche compares the passing of geological epochs to Byron's temporal succession of dream-visions (besides implying that Lyell was a mere dreamer) – but Byron's own obsession with human extinction and degeneration undoubtedly lurks behind De la Beche's choice of poet. One recalls the obverse scenario in which mankind's successors gaze at George IV's huge bones and wonder 'where such animals could sup' (*Don Juan* IX, 39).

The refrain of 'The Dream' converges with the geologists' own dramatisations of long-gone epochs in their treatises – 'a change came over the scene' and so on.[59] Byron became the obvious poet to quote when musing on the human implications of extinction and deep time. My final example is from Broderip's 1847 treatise, which concludes by meditating on the 'visions' which fossils of 'Preadamite Saurians … call forth'. The 'old dragon times' are colourfully evoked, leading to a 'Dream'-like exclamation – 'Now, how changed the scene!' – and, ending the book with a salutary *memento mori* for Victorian man:

> In future ages *his* remains will fill the bosom of the earth; and the traveller in some far distant century will feel the full force of Byron's lines wherever he sets his foot: –
>
> > Stop! – for thy tread is on an Empire's dust!
> > An Earthquake's spoil is sepulchred below![60]

Again, this quotation from *Childe Harold* is not merely illustrative: Broderip seems to imply that an emotional response to geological phenomena will always be shaped by Byron's immortal poetry, even after the extinction of his own civilisation. After all, *Childe Harold* was still the definitive expression of the sensibility of ruin on which geology's massive popularity was founded. Broderip was right: the Victorians are long gone, but Byronic sentiments and narrative models continue to underpin geological spectacle today.

Byron, then, was repeatedly invoked, both when the geological imagination was most heavily taxed, and when a 'system' needed dramatically debunking. But with one (anonymous) exception, geologists in the 1820s and 1830s avoided quoting directly from the notorious *Cain*, despite – or because of – their deeper alignment with it. As we have seen, they became bolder in the 1840s, during and after which evolution and early man replaced deep time and extinction as the new bones of contention. By now the torrent of anti-*Cain* literature had dwindled to a tired trickle,[61] and the reworkings of the 'Spasmodics' and other sanitising Byromaniacs were gradually eroding the shock-value of Byron's later dramas.[62]

Perhaps we are now closer to understanding the surprising alliance between Byron and the geologists. In any case, the *Cain*-like strategies of 'poetical geology' impressed many readers with feelings of enlightened piety, reconciling the new science with Christianity.[63] Worldly success followed: the period between Byron's death and Tennyson's rise to fame is often seen as a literary desert, but these books – and other new breeds of non-fiction – sold like novels.

Ironically, the versatility of 'poetical geology' seems to have given it it a life of its own, endangering the natural-theological framework within which it had flourished and whose fragility was becoming clear. Natural theology, observed Buckland's former pupil John Henry Newman, could just as logically lead to atheism.[64] Such critiques of natural theology were not new in this period, but they certainly intensified. 'Poetical geology' was far too powerful to be contained by this weak framework. Its visionary breadth made it potentially devastating as well as potentially uplifting, depending wholly upon the reader's prior inclination. For Edward Fitzgerald in 1847, geology 'wither[ed] the Poet's hope of immortality', being 'more wonderful than all the conceptions of Dante and Milton'.[65] Newman identified this dangerous potency in 1854, asserting that geology could lead its intoxicated devotee to view Christian narratives with 'a most distressing revulsion of feeling ... his imagination is bewildered, and swims with the ineffable distance of that faith ... contrasted with the exuberant life and reality of [science]'.[66] Newman's essay would make a superb gloss on Act II of *Cain*. Lucifer, one might say, was avenging himself for the pious uses to which his soul-wrecking strategies had been put.

The Satanic 'sea-dragons' impressed Thomas Hawkins so much that he simply had to worship them: the resurrect[ed] beast 'lay like a new creation before me – and I was the creator. I worshipped it for hours in my mad intoxication of spirit'. His overheated rhapsodies provide a disconcertingly literal example of what Newman found disturbing about geological enthusiasm. Hawkins explains his idolatry in similar terms of imaginative intoxication: 'these gone-by things ... concentrate infinity and identif[y] it, a something that the human understanding can grasp bodily and be satisfied therewith, like the opium-eater, and his drug, for awhile.'[67] Leaving aside De Quincey, this conclusion to Hawkins' strange book recalls Byron's attraction towards Catholicism, which he mentions in the context of *Cain* as being a reassuringly 'tangible religion' (*BLJ*, 9, 123). Byron's personal doubts were exacerbated both by the increasingly politicised abstractions of Protestant theology (as allegorised in *Cain*) and by the increasing distance between God and his creation which the sciences seemed to open up. The geologists' enraptured narratives focused not upon this distant Designer, but upon the evocative power of the designs themselves. The culmination of this aesthetic of natural theology would therefore be a self-generating design. Charles Darwin's final defence of evolution was expressed, tellingly, in aesthetic terms: 'there is grandeur in this view of life'.[68]

The literalist and Tractarian outrage which 'poetical geology' provoked in the 1830s and 1840s resembled the response to *Cain*. The very same four qualities which had made *Cain* so dangerous in 1821 now resurfaced in the response to the new emancipated geology. Again, thundering sermons were not the only response: many tried to silence it on its own terms, producing philosophical 'antidotes' in the form of 'scriptural geology'.[69] Thus began a new phase of the same cycle.

In various capacities, then, Byron's poetry stimulated, sustained, and popularised the science. These processes were complex, and require more detailed research than this brief account perhaps suggests. It is, however, clear that Byron contributed far more after his death than he had in his lifetime towards popularising the shocking new science of geology – albeit in ways he could not have foreseen. *Cain* and the associated controversy posed a formative challenge to geologists, forcing them to close ranks and come up with their own vivid 'poetical geology', which used the same imaginative arsenal as *Cain* (consciously and unconsciously); and they directly quoted Byron's less inflammatory and more popular works in the same cause. We can only conclude that there was that within him

> which shall tire
> Torture and Time, and breathe when I expire.
>
> (*Childe Harold's Pilgrimage* IV, 137)

Notes

1   Since this essay was delivered in 2000, I have published a fuller account in my book *The Earth on Show: Fossils and the Poetics of Popular Science, 1802–1856* (Chicago, IL:

University of Chicago Press, 2007). The present essay does not take account of the many relevant scholarly studies published in the interim, and I wish to draw particular attention to the following: Noah Heringman, *Romantic Rocks, Aesthetic Geology* (Ithaca, NY: Cornell University Press, 2004); Martin J. S. Rudwick, *Bursting the Limits of Time: The Reconstruction of Geohistory in the Age of Revolution* (Chicago, IL: University of Chicago Press, 2005); William St Clair, *The Reading Nation in the Romantic Period* (Cambridge: Cambridge University Press, 2004); and Marianne Sommer, 'The Romantic Cave? The Scientific and Poetic Quests for Subterranean Spaces in Britain', *Earth Sciences History*, 22 (2003), pp. 172–208. I would like to offer my warmest thanks to Anne Barton, Harriet Truscott, Jim Secord, Tony Howe, and William and Sandra Truscott for their invaluable advice concerning previous versions of this essay.

2   Stephen L. Goldstein, 'Byron's *Cain* and the Painites', *Studies in Romanticism* 14 (1975), pp. 391–410; Peter A. Schock, 'The "Satanism" of *Cain* in Context: Byron's Lucifer and the War against Blasphemy', *Keats-Shelley Journal* 44 (1995), pp. 182–215, pp. 209–11; William D. Brewer, *The Shelley–Byron Conversation* (Gainesville, FL: University Press of Florida, 1994), pp. 27–36; Fiona J. Stafford, *The Last of the Race: The Growth of a Myth from Milton to Darwin* (Oxford: Clarendon Press, 1994), pp. 185–96.

3   Ralph O'Connor, 'Mammoths and Maggots: Byron and the Geology of Cuvier', *Romanticism* 5 (1999), pp. 26–42; Christine Kenyon Jones, '"When this world shall be *former*": Catastrophism as Imaginative Theory for the Younger Romantics', *Romanticism on the Net* 24 (November 2001), http://www.erudit.org/revue/ron/2001/v/n24/006000ar.html.

4   In this limited space I have flattened out the heterogeneity of the British reading 'public', using the term 'popular geology' in its broadest sense, to mean any writing aimed at a wider audience than that of practising geologists. Many texts operated on both levels, popularising the science among the middle and upper classes while engaging polemically with colleagues or presenting new research.

5   *The Letters and Diaries of John Henry Newman*, ed. by I. T. Kerr *et al.*, 31 vols (Oxford: Clarendon Press, 1973–1984), I, 109.

6   For examples see *Fugitive Poems Connected with Natural History and Physical Science*, ed. by Charles Daubeny (Oxford: James Parker, 1869).

7   William Buckland, *Vindiciæ Geologicæ* (Oxford: Oxford University Press, 1820), pp. 13–14.

8   See Martin J. S. Rudwick, *Georges Cuvier, Fossil Bones, and Geological Catastrophes* (Chicago, IL: University of Chicago Press, 1997), p. 254.

9   The idea that Buckland and others were expediently betraying their 'scientific' integrity by such 'compromises' with 'religion' has long been defunct among historians of science, but not among literary critics: see Philip W. Martin, *Byron: A Poet before His Public* (Cambridge: Cambridge University Press, 1982), pp. 169–70.

10   For Byron's annoyance see *BLJ*, 9, 123.

11   Richard Carlile, '*Queen Mab, Cain, A Mystery*, and a Royal Reviewer', *The Republican* 5 (1822), p. 192.

12   See *The Letters of Thomas Moore*, ed. by W. S. Dowden, 2 vols (Oxford, 1964), II, 620; Truman Guy Steffan, *Lord Byron's Cain* (Austin, TX: University of Texas

Press, 1968), pp. 305–473.

13 *Letters of Harriet Countess Granville*, ed. by F. Leveson Gower, 2 vols (London: Long-mans, 1894), I, 219.

14 John Styles, *Lord Byron's Works Viewed in Connexion with Christianity* (London: Knight and Lacey, 1824), p. 15.

15 'Uriel', *A Poetical Address to the Right Honourable Lord Byron* (London: Hatchard, 1822), p. 76.

16 Anon., *Another Cain* (London: Hatchard, 1822); Adams, *A Scourge for Lord Byron* (London: T. Adams, 1823); William Battine, *Another Cain* (London: John Cahuac, 1822), pp. 63–4; 'Uriel', *A Poetical Address*.

17 Harding Grant, *Lord Byron's Cain* (London: William Crofts, 1830).

18 Battine, *Another Cain*; William Blake, 'The Ghost of Abel' [1822], in *William Blake: The Complete Poems*, ed. by Alicia Ostriker (London: Penguin, 1977), pp. 864–7; John Edmund Reade, *Cain the Wanderer* [1829], in his *Poetical Works*, 3 vols (London: Longman et al., 1865), II, pp. 71–131.

19 Henry Wilkinson, *Cain, a Poem* (London: Baldwin, Cradock, and Joy, 1824). Page references are to this edition.

20 Kirkdale Cave was by no means the best or most detailed of European 'bone caves'. It was simply the first one to which Buckland applied his uniquely recon-structive reasoning.

21 *BLJ*, 9, 46.

22 Humphry Davy, *Six Discourses Delivered before the Royal Society* (London: John Murray, 1827), p. 51. See Martin J. S. Rudwick, *Scenes from Deep Time: Early Pictorial Representations of the Prehistoric World* (Chicago, IL: University of Chicago Press, 1992), p. 39.

23 Quoted with the kind permission of Mr Roderick Gordon and Mrs Diana Harman. The Devon Record Office, Exeter, holds a microfilm of this manuscript: MFC 97/37, 138 M/F 711. I am currently preparing an edition of 'The Professor's Descent' for publication.

24 For example, Philip B. Duncan, 'The Last British Hyæna' [c. 1823], in Daubeny, ed., *Fugitive Poems*, pp. 119–20.

25 John Fleming, 'The Geological Deluge', *Edinburgh Philosophical Journal* 14 (1826), pp. 205–39, p. 208.

26 Nicolaas A. Rupke: *The Great Chain of History: William Buckland and the English School of Geology (1814–1849)* (Oxford: Clarendon Press, 1983), p. 39.

27 The 'warfare' model of the relations between geology and Biblical literalism in the 1820s and 1830s turns out, on closer examination, to be less universally applicable than I have suggested here. See chapters 3 and 5 of my book *The Earth on Show*, and, for a fuller account, my article 'Young-Earth Creationists in Early-Nine-teenth-Century Britain? Towards a Reassessment of Scriptural Geology', *History of Science* 45 (2007), pp. 357–403.

28 Adam Sedgwick, 'Address to the Geological Society' [1831], *Proceedings of the Geolog-ical Society of London* 1 (1826–1833), pp. 281–316, p. 313, and [William Whewell], review of Lyell's *Principles of Geology*, *British Critic* 9 (1831), pp. 180–206, p. 180.

29 Unlike Goethe, Pushkin, and his other European admirers, Byron's numerous early Victorian British worshippers (P. J. Bailey and the 'Spasmodics', for instance)

have long since passed into a perhaps deserved obscurity: commentators tend therefore to overplay the British reaction against Byron in this period.

30 Andrew Elfenbein, *Byron and the Victorians* (Cambridge: Cambridge University Press, 1995), pp. 88–9.

31 N. Stephen Bauer, 'Romantic Poetry and the Unstamped Political Press, 1830–1836', *Studies in Romanticism* 14 (1975), pp. 411–25, p. 417.

32 For example, Bailey's vast and vastly popular *Festus* (1839): see Alan McKillop, 'A Victorian *Faust*', *Publications of the Modern Language Association* 40 (1925), pp. 743–68, pp. 753–5.

33 Even some who admired Byron's dramas dismissed *Cain*: see Allan Cunningham, *Biographical and Critical History of the British Literature of the Last Fifty Years* (Paris: Baudry, 1834), p. 290.

34 Gideon Mantell, 'The Geological Age of Reptiles', *Edinburgh New Philosophical Journal* 11 (1831), pp. 181–5.

35 See *The Journal of Gideon Mantell, Surgeon and Geologist*, ed. by Cecil A. Curwen (London: Oxford University Press, 1940), pp. 93, 95, 109, 111, 125, 133, 138, and 146.

36 Gideon Mantell, *The Medals of Creation* (London: Bohn, 1844), p. 874.

37 [George Poulett Scrope and William Broderip], review of Buckland's *Geology and Mineralogy*, *Quarterly Review* 56 (1836), pp. 31–64, p. 43.

38 Gideon Mantell, *The Wonders of Geology* (London: Relfe and Fletcher, 1838), pp. 604–5; *Medals of Creation*, p. 874.

39 Thomas Hawkins, *The Book of the Great Sea-Dragons* (London: Pickering, 1840), p. 22. On Hawkins's literary techniques see Ralph O'Connor, 'Thomas Hawkins and Geological Spectacle', *Proceedings of the Geologists' Association* 114 (2003), pp. 227–41.

40 See William Buckland, *Geology and Mineralogy Considered with Reference to Natural Theology*, 2 vols (London: Pickering, 1836), I, 224; Thomas Hawkins, *Memoirs of Ichthyosauri and Plesiosauri* (London: Relfe and Fletcher, 1834), p. 51; Charles Lyell, *Principles of Geology*, 3 vols (London: John Murray, 1830–1833), III, 89.

41 [Scrope and Broderip], review of Buckland, p. 47.

42 William Broderip, *Zoological Recreations* (London: Henry Colburn, 1847), p. 369.

43 Mantell, *Wonders of Geology*, p. 31.

44 Mantell, *Wonders of Geology*, pp. 604–5.

45 Curwen, ed., *Journal of Gideon Mantell*, p. 134.

46 Hawkins, *Sea-Dragons*, p. 9.

47 Lyell, *Principles*, I, 166. Compare Hawkins, *Memoirs*, p. 29.

48 Whewell, review of Lyell's *Principles*, p. 193.

49 See *Balzac: La Peau de chagrin* [1831], ed. by Maurice Allem (Paris: Garnier, 1964), p. 25; Daubeny, ed., *Fugitive Poems*, p. 78.

50 On their composite appearance see Buckland, *Geology and Mineralogy*, I, 221. On Hawkins' 'creation' of genuinely composite fossils, see Christopher McGowan, *The Dragon Seekers* (Cambridge, MA: Perseus, 2001), pp. 117–48; M. A. Taylor, 'Hawkins, Thomas', in *The Oxford Dictionary of National Biography: From the Earliest Times to the Year 2000*, ed. by H. C. G. Matthew and Brian Harrison, 61 vols (Oxford: Oxford University Press, 2004), citing online edition at www.oxforddnb.com.

51 Report of an 1834 lecture, quoted in Dennis R. Dean, *Gideon Mantell and the*

Discovery of Dinosaurs (Cambridge: Cambridge University Press, 1999), p. 131.

52 See the poems about Mantell by Horace Smith in Charles Daubeny, *Literary Common-place Book*, Magdalen College, Oxford, MS 377, I, 157–9, and Daubeny, ed., *Fugitive Poems*, pp. 123–6.

53 These quotations litter the pages of Hawkins' *Memoirs* and *Sea-Dragons*.

54 Lyell, *Principles*, I, 459, quoting from *Childe Harold's Pilgrimage* IV, 182.

55 Gideon Mantell, *Thoughts on a Pebble* (London: Relfe and Fletcher, 1836), pp. 16–17; *Wonders of Geology*, pp. 99–100.

56 Mantell, *Thoughts on a Pebble*, 8th edn (London: Reeve, Benham, and Reeve, 1849), pp. 29–31. This also contains oceanic quotations from *Childe Harold* (p. 26) and *The Island* (pp. 19–20).

57 Lyell, *Principles*, I, 123.

58 See Martin J. S. Rudwick, 'Caricature as a Source for the History of Science: De la Beche's Anti-Lyellian Sketches of 1831', *Isis* 66 (1975), pp. 534–60; Rudwick, *Scenes*, pp. 48–49.

59 Mantell, *Wonders of Geology*, I, 262. This technique was much used by the Scottish geologist Hugh Miller: see Ralph O'Connor, 'Hugh Miller and Geological Spectacle', in *Celebrating the Life and Times of Hugh Miller: Scotland in the Early 19th Century*, ed. by Lester Borley (Cromarty: Cromarty Arts Trust, 2003), pp. 237–58.

60 Broderip, *Zoological Recreations*, pp. 379–80. The Byron quotation is from *Childe Harold's Pilgrimage* III, 17.

61 The only example I have found is a poem entitled 'Abel', written by Owen Howell and printed in 1843.

62 Part of Caesar's 'mammoth song' in Byron's *The Deformed Transformed* (III.i.54–61) heads the anonymous story 'Archæanthrope: A Fragment of a Geological Romance' [1867] (Daubeny, *Literary Commonplace-book*, I, 523–4).

63 Rupke, *Great Chain of History*, pp. 206–7. Literalist 'scriptural geology', however, still held an even wider readership in this period.

64 John Hedley Brooke, *Science and Religion: Some Historical Perspectives* (Cambridge: Cambridge University Press, 1991), pp. 203–9, 224.

65 Letter to E. B. Cowell, 24 July 1847, printed in *The Letters of Edward FitzGerald*, ed. by Alfred McKinley Terhune and Annabelle Burdick Terhune, 4 vols (Princeton, NJ: Princeton University Press, 1980), I, 566, and briefly discussed in *Charles Lyell: Principles of Geology*, ed. by James A. Secord (London: Penguin, 1997), pp. xxxviii–xl.

66 Quoted in J. M. I. Klaver, *Geology and Religious Sentiment: The Effect of Geological Discoveries on English Society and Literature between 1829 and 1859* (Leiden: Brill, 1997), pp. 165–6.

67 Hawkins, *Memoirs*, pp. 27, 51.

68 Charles Darwin, *On the Origin of Species by Means of Natural Selection* (London: John Murray, 1859), p. 490.

69 Rupke, *Great Chain of History*, pp. 216–18 and 267–74. See, however, note 27 above.

Byron and Grammatical Freedom

GAVIN HOPPS

'– Bosh!' Stephen said rudely. 'A man of genius makes no mistakes. His errors are volitional and are the portals of discovery.'[1]

If we were to apply Stephen's comment on Shakespeare to Byron's use of grammar, I would have to say: I disagree; it is partly true; and it is true in more ways than one. That is to say, even though a significant number of purported errors are plainly not beyond dispute, and even though, in many cases, they may be defended on aesthetic grounds, it has to be acknowledged that Byron's poetry contains an unusually large number of grammatical errors; secondly, it appears that *some* of Byron's grammatical mistakes are 'volitional' – though one would have to add that there are, manifestly, a number of degrees and types of volition; and, thirdly, I think that on occasion, Byron's 'mistakes' might be described as 'portals of discovery' not only in terms of what they tell us about the artist but also in terms of what they tell us about reality.[2]

Stephen's 'mistakes', 'volition', and 'portals of discovery' usefully introduce the different types of grammatical freedom that I wish to suggest it is possible to distinguish in Byron's poetry.[3] The paper is, accordingly, divided into three basic sections, corresponding to each of the notional types. The first two sections will attempt to illustrate, and differentiate between, what we might describe as 'careless' carelessness and 'deliberate' carelessness, both of which confirm a familiar picture of Byron; the final section is more restricted in its focus and more speculative in its interpretations, and concentrates on what one may call, without being in the least indecorous, Byron's 'dangling participle'.

The first type of apparent carelessness or error is perhaps the least interesting but the most frequently noted – often, as Byron observed, with 'much facetious exultation'.[4] Here are some of the more notorious instances (where appropriate, the supposed mistake has been underlined):

And dashest him again to earth: – there let him <u>lay</u>.

(*Childe Harold's Pilgrimage*, IV, 180)

Place me on Sunium's marbled steep,
Where nothing, save the waves and I,
May hear our mutual murmurs sweep.

('The Isles of Greece', 16)

Let He who made thee answer that.

(*Cain*, II, ii, 88)

A lady with her daughters or her nieces
Shine like a guinea and seven shilling pieces.

(*Don Juan*, III, 60)

as smooth a vale
As ever Spring yclad in grassy dye.

(*Childe Harold's Pilgrimage*, II, 54)

E. H. Coleridge's comment on the first and famous solecism – which also occurs in '[Pignus Amoris]' and 'The Adieu' – seems to be a fair and representative assessment of the first type of error: 'The fact is', Coleridge observes, 'that Byron wrote as he spoke, with the "careless and negligent ease of a man of quality" and either did not know that "lay" was not an intransitive verb or regarded himself as "supra grammaticam."'[5]

Yet, even in such apparently compelling cases, we must beware of making assessments about grammatical propriety or acceptability according to our own historically specific notions of correctness. The intransitive use of 'lay', for example, though it has caused and, doubtless, continues to cause many to wince, was not considered a solecism in the seventeenth and eighteenth centuries.[6] Likewise, whilst some readers might object to the use of a pronoun in the nominative case with the quasi-preposition 'save' (T. G. Steffan tactfully, though one might say unnecessarily, draws the reader's attention to Byron's usage[7]), it is, according to the *Oxford English Dictionary*, 'apparently the normal construction'. Various editors and critics have similarly found fault with Byron's use of archaisms – sometimes justly, as in the example above, where a participle form is used as a preterit. But on other occasions, the criticism is more controversial, if not pedantic. G. A. Sheldon, for instance, in his edition of *Childe Harold's Pilgrimage* (London: Rivington's, 1933), objects to Byron's use of 'ygazed' (II, 71). Yet, while it is true that the word did not exist in Old English, there is nothing incorrect about its formation or function.[8] My purpose in challenging a number of those who have challenged Byron is not to suggest that, grammatically speaking, his poetry is without fault; however, I *do* wish to argue that, in this respect, he is as sinned against as sinning.

Coleridge's 'either–or' construction in his comment on Byron's use of 'lay' sensibly acknowledges that the issue of the poet's awareness is ultimately beyond our reach. Nonetheless, some of Byron's deviations are clearly meant to be noticed, whereas noticing others appears to detract from the poem's effects. We may therefore, I suggest, tentatively distinguish between deviant or non-standard constructions according to whether or not they appear to serve a purpose, and whether or not it seems that we are *supposed* to notice them. This is, obviously, more difficult where the structure in question forms part of a rhyme; however, what matters is whether or not such deviations cause us – to use Kingsley Amis's felicitous phrase – to 'pause without profit'.[9] The error in case in the quotation from *Cain*, and the incorrect archaism in *Childe Harold's Pilgrimage*, for example, appear to contribute nothing to the respective works, and in this sense might be described as 'careless' carelessness.

Although this distinction is, I think, useful and real, we may also wish to identify something which lies in between negligence and deliberate transgression. We often encounter in Byron's poetry, particularly in his octosyllabic verse, less serious solecisms or obscurities, such as those which disturbed Jeffrey in *The Corsair*:

> His [Byron's] construction … is often ungrammatical or imperfect – as when giving directions to alter the guard of his sword, he says
>
>> Last time, it more fatigued my arm than foes.
>
> To *fatigue* foes with a sabre, is at all events a very strange mode of annoyance. In a subsequent passage, it is said,
>
>> He sate him down in silence, and his look
>> Resumed the calmness which before forsook.
>
> Forsook what? – The verb is unquestionably active, and not neuter. The whole passage indeed is clumsy in diction, and, we would almost say, vulgar in expression.[10]

Jeffrey's comments make clear, if nothing else, that obscurity, like beauty, is in the eye of the beholder. This point is nicely illustrated by a manuscript exchange recorded by Coleridge, between two unidentified readers, concerning a stanza in *Childe Harold's Pilgrimage*: 'With reference to this passage [(I, 27)], while yet in MS., an early reader (?Dallas) inquires, "What does this mean?" And a second (?Hobhouse) rejoins, "What does the question mean? It is one of the finest stanzas I ever read."'[11] While the sort of imperfections – if such they be – that Jeffrey objected to do not appear to be as self-conscious or willed as those I shall consider in a moment, they are, we might say, *permitted*, in that they form part of a deliberate attempt to create an impression of rapidity or haste; as Camille Paglia has noted in her essay 'Speed and Space: Byron', it is 'this slapdash freedom [which] gives Byron his relentless forward propulsion'.[12]

Probably Byron's most unsparing critic with respect to such careless-ness was Matthew Arnold, who, talking of the passage in *The Giaour* beginning 'He who hath bent him o'er the dead' (68), was moved to exclaim with something approaching incredulity at its 'trailing relatives, that crying grammatical solecism, that inextricable anacoluthon!'[13] And though Arnold nonetheless goes on to rank Byron, alongside Wordsworth, as the greatest English poet of the century, his view of Byron's use of grammar was unforgiving: 'Byron', he writes, 'is so negligent in his poetical style, he is often, to say the truth, so slovenly, slipshod, and infe-licitous, he is so little haunted by the true artist's fine passion for the correct use and consummate management of words, that he may be described as having for this artistic gift the insensibility of the barbarian'.[14]

Scott, by contrast, was less troubled by such ungrammaticalities, and saw them as a vital and constituent part of Byron's poetry: 'Sketches from Lord Byron', he observes, 'are more valuable than finished pictures from others; nor are we at all sure that any labour which he might bestow in revisal would not rather efface than refine those outlines of striking and powerful originality which they exhibit, when flung rough from the hand of the master.'[15] To emphasise the importance of the eye of the beholder, it is worth mentioning that Ethel C. Mayne saw in the anacoluthon that gave Arnold such pain: 'that strange, slipshod loveliness, where He never fulfils his destiny as the subject of the opening phrase. Bent o'er the dead he remains immovable to the end of time.'[16]

Byron was, of course, himself the first to acknowledge his carelessness and misuse of grammar. In *Don Juan* he confesses to the 'sin' of breaking Priscian's head (XV, 24), and, we might note, agreed with Scott *as well as* Arnold, pointing out that 'No one [had] done more through negligence to corrupt the language'.[17] Indeed, Byron seems to be genuinely and pleas-antly taken aback by Gifford's comment that the first act of *Marino Faliero* is 'good, "sterling, genuine English"';[18] writing to Murray, Byron remarks: 'I am glad that I have got so much left – though heaven knows how I retain it – I *hear* none but from my Valet – and his is *Nottinghamshire*'.[19]

Even in his early verse, however, Byron clearly felt that there were more important things at stake; as he writes in 'Hints from Horace':

And must the Bard his glowing thoughts confine?
Lest Censure hover o'er some faulty line,
Remove whate'er a Critic may suspect,
To gain the paltry suffrage of 'Correct'!
Or prune the spirit of each daring phrase,
To fly from Error – not to merit praise?

(415–20)

Before moving on to our second type of grammatical freedom, it is necessary to mention an important subcategory of unintentional error for which Byron is *not* to blame (I am, of course, in doing so, trying to cut a very long story short). This consists of mistakes made in printing or copying, an example of which can be seen in the following lines:

as the home
Heart-ballads of Green Erin or Grey Highlands,
That <u>brings</u> Lochaber back to eyes that roam.

(*Don Juan*, XVI, 46)

As McGann notes: 'The reading "brings" is a mistake which originates in a lack of clarity in Byron's MS. Byron originally wrote "brings" but then overwrote the final s to correct the grammar. His correction was missed by Mary Shelley or Hunt's printer.'[20]

While the sort of mistakes which made Arnold exclaim appear to be instances of unwitting negligence or of a prioritisation of speed over technical accuracy, on other occasions, as critics such as Helen Gardner and George Ridenour have shown, Byron's carelessness is evidently the product of considerable care. This second type of carelessness, to which I now turn, is most obvious in *Don Juan*.[21]

Volitional errors in a sense cease to be errors; or, to put it another way, such errors are rather like madness in England according to one of the gravediggers in *Hamlet*: in a work such as *Don Juan*, whose 'Soul' is its 'licence',[22] they are, we might say, less likely to be seen as deviations. Indeed, Byron's abuse of grammar in *Don Juan* is more often than not a *flouting* of the rules, and a flaunting of his non-observance, and is perhaps better described as a deliberate *manhandling* of language, rather than error as such; as Goethe aptly observed, Byron 'spares his language as little as he spares humanity'.[23]

Such advertised violation or manhandling of language takes many forms and has a variety of effects. Some of these violations have what we might heuristically describe as a 'centrifugal' function, in that they direct attention towards the poet, while others may be said to have a 'centripetal' function, in that they are principally related to what is said. Let us begin with the former and the most minor violations.

Byron unconcernedly both adds words where, conventionally speaking, they are out of place, and leaves words out where, conventionally, they are required –

> henceforth no temptation
> Shall 'fool me to the top up of my bent'
>
> (*Don Juan*, XV, 94)

> for that with me's a '<u>sine quâ</u>'
>
> (*Don Juan*, XV, 86)[24]

– openly padding and contracting his verse, irrespective of what it does to his grammar.[25] More blatantly, Byron also introduces audacious morphological distortions, for the sake of rhyme or comic effect, as seen, for example, in canto XIII of *Don Juan*:

> I've seen a virtuous woman put down quite
> By the mere combination of a Coterie;
> Also a So-So Matron boldly fight
> Her way back to the world by dint of <u>plottery</u>.
>
> (82)[26]

And, perhaps most extravagantly of all, Byron is even prepared to travesty his narrative with whimsical malapropisms:

> there's nothing makes me so much grieve
> As that abominable tittle tattle,
> Which is the cud <u>eschewed</u> by human cattle.
>
> (*Don Juan*, XII, 43)

On other occasions, Byron's violations are less dramatic yet more overt, not on account of the nature of the error, but because Byron draws our attention to his transgressions himself. Here are two such examples from *Don Juan*:

> few are slow
> In thinking that their enemy is beat,
> (Or *beaten*, if *you* insist on grammar, though
> I never think about it in a heat).
>
> (VII, 42)

> the maxim for the amorous tribe is
> Horation, 'Medio tu tutissimus ibis.'

The 'tu' 's *too* much, – but let it stand – the verse
Requires it.

(VI, 17–18)

To conclude our examination of deliberate transgressions that direct attention towards the poet, I would like to cite an extract from *The Blues*, which archly alludes to an earlier mistake, and reveals something about Byron's attitude towards correction and correctness. Here is what George Ellis had to say about the error in question:

we admit that, for every ancient word employed by the modern poet, the authority of Spencer may be pleaded. … Even if these words … were always correctly inserted, their uncouth appearance would be displeasing; but Lord Byron is not always correct in his use of them. For instance, when he says,

Devices quaint, and Frolics ever new,
Tread on each other's *kibes*, –

it must be supposed that he did not mean to personify devices and frolics for the purpose of afflicting them with chilblains.[27]

And here is the allusion to the mistake in *The Blues*:

TRACY.   'Tis high time for a '*Sic me servavit Appollo.*'
And yet we shall have the whole crew on our <u>kibes</u>,
Blues, dandies, and dowagers, and second-hand scribes,
All flocking to moisten their exquisite throttles
With a glass of Madeira at Lady Bluebottle's.

(156–60)

In echoing, but subtly altering, the earlier error, Byron appears, as McGann points out, to be 'engaging in some witty self-satire, for he was painfully aware of his earlier blunder since it had been pointed out by George Ellis'.[28] Byron's satire is, however, not only directed towards himself. The virtual repetition of the exposed mistake, in a poem concerned with literary reputation and *Schadenfreude*, and spoken by a character who has just been describing the 'threshing' of a friend at the hands of a 'Review', invites a supplementary, tangential reading of the line as alluding to Byron's own (biographical) case and the painful encroachments of literary critics. In this way, Byron seems to turn what is a sort of confession into something of an accusation, since the utterance acknowledges, though also subtly defends – in criticising the criticism of – the earlier error. The poet's self-satire thus appears to evince a familiar Byronic compound of penitence and defiance.

What connects the foregoing violations and marks them off from our first category of carelessness is that they might be said to have an aesthetic or biographical function. Whilst the first type of mistakes may be a *result* of haste and a want of revision, the second sort of transgressions seem to be intended to *show* us that the author does not care about such matters and has better things to do. Such negligence, on the one hand, might there-fore be a sign of what Paul West refers to as 'the gentleman-poet's disrespect for his hobby',[29] or else suggests that Byron wants us to imagine him literally writing his poetry 'while undressing after coming home from balls and masquerades'.[30] On the other hand, Byron's witting carelessness in and towards poetry is also, of course, a sign of his aesthetic stance. Most obviously, his negligence and his privileging of rapidity are provocatively opposed to Wordsworth's 'emotion recollected in tranquillity'; yet, his disregard for, or de-prioritisation of, prose grammar additionally connects him with Pope, who, for all his celebrated propriety and polish, is habitu-ally and serenely unmindful of the rules of English grammar.[31]

Turning, then, to deviations that are related more to *what* is described, we can, I think, identify three basic types of effect. As we can see from the functional conversion in the following lines, grammatical deviation may be employed, firstly, in the *service* of the story, to vivify or defamiliarise:

> like the Rhone by Leman's waters wash'd,
> Where mingled and yet separate appears
> The river from the lake, all <u>bluely</u> dash'd.

> (*Don Juan*, XIV, 87)

Alternatively, the deviation may stand in ironic or *antagonistic* relation to what the poet is saying:

> Some kinder casuists are pleased to say,
> In nameless print – that I have no devotion;
> But set those persons down with me to pray,
> And you shall see who has the <u>properest</u> notion
> Of getting into Heaven the shortest way.

> (*Don Juan*, III, 104)

The use of the acceptable but slightly unorthodox and metrically obtrusive inflectional superlative 'properest', coming as it does after the reverent, intense, and extended prayer to the Virgin Mary, subtly skews or complicates the tone, as if the speaker's preceding reverence had precipitated its opposite. Finally, the deviation may mirror or imitate what is signified in some way. Here is an example from canto V:

> Now, if my Pegasus should not be <u>shod ill</u>,
> This poem will become a moral model.

(2)

Such poetic licence is, needless to say, conventional and relatively minor, yet it might be described as 'performative' or, to use Dr Johnson's phrase, as 'representative versification',[32] in that it enacts what it simultaneously describes. In this particular case, Byron uses a comically contorted structure to speak about the hypothetical faultiness of his verse (which is in a sense 'ill shod' in describing itself as 'shod ill'). The deviation thus illustrates – but in its ingenuity paradoxically testifies against – the defect that the conditional clause leaves as an analogously unresolved hypothesis.

To sum up, then: not only can we distinguish between deliberate and apparently unwitting error in Byron's verse, we may, it seems, also discern significant differences in function and effect *within* the category of volitional error.

I would like to introduce my third and final category with an example which is neither from Byron nor ungrammatical. At a critical moment in Wordsworth's 'There Was a Boy', we find a striking and ambiguous use of the present perfect verb form:

> And, when it chanced
> That pauses of deep silence mock'd his skill,
> Then, sometimes, in that silence, while he hung
> Listening, a gentle shock of mild surprize
> <u>Has carried</u> far into his heart the voice
> Of mountain torrents.

(16–21)[33]

Whilst the use of the present perfect in conjunction with a definite expression of completed time is not as exceptional as it might be thought, and although Wordsworth was peculiarly attached to present-perfect constructions,[34] the use of the form here is, I believe, both calculated and extraordinary: calculated, in view of the alteration from the habitual form 'Would carry', which is used in the original first-person draft of the lines, and the availability of neutral and more customary alternatives;[35] extraordinary, in that the structure carries with it certain implications with respect to time, which, from a common-sense point of view, are plainly inappropriate. To be more precise: the use of the present perfect allows a dilation of the reference of the verb into the present, which the past tense or habitual form would exclude, thereby extending the effect of the encounter with nature not only beyond the moment of its occurrence but also beyond the death of the child, which is thus robbed of its finality. On this reading, if, as Paul de Man argues, Wordsworth's use of 'to hang' indicates 'an anticipatory announcement of his death', which overshadows his sense of 'analogical correspondence between man and nature',[36] this apparently decisive eclipse is *itself* eclipsed by a disclosure of continuity. If this is the case, Wordsworth's use of the present perfect, while not ungrammatical, would nevertheless seem to be a significant avoidance of more conventional or contextually appropriate structures for the sake of its peculiar temporal implications. It might therefore be argued that the poet's choice of grammatical structure serves an ontological purpose, and that it is his view of reality rather than his attitude towards language as such that differs from the norm.

We are now, I think, in a better position to take a look at Byron's notoriously dangling participle. The offending construction occurs in the first stanza of *Childe Harold's Pilgrimage*, canto III:

> Is thy face like thy mother's, my fair child!
> Ada! sole daughter of my house and heart?
> When last I saw thy young blue eyes they smiled,
> And then we parted, – not as now we part,
> But with a hope. –
>
> Awaking with a start,
> The waters heave around me; and on high
> The winds lift up their voices: I depart,
> Whither I know not; but the hour's gone by,
> When Albion's lessening shores could grieve or glad mine eye.

The 'rule' that Byron's lines contravene may be stated as follows. A subjectless non-finite clause – in this case 'Awaking with a start' – is conventionally understood to have the same subject as the main clause to which it is attached. Byron's lines, however, depending upon our reading, appear to involve a conflation of disparate subjects – the poet (by implication) in the subordinate clause, 'The waters' in the main clause.[37] What is so interesting about Byron's breach of linguistic etiquette is that the syntax's permission of two alternative readings reflects concerns that are central to the poem.[38] In order to understand the peculiar ambiguity and general significance of Byron's construction, it will be helpful to take a step backwards to the apostrophe which immediately precedes Byron's dangling or misrelated participle – if dangling or misrelated it is.

The act of apostrophe, speaking for a moment of the trope in general, is central to the poem as a whole, both in the sheer frequency of its occurrence, and in its peculiar negotiation of contrary realities. In another context, Catherine Pickstock has observed: 'Every invocation betrays an absence, but it also embodies the reparation'.[39] For Byron, this seems to be true in reverse: the act of apostrophe partly reveals the absence or distance it partly repairs. In this way, such utterances precariously conjoin two contrary versions of reality – one common-sensical and one counter-rational. Indeed, one might say that apostrophe, for Byron, is the cruellest figure, involving a simultaneous sense of relation and loss.

Nowhere is this more apparent than in the apostrophe at the start of canto III. Byron seems at once to be acutely aware of his separation from Ada – asking her what her face looks like – and to have a sense of relation sufficient to induce him directly to address her and to make the subsequent re-cognition of the empirical present feel like an awakening.

The significance of the space of four years in between cantos II and III has frequently been discussed; yet the more remarkable gap, I believe, occurs at the beginning of canto III, where the poet dramatically sinks into silence before us, after only four-and-a-half lines of narration. Byron is surely one of the few poets who can interest us in contemplating him in the act of *not* writing a poem in the *middle* of the poem. Byron's misrelated participle interrupts this silence, and seems at once to disavow, and reassert the validity of, the sense of counter-rational relation announced by the apostrophe. Let us return then to and look a little more closely at the structure in question.

The syntactic relation of the clauses and the apparent inconsonance of their subjects holds in balance two radically divergent readings of the relation between the speaker and the external world. Pragmatically speaking, the clauses (and the events they describe) are unrelated. The initial clause, according to such a reading, is a free adjunct, whose subject is recoverable from the context, and, common-sensically, other than that of the following clause. If, however, we read the lines strictly according to their syntax, and suspend our disbelief, the initial clause appears to function as a subordinate adverbial, whose pragmatic subject is displaced by that of the following main clause. It is therefore the *waters* that awaken and which – along with the winds, which, in a less equivocal instance of pathetic fallacy, 'lift up their voices' – appear to be contingent upon, and in sympathy with, the consciousness of the speaker. Byron's ambiguous construction thus, on the one hand, reinforces the preceding sense of counter-rational relation, in appearing to validate such modes again, and, on the other hand, resolutely *disaffirms* such claims in its stark description of the alienating empirical world.

Although the implications of a 'related' reading are, plainly, absurd – which is to say, a stumbling-block to reason – occurring at the beginning of a canto which explores the nature of the relationship between the self and the external world, and which treats such radical positions – even if it ultimately fails to endorse them – with unembarrassed seriousness, they are clearly not out of place. Indeed, Byron is evidently reluctant to believe that what was to become known as pathetic fallacy is in fact fallacious. As he writes later on in the canto:

> And Ardennes waves above them her green leaves,
> Dewy with nature's tear-drops, as they pass,
> Grieving, if aught inanimate e'er grieves,
> Over the unreturning brave.
>
> (27)

And similarly in *Don Juan*:

> the far bell of vesper makes [the pilgrim] start,
> Seeming to weep the dying day's decay;
> Is this a fancy which our reason scorns?
> Ah! surely nothing dies but something mourns!
>
> (III, 108)

The if-clause in the first extract and the question in the second bespeak the same equivocal conjunction of faith and doubt respecting the sense of sympathetic continuity between man and nature that I am suggesting is figured in the ambiguous syntax of the lines we have been examining.[40] It may for this reason be argued that it is the *view of reality*, as it was in Wordsworth's poem, rather than Byron's use of grammar, which is extraordinary.

Peter Cochran has drawn attention to another well-known, supposed solecism in *Childe Harold's Pilgrimage* which may similarly be seen as the expression of an extraordinary view of reality rather than a misuse of language. Referring to the opening lines of canto IV – 'I stood in Venice, on the Bridge of Sighs; / A palace and a prison on each hand' – Cochran points out that the apparently ungrammatical construction carries the 'bold implication … that the prison *is* a palace and the palace *is* a prison, and that Byron stands trapped between the two'.[41] He is surely right in this.

To conclude, I would like to invoke a distinction – popularised by Isaiah Berlin (though a version of it is to be found in Anselm's treatise *On Free Will*) – between 'positive' and 'negative' freedom, which might be applied to Byron's practice. In the first instance, Byron's 'creatively illicit' use of grammar seems to advertise a deliverance from restraint, and may therefore be described as *negative* freedom, or freedom *from*. Yet, on other occasions, or looked at from a different point of view, his transgressions seem to exist in order to achieve a fidelity of a greater kind, as seen in the way his syntax is open and faithful to different experiences of reality, however extraordinary. His use of grammar might thus be described as a form of *positive* freedom, or freedom *for*, since his concern in such cases is not so much for the shackles being cut, but for what he is freely, that is, wholly and faithfully, attending to.

Earlier I suggested that Stephen's point about the errors of a man of genius being 'portals of discovery' was true in more ways than one. Some 'mistakes', as I hope I have shown, not only tell us something about the artist, but also tell us something about reality. Hence, while the constructions used in our final examples may be described as deviant from a prescriptive point of view, they are, we might say, impressionistically correct, in that they accurately represent what seem to be the feelings of the poems' speakers, as Ruskin famously argued; secondly, and more controversially, without disallowing the claims or reality of the common-sensical view of the world, this third type of poetic licence suggests that this is not or not always the only or most compelling view of things.[42]

Notes

1   James Joyce, *Ulysses* (London: The Bodley Head, 1964), p. 243.
2   It is perhaps worth recalling that when Stephen Dedalus is asked who he thinks is the greatest poet, he replies, 'Byron, of course' – an opinion he refuses to retract in spite of being pinned against a barbed-wire fence and beaten with a cabbage stump. James Joyce, *A Portrait of the Artist as a Young Man* (London: Penguin, 1992), pp. 85–6.
3   The issue of grammaticality is, of course, a highly contentious matter, which is given added piquancy in the present case by the fact that the currently dominant standpoint in such discussions is different from that of the period with which we are concerned. Crudely, if it is nowadays typical to prioritise working sense and the fluidity of things, when Byron was writing, it was customary to prioritise

prescriptive forms. However, notwithstanding modern linguists' rightful insistence that grammaticality is subject to gradience, and is neither synchronically nor diachronically fixed but is continually assailed and modified by the generation of new forms, language at any given time recognises a distinction between regular and irregular, correct and incorrect forms; or, as George Steiner puts it, there is always a 'dynamic tension between that in language which is conservative, which seeks legitimacy in precedent and the useful fiction of "correctness," and that which is innovative and creatively illicit'. *Real Presences* (Chicago, IL: Chicago University Press, 1989), p. 159. It is this normative presumption or 'useful fiction of "correctness"' which I wish to retain in order to highlight Byron's inventive subversion of it. There is an important relation, upon which it is unfortunately not possible to elaborate here, between Byron's concern for – even as he transgresses – notions of 'correctness' in language, and his larger, class-related interest in social and aesthetic propriety, as seen, for example, in his criticism of Keats and Hunt, which exists alongside the will to transgress. In social as well as linguistic matters, Byron's penchant for transgression and ability to relax in relation to the 'rules' is predicated upon an intimate knowledge of – and suggests a covert attachment to – notions of 'correctness'.

4   Notes to *Childe Harold's Pilgrimage, CPW*, 2, 294.
5   *The Works of Lord Byron*, ed. by Ernest Hartley Coleridge, 7 vols (London: John Murray, 1904); II, 458, 2. Hereafter cited as *WLB*.
6   See the *OED*, sense 43.
7   *Don Juan*, ed. by T.G. Steffan, E. Steffan, and W.W. Pratt (London: Penguin, 1996), p. 14.
8   Coleridge similarly censures the formulation 'Childe Harold was he hight', only to acknowledge immediately afterwards that such a construction is in fact permissible and precedented (*WLB*, II, 17, 1).
9   Kingsley Amis, *The King's English* (London: HarperCollins, 1998), p. 40.
10 Francis Jeffrey, *Byron: The Critical Heritage*, ed. by Andrew Rutherford (London: Routledge, 1970), p. 63.
11 *WLB*, II, 42, 1.
12 Camille Paglia, *Sexual Personae* (London: Penguin, 1991), p. 356.
13 Matthew Arnold, *Poetry and Prose* (London: Rupert Hart-Davis, 1954), pp. 719–20.
14 Arnold, *Poetry and Prose*, p. 719.
15 Walter Scott, in Rutherford (ed.), *Byron: The Critical Heritage*, p. 87.
16 Ethel Colburn Mayne, *Byron* (London: Methuen, 1969), p. 177.
17 *BLJ*, 7, 182.
18 *BLJ*, 7, 194.
19 *BLJ*, 7, 175.
20 *CPW*, 5, 767. P. E. More suggests that part of the blame for ungrammaticalities in Byron's work should, in any case, be laid upon Gifford and Murray; referring to the solecism cited earlier in *Cain*, he writes: 'Byron apparently had a genius for bad grammar. The curious thing is that Gifford and Murray should have let such solecisms slip through the press'. *The Complete Poetical Works of Byron* (Boston, MA: Houghton, Mifflin and Co., 1933), p. 1032.
21 It is worth reminding ourselves that in choosing to write in ottava rima, and

committing himself to what Gifford described as the 'wicked necessity of rhyming' (*CPW*, 5, 754–5), Byron was wilfully submitting to considerable constraints, which would pull him and his language in all sorts of directions. In this more general sense, his transgressions may be said to be both anticipated and unforeseen, and the product of both volition and chance. Indeed, one might go so far as to say that his poetic licence is not only accompanied but is to a certain degree *prompted* by discipline and restraint.

22 *BLJ*, 6, 208.

23 Goethe, *Byron: The Critical Heritage*, p. 164.

24 Byron in this case included a note on his omission: 'Subauditur "*Non*"; omitted for the sake of euphony' (*CPW*, 5, 756).

25 There is arguably another, even more subtle, way in which Byron's verse pulls against grammatical norms. Although the use of enjambment obviously does not affect the grammar of a sentence, it may, especially in conjunction with rhyme, create temporary contrapuntal disruptions of grammar, passingly separating or conjoining constituents which, syntactically, belong together or apart. And whilst Byron is, to be sure, also attached to a Popean synchronicity of metrical and grammatical boundaries, he clearly enjoys the way enjambment and rhyme may be used to isolate and contrapuntally suspend nonsensical fragments or combinations of words, without, in fact, doing anything wrong or any harm to his syntax. Memorable examples occur in *Don Juan*, VIII, 105 ('bigamy/twig.—Am I) and XII, 75, in which we find a mid-word enjambment ('warb-/le'). For an illuminating general discussion of this issue, to which my point is indebted, see Roger Fowler, '"Prose Rhythm" and Metre', in *Essays on Style and Language*, ed. by Roger Fowler (New York: The Humanities Press, 1966), pp. 82–99.

26 Auden wittily imitates Byron's practice in this respect in his *Letter to Lord Byron*: 'The south of England before very long / Will look no different from the Continong' (II, 16).

27 George Ellis, in Rutherford (ed.), *Byron: The Critical Heritage*, pp. 45–6.

28 *CPW*, 6, 666–7.

29 *Byron: A Collection of Critical Essays*, ed. by Paul West (Englewood Cliffs, NJ: Prentice-Hall, 1963), p. 3.

30 *BLJ*, 9, 168.

31 For an interesting discussion of Pope's 'deliberate mistaking', see Allan Rodway, 'By Algebra to Augustanism', in Fowler, ed., *Essays on Style and Language*.

32 Samuel Johnson, *The Lives of the Poets* (London: Oxford University Press, 1964), p. 51.

33 Wordsworth, *Lyrical Ballads*, ed. by R. L. Brett and A. R. Jones (London: Methuen, 1965).

34 See, for example, John Alexander Alford, 'Wordsworth's Use of the Present Perfect', in *Modern Language Quarterly* 33 (1972), and Julian Boyd and Zelda Boyd, 'The Perfect of Experience', in *Studies in Romanticism* 16, no. 1 (1977).

35 Interestingly, De Quincey, in quoting from memory, normalises Wordsworth's verb form (to 'Was carried') in his famous remarks upon these lines.

36 *The Rhetoric of Romanticism* (New York: Columbia University Press, 1984), pp. 54, 51.

37 As my use of quotation marks suggests, the ordinance of the 'rule' is open to question. Where the implied subject is obvious, the breaking of such a rule, according to Geoffrey Leech *et al.*, is only as objectionable as 'putting one's elbows on the table or eating peas with the underside of one's fork'. *English Grammar for Today* (London: Macmillan, 1985), p. 182. For a detailed objection to the objection to such usage, see Bernd Kortmann, *Free Adjuncts and Absolutes in English* (London: Routledge, 1991).

38 Geoffrey Ward makes a similar point in 'Byron's Artistry in Deep and Layered Space', in *Byron and the Limits of Fiction*, ed. by Bernard Beatty and Vincent Newey (Liverpool: Liverpool University Press, 1988), pp. 199–200.

39 'Liturgy and Language: The Sacred Polis', in *Liturgy and Dialogue*, ed. by Paul Bradshaw and Brian Spinks (London: SPCK, 1993), p. 115.

40 For an 'ontological defence' of pathetic fallacy, see Gavin Hopps, 'When Might Pathetic Fallacy Be Neither Pathetic nor Fallacious?' (in preparation).

41 The point was made in an unpublished talk given at Newstead Abbey in 1988, entitled 'Byron and the Essence of Imprisonment.'

42 I would like to thank my friend and colleague Peter H. Marsden for his expert reading of and comments upon an early draft of this paper, and Thorlac Turville-Petre for his invaluable advice concerning historical grammar.

Byron, Napoleon, and Imaginative Freedom

JOHN CLUBBE

The obsession was Byron's, and its object was Napoleon. One conquered Europe by words, the other by might; but the nineteenth century's two most spectacular figures never met, and Napoleon left no recorded pronouncements on Byron.[1] Why did the French Emperor seize Byron's imagination more than any other living human being, seize it overwhelmingly, seize it at the onset of his life, and never relinquish his grasp until Byron's dying hour? In Byron's day-to-day life other friends and lovers – Augusta, Lady Byron (negatively), John Cam Hobhouse, Thomas Moore, Douglas Kinnaird, Lady Melbourne perhaps – held sway; in his imagination, there was, first and foremost, Napoleon.

The most confessional of poets, Byron, paradoxically, is the most reticent. He tells us much in his seven volumes of poetry, one of prose, and thirteen of letters and journals. But he also tells us little: his writings cover his tracks as much as reveal them. The Napoleonic current in Byron proceeds, like the mysterious stream in 'Kubla Khan', in a mazy motion. Its subterranean course lies beyond our normal line of vision. But when the current abruptly bursts into view 'with ceaseless turmoil seething', as it frequently does across Byron's writings, the effects can be stunning.

Why should the Emperor of the French appeal so strongly to Byron? After all, except for fourteen months in 1802–1803, the country of Byron's birth, and of which he was a peer of the realm, was continuously at war with France, with one brief interval, from 1793 to 1815. To understand Byron's obsession, to discover what drew him irresistibly to Napoleon and held him in thrall, clarifies much that puzzles us about this enigmatic poet. Politics dominated Byron's life, and his idea of Napoleon dominated his politics. But that is only part of it. Remove Napoleon from Byron's imagination, and the man – and his writings – become less vital things.

For Byron, in life as in poetry, Napoleon was an obsession. In Scotland as a child, in England during his growing-up years, in the East on his first pilgrimage, in England again during his years of notoriety, in Switzerland in 1816, in Italy until 1823, even in Greece during the fraught final year, Napoleon rarely receded far beneath the surface of Byron's consciousness. Within the Byronic imagination he serves as a *basso continuo*, barely audible at times, defiantly plangent at others. In neither range, however, and at no time in his life does Byron respond to Napoleon consistently. His obsession waxed and waned, running through adulation, disdain, attraction, and repulsion; contrary emotions appear and disappear, and then reappear, sometimes within the same week, the same day, even the same hour.

The French Emperor captured Byron's imagination early. A student at Harrow in 1803, the young Byron ferociously defended his prized bust of Napoleon against 'rascally time-servers' – presumably referring to certain of his fellow Harrovians.[2] As this incident indicates, Byron was already, at age fifteen, openly defiant. Defiant he remained all his life. Actually, Byron's lifelong involvement with Napoleon began even earlier, when the young general triumphed at the battle of Lodi on 10 May 1796. That stunning victory impressed Napoleon Bonaparte upon the European consciousness: the man with the odd name became a household word. For Byron Lodi became a defining moment, one to which, as a mature poet, he would return again and again.

Napoleon died in 1821, but Byron's involvement with the Emperor continued until his own death three years later. On Cephalonia in 1823, recalling the victory at Lodi and the spectacular Italian campaign of 1796, Byron apostrophised Napoleon as 'the Emperor of Emperors'. This was in fact eight years before General Bonaparte became the Emperor Napoleon, but such a detail mattered little in Byron's imagination. It was in Napoleon's campaign in Italy that he sought a model for his own fantasy of victory in Greece.

As he followed with rapt attention Napoleon's activities in France and subsequently in his island exile on St Helena, Byron kept Napoleon's words in constant dialogue with his own. We can only understand what Byron says about Napoleon by involving ourselves fully in the historical record of this dialogue and these activities. Byron responded passionately to Napoleon, and to come to grips with that response requires involvement with the psychology of both figures; it requires of us emotional empathy, a critical kind of passion. By passion I do not mean the emotion that blinds us, but the emotion that enthrals our being, that makes us desperately want to know and to understand, to explain why these things happened the way they did; and why, two hundred years later, they still resonate; why they are still tremendously important.

Obsessions defy reason. They are fundamentally irrational. How can we make sense of them? What makes Byron's Napoleonic obsession unusual is its extent and duration. Byron's comments about Napoleon differ in intensity and in kind from anything he says about anyone else. His feelings for Napoleon involve more than admiration or even veneration. He admired and venerated Walter Scott more than he did Napoleon, but Scott did not obsess him. Napoleon, unlike Scott, provoked a certain kind of imaginative reaction from Byron, one that seized the deepest level of his mind and being; and, however frustrated and even disillusioned Byron would become with him, it did not let go of its grip.

One reason Napoleon riveted Byron is because he appeared to live life with such intensity. Passionate characters fascinated Byron. Ali Pasha was one; Rousseau, another; Curran, a third. There was something about these figures, Napoleon pre-eminently, that prompted Byron into mimicry and hero worship: the almost incomprehensible vitality of his own life was modelled largely on his own imaginative reconstruction of the most passionate men of his day.

Napoleon fired Byron's imagination chiefly as a gigantic, though flawed, human being *and* as a parallel figure against whom to measure his own development. Byron saw himself, in distorted and elliptical form, reflected in Napoleon. Napoleon showed Byron what, for good or for ill, he might become. Byron compared Napoleon to others on several occasions, but found only the mythical Prometheus worthy to stand alongside Napoleon. Napoleon was thus both rival and stimulus. At times Byron imagined himself as Napoleon, at others as Napoleon's successor. His imaginative immersion in an imagined version of Napoleon was almost frighteningly total.

Napoleon's mind, for Byron, was distinguished by a kind of omnipresence. In thought and deed he seemed to Byron to push back the earthbound frontiers of human existence. He embodied an element of immeasurability that Byron associated with the ocean or the Alps, which are, in turn, key images in Byron's poetics. 'Immensity', one of Napoleon's favourite words, early became Byron's goal as a poet.[3] Byron's response to Napoleon parallels his response to Shakespeare but in its consequences has effects even more far-reaching. He denigrates and belittles both Shakespeare and Napoleon, but neither response conceals his desire to emulate and surpass, to achieve comparable immensity himself.

Contemporaries, whether aware or not of Byron's self-identification with the Emperor, rightly linked the two. Byron and Napoleon together encapsulate the energy of the decades after 1789, a time when stupendous historical events followed each other in pulse-quickening succession. 'Events may be so extraordinary that they can hardly be established by testimony', sighed a contributor to the *Edinburgh Review* in September 1814, soon after it appeared that the Allies had safely stashed Napoleon away on Elba.[4] Events in the political and military arena left people breathless, but events equally extraordinary took place in the realms of literature, the arts, music, science, and philosophy. The energy generated during the Napoleonic era vibrated across Europe, in the Americas, in India, indeed over most of the globe known to Europeans. Byron, in imagination at least, and often enough in creativity, embraced much of that globe.

Throughout this period Napoleon – as symbolic inheritor of the French Revolution, as Europe's dominant figure, as human colossus – alternatively entranced and repelled others as well as Byron. The most celebrated man in the world, an overwhelming presence in person, Napoleon amazed Byron's contemporaries. For Chateaubriand, Stendhal, and Mme de Staël in France; Goethe, Beethoven, and Heine in Germany; Hazlitt and Moore, Scott and Coleridge in England, the diminutive Emperor assumed a larger-than-life stature. He *was* larger than life. As did Byron, these figures liked *and* disliked Napoleon vigorously and eloquently, often passionately. Sometimes they displayed all of these responses at the same time. Looking at Napoleon through their eyes, probing their words and images, hones our understanding of Byron's own obsession. Even those who abhorred Napoleon, who rejected vehemently what he stood for, who fought him tooth and nail, found themselves mesmerised by the man and the huge swathe he cut through history.

Viewed positively, Napoleon was the man who attempted to build on the ideals of the French Revolution, who gave purpose and focus to hopes for the betterment of European life, who fostered belief in a new era shorn of legitimist monarchs. Napoleon proclaimed himself the liberator of oppressed countries. For Byron, he was the one individual who could have fulfilled the promise of Revolution.

Goethe was mesmerised by both Byron and Napoleon. The enormous energy unleashed by the French Revolution had amazed him. At the battle of Valmy in 1792 Goethe witnessed hardscrabble French troops, fearless and enthusiastic, shouting 'Vive la nation' as they charged King Frederick William's disciplined Prussian regulars. That evening Goethe in the Prussian camp remarked, 'From this time and place a new epoch is beginning, and you will be able to say that you were there.'[5] Goethe's rhetoric is a telling instance of how the artistic cultures of Romanticism crossed over into the realm of hard warfare.

Faust, Erster Teil, which appeared in 1808, consolidated Goethe's stature as Europe's major man of letters. On 2 October of that year he and Napoleon met, at the Emperor's request, at Erfurt, twenty-four miles from Weimar where Goethe had lived since 1775. Napoleon had defeated Austria and Russia at Austerlitz in 1805; the next year it was Prussia's turn at Jena and Auerstadt. Napoleon, now master of Europe, had called the Congress of Erfurt to reshape its boundaries.

They talked for an hour, about literature and politics and theatre, but chiefly about *The Sorrows of Young Werther* (1775). As a youth Napoleon had succumbed to the melancholia of late Enlightenment Europe. He probably first read *Werther* in the 1780s when he wrote imitative dialogues full of Rousseauian and Wertherian sentiments. But it was only on his way to Egypt in 1798, aboard the *Orient*, that Napoleon first revealed his deep appreciation for, and amazing grasp of, Goethe's novel. He told Goethe he had read it seven times. However that may be, he certainly knew it well enough to discuss with him fine points of detail. Chiefly he chided Goethe, not unreasonably, for giving no clear motivation for Werther's suicide.[6] As Goethe left the room, Napoleon said of him, words which would resonate in Goethe's imagination, 'Voilà un homme!'[7]

Four days later they met again at Goethe's theatre in Weimar. On the boards was Voltaire's *La Mort de César*, with Talma in the title role. Napoleon took Goethe aside after the performance and they discussed tragedy. He counselled Goethe:

> You ... ought to write a tragedy about the death of Caesar – one really worthy of the subject, a greater one than Voltaire's. ... You would have to show the world how Caesar would have been its benefactor, how everything would have turned out quite differently if he had been given time to carry out his magnificent plans.

It would not be far-fetched to suggest that Napoleon was thinking more of himself than his great Roman predecessor here. Napoleon even invited Goethe to live in Paris. Goethe would find 'a larger view of things' and 'abundant material there to inspire your works'.[8] Though tempted, Goethe politely declined. Passing through Weimar again on his way back from Russia in 1812, Napoleon asked the French ambassador to convey his greetings to Goethe.

Goethe's brief encounters with Napoleon impressed themselves indelibly on his mind. The German sage recognised the power of the man and confessed that life held 'nothing higher or more pleasurable than meeting the Emperor'. The Holy Roman Empire had disappeared in 1806; but now Napoleon ruled Germany, what had been a farrago of small city states, more efficiently. 'Shake your chains if you will', Goethe told his countrymen fighting against Napoleon in 1813; 'you will not break them. That man Napoleon is too strong for you!'[9] He was wrong, but men such as Gentz and Fichte, agitating to arouse German nationalism, found his words chilling.[10]

Napoleon's fall from power in 1815 did not diminish Goethe's regard. Both as a man of action and as a human exemplar Napoleon remained the perfect hero. Napoleon struck him, as he struck Byron, 'as a natural phenomenon beyond the laws of men'.[11] Goethe kept a bust of Napoleon in his study, as did, among numerous other contemporaries, Thomas Hope and Thomas Jefferson. The busts were there, not because these individuals thought Napoleon (in Aldous Huxley's phrase) 'the world's most spectacular militarist', but because they thought him a genius.[12]

Like Byron, Goethe devoured every book that came his way about Napoleon. In 1823 he raced through Las Cases's *Mémorial de Sainte Hélène* – eight massive volumes – in a month. The next year he remarked, with only slight exaggeration, that to 'everyone who has served under Napoleon ... nothing appears impossible'. In 1825 he devoured another biography of Napoleon. In 1827 Scott sent him his nine-volume *Life of Napoleon Buonaparte*, which Goethe 'greatly looked forward' to reading and was not disappointed with when he did.[13] The next year, when his son August announced he wished to decorate a large room with 'good pictures or engravings of all Napoleon's deeds', Goethe told him that 'the room must be very large, and even then it would not hold the pictures, so great are the deeds'.[14]

It was Las Cases's *Mémorial* that gave Goethe the idea for the *Conversations with Eckermann*. Set down in the late 1820s, the *Conversations* contain Goethe's most intriguing *obiter dicta* on Napoleon. 'What a compendium of the world!' he observed of the Emperor – enigmatically, and indeed rather Byronically, for the phrase mirrors his own achievement. Goethe thought Napoleon's mind the most perfect the world had ever seen. The man himself was worth looking at, the poet told Eckermann. When Eckermann, who had never seen him, asked 'Did he look like something?' Goethe became still more succinct: 'He *was* something' (*Er war es*) (p. 169). A stanza by Goethe captures both Napoleon's mental penetration and the immensity of his vision:

What centuries have dimly meditated
His mind surveys in brightest clarity;
All that is petty has evaporated,
Here nothing is of weight save earth and sea.[15]

The emphasis on vastness ('earth and sea') and the insistence on the immensity of the warrior's mind rather than the strength of his arm closely recall Byron. Goethe also admiringly noted Napoleon's 'passionate desire to know and understand everything', the solidity and sense that marked his every pronouncement, what J. Christopher Herold calls the 'radiant power of the mind that cut through and dispelled the mists of speculation … discarding all obstacles to action.'[16] A character of such eminence had never existed before, Goethe felt, and probably would never come again.

For Goethe, the quality of 'productiveness' (*Produktivität*), defined as that power from which deeds arise, was Napoleon's defining characteristic. Productiveness combined strength of body with strength of mind. Napoleon was, physically, 'a man of granite'.[17] Productiveness was a quality Goethe associated with genius, particularly with Mozart. For Goethe it was Byron who embodied productiveness in the sphere of 'poems and plays'; he was, Goethe told Eckermann, 'one of the most productive men who ever lived'.[18] Napoleon was the corresponding exemplar of 'productiveness of deeds'. They balanced each other out; they were the opposing yet essentially similar poles of human greatness in an age of genius.

Goethe often associated Byron with Napoleon. They never met, but Goethe followed Byron's career closely, read his poems eagerly, and as he grew older yearned to know more about the poet whom he felt had brought back to him his long-ago youth. In a brilliant interpretation of the imaginative engagement of the two poets with each other, E. M. Butler observes that Goethe felt for Byron less admiration than passion, passion 'oblivious of everything but its own need to arouse a response, a hopeless passion'. From Byron there went out 'a power for which there is no rational accounting'.[19]

Goethe also associated Byron and Napoleon as embodiments of the *daimonisch*, or daimonic. Goethe's evolving concept of the daimonic, one crucial to his thought, Butler defines as 'something irrational, powerful, dangerous, destructive and irresistible' (p. 214).

Goethe was not alone in Germany in admiring Napoleon's greatness. Beethoven, believing Napoleon deserved music correspondent to that greatness, composed in his honour the *Eroica* symphony, initially entitled *Bonaparte*. In 1806, as Napoleon, after humiliating the Prussian armies at

Jena and Auerstadt, entered Berlin, Hegel saluted the French Emperor as a 'soul of worldwide significance ... an individual who ... encompasses the world and rules it'.[20] The young Heine, who thought St Helena would be a pilgrimage site long after perfidious Albion had slipped into oblivion, elevated Napoleon to 'a tragic hero of epic proportions'.[21] Nietzsche, who valued the Emperor's vision of a united Europe, speculated that Napoleon's ascendancy had moved Goethe to rethink *Faust*, 'indeed the whole problem of man'.[22] Goethe himself, in a moment of irony, likened the burgeoning Napoleonic legend to the Revelation of St John the Divine: 'Everyone feels that there is something in it, but nobody quite knows what it is.'[23]

Myth acts upon the imagination far more powerfully than fact. From the first, Napoleon's career took on the qualities of myth. After Waterloo and especially after his death on St Helena in 1821, the myth proved a potent force, in literature, and even on the political stage. Throughout the nineteenth century the idea of Napoleon excited the English and European imagination with seemingly unabated intensity. Byron's tormented trajectory regarding Napoleon adumbrated the course that legions would follow.

Many of the great figures of the age used Napoleon as a touchstone in shaping their lives. Hazlitt and Scott were Napoleon-obsessed to their dying day. Scott vilified Napoleon in nine volumes, Hazlitt offered homage in four. In their massive biographies, completed shortly before their deaths, Scott and Hazlitt sought to exorcise the Napoleonic demon that haunted them. No less than Byron they stood under the Emperor's spell. Few alive at the time could put Napoleon into perspective. He was too close to them. After he departed the scene, the hopes of the coming generation to attain glory and greatness seemed to vanish with him. Born barely a decade after Byron, Hugo, and Balzac, Lamartine and Vigny felt they had entered the world a little too late. Nonetheless they sought to capture the impact Napoleon had left on the European psyche. Later came novels by Dostoevsky and Tolstoy, poems by Pushkin and Hardy, dramas by Rostand and Sardou. Abel Gance, a century after Napoleon's death, interpreted the youthful hero's greatness in an incomparable film. If Napoleon does not obsess us as he did Byron, few remain indifferent to the Emperor of the French. He still – after two centuries – towers above his contemporaries. Historians often fail to recapture the effect upon others of Napoleon's presence. That presence lives on, often in popular forms. The stock nutcase in movies or on TV is still the guy who thinks he's Napoleon. The concept may even remotely fit Byron. Given the lasting appeal their complex natures continue to exert, it is thus not surprising that both Byron and Napoleon have riveted students of psychiatry.

'The truth about us', wrote W. B. Yeats, 'though it must exist, though it must lie all around us every day, is mostly hidden from us, like birds' nests in the woods.' The truth of Byron's psyche seems particularly well hidden. Byron famously detested all systems. 'When a man talks of his system', he wrote, 'his case is hopeless' (*BLJ*, 6, 46). 'Create a concept', says Ortega y Gasset, 'and reality leaves the room.' Systems can be alluring, Byron well knew, but they falsified, as he also knew, the idiosyncrasy of human experience. And, at least for himself, he was right. No psychological framework – whether Freudian, Jungian, or other – holds Byron convincingly or for long. It is thus, inevitably, a risky business to introduce psychiatric speculation about what might be called Byron's Napoleon complex. I will, nonetheless, venture to do so.

Kay Redfield Jamison, trained in clinical psychiatry and author of *Touched with Fire: Manic-Depressive Illness and the Artistic Temperament*, considers Byron a being of enormous complexity, 'a veritable city of selves'.[24] Lady Byron spoke of her husband's 'chameleon-like character', and in *Don Juan* Byron seizes upon 'mobility', which he defines as 'an excessive susceptibility of immediate impressions'. Mobility is the closest Byron, in his ceaseless effort to understand how human beings (and by implication himself) function, comes to a system. Jamison goes further. In Byron's volatile temperament and extraordinary swings of mood she sees symptoms of manic depression. In her discussion of Byron as a manic-depressive personality, Jamison does not consider his responses to Napoleon, though in the often rapid shifts of these responses, Napoleon would seem the ideal subject to activate Byron's manic depression.

Transference, a complex, much-studied, and yet elusive concept, may also afford us help in understanding Byron's obsession with Napoleon. Human beings, according to Freud, need illusions. 'The real world', writes Ernest Becker in *The Denial of Death*, 'tells man that he is a small, trembling animal who will decay and die. Illusion changes all this, makes men seem important, vital to the universe, immortal in some way.'[25] This process Freud calls transference, and Janet Malcolm, for one, believes it to be his 'most original and radical discovery'.[26]

Focusing on the heroic in contemporary society, Becker lucidly develops Freud's ideas about transference. Through transference, Becker explains, human beings, adrift in a universe deemed godless, endow others with the virtues and qualities they believe they lack. They escape their sense of isolation by transferring a sense of greatness onto others whom they think greater, more gifted, than they. Becker writes of mankind's innate

> desire to stand out, to be *the* one in creation: in our culture anyway, especially in modern times, the heroic seems too big for us, or we too small for it. ... But underneath throbs the ache of cosmic specialness, no matter how we mask it in concerns of smaller scope. ... The urge to heroism is natural, and to admit it honest.

Heroism for Becker 'is first and foremost a reflex of the terror of death. We admire most the courage to face death.'[27]

Transference we may regard 'as the enduring monument of man's profound rebellion against reality'; its essence is 'a *taming of terror*'.[28] Transference involves a 'total and desperate focalization of horror and wonder in one person and complete worship in him in a kind of dazed, hypnotic way'. The subject, Byron in this case, regards the human transference object, Napoleon, 'in all of its awe and splendor'. 'Most people', notes Becker, 'can hide and disguise their inner urge to merge themselves with power figures'. Much of the time Byron hid and disguised his inner urge to merge himself with the seemingly all-powerful being that was the French Emperor.[29]

In transference, as Freud and Becker both knew, lurks an erotic element. It may well have come into play in Byron's response to Napoleon. In what ways did Byron fantasise about Napoleon? Did he find Napoleon, the great man of his imagination, physically, even sexually attractive? This is hard to gauge, but what seems beyond doubt is that the Emperor provoked and stimulated him enormously. Napoleon, if we adopt Becker's argument, made possible for Byron 'a new experience, the expression of forbidden impulses, secret wishes, and fantasies' (p. 135).

Early in *Childe Harold* III Byron insisted that imagination created its own reality. The idea of Napoleon was for him a real thing, as real as anything out there, and in Byron's imagination his awe before Napoleon shaped how he understood the world. Although, like Jamison, Becker does not mention Napoleon, his analysis of transference casts light on Byron's obsession with the Emperor. As he sought to break the spell cast over him by Napoleon, Byron often lashed out at his transference object. But at no time could he sever the tie binding him to the Emperor. Only after Napoleon's death in 1821 did Byron obtain a measure of perspective on him. The tie itself remained as strong as ever.

Napoleon provided Byron, at crucial moments in his life, with a bulwark against what appeared to him to be a terrifying, enveloping chaos. One such moment occurred when he returned from the East in 1811. With both parents now dead, his gifted contemporaries dying about him, and tormented about his future, Byron felt adrift in an indifferent world. The idea of Napoleon, a man seemingly above common mortality, he found an irresistible lodestone. Uncertain about a political career in England, uneasy about a vocation as poet that seemed to offer him little more than a second-best career, Byron increasingly dreamt of Napoleon and Napoleonic grandeur. In Napoleon at least was a man fearless of death, a man not shackled by convention, a man who acted decisively, who strode from conquest to conquest, who bent empires to his will, who surrounded himself with beautiful men and women: a man, in short, very much like the man Byron wished to become. For Byron, Napoleon embodied all the attractions and ambiguities inherent in a Promethean force of will.

Napoleon transformed the politics of Europe. This could be seen as bringing liberty to subjugated peoples or as the foundation of a new imperialism at the service of a titanic egoism. Byron, as ever, was on both sides of this divide. Napoleon was, in a sense, a realisation of the form of freedom that energised Byron's imagination but, in another sense, he was a disappointing, even a betraying exemplar of that form. Alike in the energies and contradictions that marked them, the forms of their achievements and personalities represented back to Napoleonic and Byronic Europe a compelling image of the liberties of their time.

Notes

1   It is difficult to imagine Napoleon unaware of Europe's most talked-about poet. They had friends in common, notably Lord and Lady Holland as well as several Holland House devotees; and Napoleon owned numerous English books.

2   *BLJ*, 3, 210.

3   *The Mind of Napoleon*, ed. by J. Christopher Herold (New York and London: Columbia University Press, 1955), p. xxxv.

4   *Edinburgh Review* (September 1814), p. 327, cited from Richard Whateley, *Historic Doubts Relative to Napoleon Buonaparte* (1819; New York: Robert Carter, 1871), p. 50n.

5   *Campaign in France 1792*, cited from Goethe, *From My Life. Poetry and Truth. Campaign in France 1792. Siege of Mainz*, ed. by Thomas P. Saine and Jeffrey L. Sammons (New York: Suhrkamp, 1987), p. 652.

6   F. G. Healey, *The Literary Culture of Napoleon* (Geneva: Droz; Paris: Minard, 1959), p. 127 and 'Appendix E', pp. 160–1.

7   'Voilà un homme', in *Goethe. Conversations and Encounters*, ed. by David Luke and Robert Pick (Chicago, IL: Henry Regnery, 1966), p. 72. For a variation on the

phrase ('Vous êtes un homme, monsieur de Goethe'), see Pieter Geyl, *Napoleon For and Against* (London: Jonathan Cape, 1949), p. 105.

8   *Goethe. Conversations and Encounters*, p. 72.

9   Cited from E. M. Delderfield, *Imperial Sunset: The Fall of Napoleon, 1813–1814* (Philadelphia, PA: Chilton, 1968), p. 27.

10   Even today they can strike biographers as an anomaly. See John R. Williams, *The Life of Goethe. A Critical Biography* (Oxford: Blackwell, 1998), and *Times Literary Supplement* review, 2 October 1998, p. 9.

11   Herold, introduction to *The Mind of Napoleon*, p. xxxiii.

12   Aldous Huxley, *The Olive Tree* (London: Chatto & Windus, 1936), p. xx.

13   *Goethe. Conversations and Encounters*, p. 163.

14   *Conversations of Goethe with Eckermann and Soret*, trans. by John Oxenford, new edn (London: George Bell, 1874), p. 194. German texts when given from *Gespräche mit Goethe*, ed. by Hellmuth Steger (Munich: Deutsches Verlagshaus Bong, 1949).

15   Cited from *The Mind of Napoleon*, ed. Herold, p. xvii.

16   Georges Lefebvre, *Napoleon: From 18 Brumaire to Tilsit 1799–1807*, trans. by Henry F. Stockhold (New York: Columbia University Press, 1969), p. 65; *The Mind of Napoleon*, ed. Herold, p. xvii.

17   *Conversations with Eckermann*, pp. 305, 306.

18   *Conversations with Eckermann*, p. 312.

19   E. M. Butler, *Byron and Goethe* (London: Bowes & Bowes, 1956), pp. 5, 97.

20   Cited from Maynard Solomon, *Beethoven*, 2nd edn (1977; New York: Schirmer Books, 1998), p. 175.

21   Jeffrey L. Sammons, *Heinrich Heine. A Modern Biography* (Princeton, NJ: Princeton University Press, 1979), p. 118.

22   *Beyond Good and Evil*, cited from *Basic Writings of Nietzsche*, trans. and ed. by Walter Kaufmann (New York: The Modern Library, 1992), p. 368.

23   Cited from James Marshall-Cornwall, *Napoleon as Military Commander* (1967; New York: Barnes & Noble, 1998), p. 11.

24   Kay Redfield Jamison, *Touched with Fire: Manic-Depressive Illness and the Artistic Temperament* (New York: The Free Press, 1993), p. 151. Jamison's *An Unquiet Mind: A Memoir of Moods and Madness* (New York: Knopf, 1995) offers a riveting account of the author's own struggle with depression.

25   Ernest Becker, *The Denial of Death* (1973; New York: The Free Press, 1975), p. 133.

26   Janet Malcolm, *Psychoanalysis: the Impossible Profession* (1981; New York: Random House, 1982), p. 6.

27   Becker, *The Denial of Death*, pp. 3, 4, 11.

28   Becker, *The Denial of Death*, p. 143, cites W. V. Silverberg, 'The Concept of Transference', *Psychoanalytical Quarterly* 17 (1948), pp. 319, 321.

29   Becker, *The Denial of Death*, pp. 145, 147, 131.

Slaves of Passion: Byron and Staël on Liberty

JONATHAN GROSS

'Officialese is my only language', Adolf Eichmann informed the prosecutor during his trial for 'crimes against humanity' in Jerusalem.[1] Covering this event for *New Yorker* magazine, Hannah Arendt described Eichmann's strange penchant for 'winged words'. Eichmann borrowed his metaphor from Homer to explain the official 'language rules' (*Sprachregelung*) which led him to describe the deportation of 4 million Jews to gas chambers as 'labor in the East' (p. 85). A language rule is a manufactured phrase that conceals a murderous intention: 'final solution' for extermination, 'typhoid epidemic' for gassing. Linguistic corruption affected every aspect of Nazi ideology, according to Arendt. Eichmann's 'incapacity for normal speech', his penchant for catchphrases, epitomised this ideology, for it shielded him from the truth of what he was doing. Or to put it more precisely, 'The net effect of this language system was not to keep these people ignorant of what they were doing but to prevent them from equating it with normal knowledge.' For Eichmann,

> the … lies changed from year to year, and they frequently contradicted each other; moreover, they were not necessarily the same for the various branches of the Party hierarchy or the people at large. But the practice of self-deception had become so common, almost a moral prerequisite for survival, that even now, eighteen years after the collapse of the Nazi regime, when most of the specific content of its lies has been forgotten, it is sometimes difficult not to believe that mendacity has become an integral part of the German national character.
>
> (*EJ*, 52)

Yet lies are nothing new in politics, and in a later essay, 'Lying in Politics', Arendt traced its illustrious history. To the two-thousand-year history of lies and euphemisms, she wrote, must now be added the lies of the public-relations man and Madison Avenue, the lies of H. R. Haldemann and John Ehrlichmann, who designed phrases ('search and destroy mission') to conceal the innocent massacre of women and civilians in Vietnam.[2]

What distinguishes Eichmann from others, according to Hannah Arendt, is the 'elation' he experienced whenever he uttered such phrases:

> The striking consistency with which Eichmann, despite his rather bad memory, repeated word for word the same stock phrases and self-invented clichés (when he did succeed in constructing a sentence of his own, he repeated it until it became a cliché) each time he referred to an incident of importance to him … The longer one listened to him, the more obvious it became that his inability to speak was closely connected with an inability to think, namely, to think from the standpoint of somebody else. No communication was possible with him, not because he lied but because he was surrounded by the most reliable of all safeguards against the words and the presence of others, and hence against reality as such.
>
> (*EJ*, 49)

When Mme de Staël and Lord Byron attacked British Foreign Secretary Viscount Castlereagh for his role in European politics – a man also eminently concerned with advancing his own career – they anticipated Arendt's (perhaps dubious) strategy of attacking his deficiencies of language. Staël viewed Castlereagh's Parliamentary speeches as 'stamped with a sort of glacial irony, singularly baneful when applied to everything fine in this world';[3] he treats liberty with mockery, or, as at the Congress of Vienna, with a sarcastic smile (perhaps comparable to Eichmann's 'elation'). Byron describes him as 'An orator of such set trash of phrase, / Ineffably, legitimately vile', such that his language 'turns and turns, to give the world a notion / Of endless torments, and perpetual motion' ('Dedication' to *Don Juan*; *CPW*, 5, 13). The period of his power represented 'the first time indeed since the Normans, that England had been insulted by a *Minister* (at least) who could not speak English, and that Parliament permitted itself to be dictated to in the language of Mrs. Malaprop' (Preface to Cantos VI–VIII, *DJ; CPW*, 5, 295). As Joanne Wilkes observes, 'both writers often made links between the quality of language and the moral stature of the people who used it, but were disturbed by the power of discourse which was obscure, jargon-ridden, deluded, frivolous, or sophistical'.[4]

For Byron, language rules, of the type devised for Eichmann, were the natural counterpart to moral degeneration; he referred to such language as 'cant'. At Castlereagh's funeral, one hears the '"Syllables of Dolour yelled forth" by the Newspapers, – and the harangue of the Coroner in an eulogy over the bleeding body of the deceased – (an Anthony worthy of such a

Caesar) – and the nauseous and atrocious cant of a degraded Crew of Conspirators against all that is sincere and honourable' (Preface to Cantos VI–VIII, *DJ*; *CPW*, 5, 296). Byron describes his own nemesis, Castlereagh, more bluntly, as a 'felon' or a 'madman'. *Don Juan* cannot be understood, Byron suggests, because words, especially English words, have been corrupted to such an extent that they have no meaning at all. He welcomes the title of 'Blasphemer', which he shares with Socrates and Jesus Christ, preferring it to the role of 'overpensioned Homicide' which he connects with Lord Castlereagh and the Duke of Wellington. Byron begins Canto 6 by turning words around, comparing French and English versions – the English Wellington is pronounced 'Villainton' in France. Morality, Byron suggests, is more than a matter of words; it relates to actions, deeds, and, most of all, to one's nationalistic perspective. Nationalists (and paid employees of governments) can fall prey to cant, an imprecise language, which vitiates their capacity for understanding and empathy. English readers of *Don Juan*, for example, reject his poem because their degraded language prevents them from recognising its truth. Like Eichmann, they cannot think because they cannot speak. In his preface to Canto 6 of *Don Juan*, Byron makes the connection between language and liberty explicit by quoting Voltaire: 'La pudeur s'est enfuite des cœurs, et s'est refugiée sur les lèvres... Plus les mœurs sont dépravés, plus les expressions deviennent mesurées; on croit regagner en langage ce qu'on a perdu en vertu.'[5] 'You are not a moral nation and you know it', he warns the English (*CPW*, 5, 11, 695).

It would be comforting to believe, with Arendt, Byron, and Staël, that truth is on the side of those who do not corrupt language. Perhaps the use and misuse of language is alone the 'efficient causes of our political disorders', as Noah Webster speculated; perhaps language 'becomes ugly and inaccurate because our thoughts are foolish', George Orwell reasoned.[6] Can language really be separated from those who employ it, however? From *eros* itself? 'It is a fact, and in some ways a melancholy fact', Paul Johnson argues, 'that massive works of the intellect do not spring from the abstract workings of the brain and the imagination'.[7] *Eros*, as the Greeks believed, controls even the intellect. Thus Arendt's affair with Martin Heidegger; Byron's homoerotic friendships with young boys; and Staël's flirtation with Napoleon cannot be separated from the tone and tenor of their attacks on Eichmann, Castlereagh, and Napoleon. 'The degree and kind of a man's sexuality reach up into the ultimate pinnacle of his spirit', Nietzsche observed in *Beyond Good and Evil*; or, to reverse the opening line of J. M. Coetzee's novel, one never solves the problem of sex 'rather well'.[8] In the same way that Byron's anxieties about his own homosexual practice informs both what he says and does not say about Castlereagh, his fear of not being considered a gentleman leads him both to dismiss and to refine English gentlemanliness in the Pope–Bowles controversy. Byron wishes to belong to the club that he excoriates. Byron's self-interested attack on Castlereagh (his sense of class anxiety prompted by Castlereagh's Westminster burial and his own diminished reputation after publishing the first five cantos of *Don Juan*) reminds us of Mme de Staël's extended criticisms of Napoleon in *De l'Allemagne* and *Considerations on the French Revolution*, which occurred during her own exile by the Emperor. She concealed her real *animus* against Napoleon in these works even as she represented her critique of him as dispassionate and purely political.

That Mme de Staël was persecuted by Napoleon is well known. Less well known, perhaps, is her early flirtation with him. Alan Schom describes how 'the perspicacious Madame de Staël, ... la[id] unsuccessful amorous siege to General Bonaparte'.[9] What evidence is there for this 'amorous siege'? They first met on 6 December 1797. Napoleon had just returned from Italy, having made a victorious peace which changed the map of Europe. Talleyrand arranged a grand reception. 'He paid little attention to her', Talleyrand recalled. 'She paid a great deal of attention to him, and his brief, modest speech impressed her as sublime', Herold (her biographer) notes.[10] Four days later, she met him again at the Luxembourg Palace. 'There can be no question that, at least until 1800, Germaine wooed Bonaparte and praised him hyperbolically', Herold writes. In an article, she called him 'the intrepid warrior, the most reflective thinker, the most extraordinary genius' in history, and was always 'overwhelmed in his presence, often reduced to silence'.[11] When she turned against him, she wrote that 'there is something like a physical pleasure ... in resistance to an unjust power'.[12] Perhaps the 'physical pleasure 'of resisting Napoleon compensated, in part, for the pain of Staël's unrequited passion and her political ambition in attempting to join forces with the Corsican parvenu.

Byron, who loudly proclaimed the connection between the public and the private, would have been delighted to know of Staël's 'amorous siege' of Napoleon (if he did not already know), but Byron's own relationship with the French Emperor was itself vexed by a similar blurring of boundaries between public and private: both Staël and Byron, in other words, flirted with the French General in more than one sense. Byron defended

Napoleon's bust as a fifteen-year-old schoolboy at Harrow; followed his career closely in his letters and journals of 1813 (even mentioning him, repeatedly, in letters to his prospective wife); rode in a carriage modelled on Napoleon's when he left England in 1816; approved of Napoleon's lack of bonhomie in a letter to Hobhouse ('How should he, who knows mankind well, do other than despise and abhor them?' he wrote) and in *Childe Harold* III:

> 'twas wise to feel, not so
> To wear it ever on thy lip and brow.
>
> (*CPW*, 2, 3:40)

After his mother-in law's death in 1822 he styled himself 'Noel Byron' or just 'NB', the initials he had come to share with Napoleon; in *Don Juan* he called himself 'the grand Napoleon of the realms of rhyme' (*CPW*, 5, 11, 55). If Byron's famous 'ode' criticises Napoleon, this poem needs to be placed in the context of his wider admiration. One only becomes passionately disappointed with those one once admired. Edward Tangye Lean, in *The Napoleonists*, suggests that the absence of a father figure or a father (as in the case of Hazlitt) who could not be rebelled against, led several English intellectuals, such as Byron, Hazlitt, and Leigh Hunt, to identify with the French ruler no matter how despotic he became.[13] Joanne Wilkes goes further and notes that

> There may even be as well a hint of erotic attraction which expresses part of Byron's bisexuality, and which, if we credit Lady Blessington's account, he was aware of himself. According to her, he said that when he found fault with Napoleon, it was 'as a lover does with the trifling faults of his mistress, from excessive liking, which tempts [Byron] to desire that he had been all faultless', such that he 'returns with renewed fondness after each quarrel'.[14]

If Byron and Staël's relationship to Napoleon was ambiguous, in other words, their erotic attraction to him and what he represented played no small role in this ambivalence.

Any political analysis that is purely linguistic, then, is doomed to failure. Linguistic critique of an opponent, one might conclude, is bad faith, a dubious strategy that often conceals erotic (as well as other) motivations. One thinks of Arendt and Eichmann, Staël and Napoleon, and Byron and Staël (here I am thinking particularly of his dismissal of her as 'frightful as a precipiece' [8 June 1814; 4, 122], with 'pen behind the ears and her mouth full of ink' [*BLJ*, 3, 19]). Far more than Castlereagh, Napoleon exposes how *eros* informs Byron and Staël's political judgement. Precisely because intellectuals are so adept at using language to conceal *eros* and *animus*, verbal facility alone can never be a measure of truth.

Mme de Staël's relationship with the Vicomte de Narbonne offers a second example of how erotic politics can inform liberal critique.[15] Here some background may be necessary, for my argument is as much about literary influence of Staël on Byron as about erotic politics. At the end of her life, Staël projected a drama based on 'Richard Coeur de Lion. Asked whether her hero would be "un Lara", she replied, "Perhaps… but I promise you that no one in the world will suspect it".'[16] Though Staël never lived to write this drama, having died in 1817, her facetious reference to Byron's *Lara* provokes speculation. Jerome McGann suggests that the title of *Lara* was perhaps taken from Southey's *Chronicles of the Cid (1808)* (*CPW*, 3, 453). Yet Narbonne's own surname was *Lara*. Byron's extended exposure to Staël's writings and personality would make her affair with Narbonne as interesting to him as any literary document by Southey. Having advised him to 'Stick to the East; … it [was] the only poetical policy' (*BLJ*, 28 August 1813; 3, 101), she may also have unwittingly alerted him to the dramatic potential of events in her own life. For Staël exchanged traditional gender roles in her relationship with Narbonne, much like Gulnare unmans Conrad through her precipitous murder of Seyd (the basis for Byron's sequel in *Lara*).

Louis, Vicomte de Narbonne-Lara, was thirty-three when Germaine met him. He was handsome, intelligent, and 'cloaked in mystery', Herold writes.[17] Born in Italy, in a castle belonging to the Duke of Parma, Narbonne-Lara (and the surname here is crucial) was rumoured to be the son of Louis XV and the Comtesse de Narbonne-Lara; or even of Louis XV's daughter, Mme Adélaïde. Married in 1782, Narbonne enjoyed the benefits of a military career he never quite earned. 'There was no need for him to give himself the trouble of serving in the American war', Herold writes. 'By 1786 he commanded a regiment without ever having fought a battle except on sofas and beds.'[18] Narbonne met Staël in the Rue du Bac; her salon catered to the liberal aristocracy which carried out the first phase of the revolution. Governor Morris, who witnessed their growing attachment, described Germaine to George Washington as 'a woman of wonderful wit, and above prejudices of every kind'. Narbonne found himself uncomfortable in the libertarian tone that reigned at Staël's salon, but she inspired him to serve the cause of freedom and progress.[19]

By July 1789, Staël and Narbonne were lovers, though her husband tried to forbid him access to his house. In December 1789 she was pregnant by

Narbonne; and Herold assumes that Narbonne was the father of both sons, Auguste and Albert. On 2 October 1792 she informed Narbonne how her husband's references to Auguste as his own son enraged her: 'tout mon sang se révoltait d'une telle idée', she wrote, 'que d'ailleurs je voyais qu'on voulait tendre à nous rapprocher et que j'étais decidée à l'époque du 15 janvier à deux voyages seulement: celui de L'Angleterre ou du fond du lac'.[20] Auguste already reminded her of her divine friend, she added later in the same letter.[21] As Staël betrayed her husband in her affair with Narbonne, Gulnare betrays Seyd in her rescue of Conrad in *The Corsair* and her subsequent service to him as a page in *Lara*.

Perhaps the most striking resemblance between Staël's relationship with Narbonne and the *The Corsair* and *Lara* occurs in Staël's rescue of Narbonne after the overthrow of the monarchy on the 10 August 1792. 'One day late in August a search patrol appeared at the Swedish embassy', Herold records:

> detachments of soldiers were stationed at either end of the block. Monsieur de Narbonne, the officer in charge explained, was said to be hiding on the premises. Germaine, who with the help of the embassy chaplain, Pastor Gambs, had just hidden her lover under the altar before which she had been married (by the same pastor), planted herself at the entrance of the embassy and began to lecture the patrol on the sanctity of international law, the inviolability of embassies, and the extraterritoriality of their occupants. Sweden, she asserted with bravura, was one of the mightiest nations of Europe, situated directly across the Rhine from France; its friendship for France was known, but if the patrol dared set foot in the house, Sweden would wreak terrible vengeance.[22]

The men seemed undecided. In *Considerations on the Principal Events of the French Revolution*, Staël recalled how

> I had the courage, with anguish in my heart, to jest with them on the injustice of their suspicions. Nothing is more agreeable to men of this class than a tone of pleasantry; for, even in the excess of their fury against the upper ranks, they feel a pleasure in being treated by them as equals. I led them back in this manner to the door, and thanked God for the extraordinary courage with which he had endowed me at that moment.

(II, 67)

Through Mme de Staël's contrivance, a Hanoverian physician, Erich Bollmann, provided Narbonne with the passport of one of his friends and both men reached England on 20 August. In a letter written one month afterwards, Bollmann remembered how 'extraordinar[ily]' theatrical the incident was: 'Une femme enceinte et prête d'accoucher, qui se lamente sur le sort de son amant, fit une vive impression sur mon imagination. Ses larmes, un homme en danger de mort, l'éspoir de le sauver, l'idée de gagner l'Angleterre et d'ameliorer ma situation, le charme de l'extraordinaire, tout cela agit à la fois.'[23]

Though successful in pleading her cause with Bollmann – who could not resist noting that 'elle est laide' and that this played no motive in his virtuous deed – Staël exhibited a wilfulness that soon melted her lover's resolve. Her relationship with Narbonne dissolved long before Staël crossed a war-torn Europe to reunite with him at Juniper Hall. She had written him beseeching letters asking him to declare his love; he responded only intermittently. 'He no longer loved her', Herold writes.

> If he had to reproach himself for having been instrumental in the King's down-fall, it was Germaine he could blame for guiding him into a political course with which, at bottom, he had never sympathized. Now she exacted love as payment for having saved his life when his honor demanded that he die with his King. Courteous, dignified, and grave, he continued to accept her money and to live under her roof.[24]

Byron may well have drawn on Staël's unusual relationship with the passive Narbonne for his tale of unrequited love in *The Corsair*. Details of it were so well known, in fact, that Fanny Burney used Staël's extramarital affair and child by Narbonne to break off her relationship with Staël in 1792, and to avoid her company when she returned to England in 1813.[25] Byron may have had Narbonne in mind when he describes Conrad's reaction after Gulnare executes Seyd:

> This Conrad mark'd, and felt – ah! Could he less?
> Hate of that deed-but grief for her distress;
> What she has done no tears can wash away,
> And heaven must punish on its angry day:
> But – it was done: he knew, whate'er her guilt,
> For him that poniard smote, that blood was spilt;
> And he was free! – and she for him had given
> Her all on earth, and more than all in heaven!
> And now he turn'd him to that dark-eyed slave
> Whose brow was bowed beneath the glance he gave,
> Who now seemed changed and humbled: – faint and meek,
> But varying oft the colour of her cheek
> To deeper shades of paleness – all its red
> That fearful spot which stain'd it from the dead!

(*CPW*, 3, 3, 522–36)

'And he was free!' Byron writes, but the line falls like a lead weight, for, like Narbonne, Conrad has entered a world of moral contingency, one in which he exchanges the freedom to hate Seyd with the necessity of loving Gulnare. In the words of Isaiah Berlin, he has exchanged negative liberty (liberty from) with positive liberty (liberty for).[26] Gulnare's attachment to Conrad has unmanned him, making him incapable of performing the act of positive liberty – of loving her – that she demands. Here is the relationship from her perspective, which resembles Mme de Staël's.

> Thou lov'st another – and I love in vain;
> Though fond as mine her bosom, form more fair,
> I rush through peril which she would not dare.
> If that thy heart to hers were truly dear,
> Were I thine own – thou wert not lonely here:
> An outlaw's spouse – and leave her lord to roam!
> What hath such gentle dame to do with home?
> But speak not now – o'er thine and o'er my head
> Hangs the keen sabre by a single thread;
> If thou hast courage still, and would'st be free,
> Receive this poignard – rise – and follow me!
> Ay – in my chains! [Conrad replies] my steps will gentle tread,
> With these adornments, o'er each slumbering head!
> Thou hast forgot – is this a garb for flight?
> Or is that instrument more fit for fight?'
>
> Misdoubting Corsair! I have gain'd the guard,
> Ripe for revolt, and greedy for reward.
> A single word of mine removes that chain:
> Without some aid how here could I remain?
>
> *(The Corsair, CPW,* 3, 3, 297–315)

Like Gulnare, Staël recognised that her imaginary rival's 'form was more fair' than her own, but that she possessed greater moral courage. Like Staël, however, Gulnare 'gains the guard' only to lose her lover; her act of rescue unmans him.

Liberty, in short, is impossible without being freed from erotic constraint. Staël explored this paradox in *Treatise* and *Corinne*, as Byron did in *The Corsair* and *Lara*. Both understood that men and women are affected differently by such constraints: 'Love is the story of women's lives; it is an episode in that of men', Staël wrote in *Treatise on the Passions* (reformulating this phrase a second time in *Corinne*);[27] and Byron echoed the sentiment in *Don Juan*:

Man's love is of his life a thing apart
'Tis woman's whole existence.
(*CPW*, 5, 1, 194)

Psychological liberty is at least as important as political liberty. Certainly Benjamin Constant's *Adolphe* (he was another lover of Mme de Staël's) makes clear how liberal societies can induce the type of moral torpor that makes action next to impossible. Staël and Byron did not suffer from such moral entropy; far from it, but their works clearly show how gender roles imperil the pursuit of liberty, by imprisoning citizens in roles that are not commensurate with their freedom or happiness.

The theme I have been struggling to trace – the relationship between sexual passion and political liberty – is perhaps best illustrated by J. M. Coetzee's *Disgrace*. In this novel, set in contemporary South Africa, a professor at a polytechnic university finds his taste for English Romantic poetry challenged by dwindling budgets and the end of apartheid. The Department of English has become a Department of Communications and he is given his course on Romantic poetry only to keep up his morale. But that is the least of his problems. His primary problem is erotic, as the first line of the novel reveals: 'For a man of his age, fifty-two, divorced, he has, to his mind, solved the problem of sex rather well.'[28] This unsavoury figure pays a young black woman named Soroya to sleep with him; until he discovers her one day walking down the street with her two sons, and their affair, spoilt by such contingencies, quickly ends; at this point he seduces a young student named Melanie Isaacs and is dismissed (or resigns) from his faculty position rather than face an academic committee that wishes him to repent his actions. What he most objects to is the linguistic corruption that has spread from the curriculum to the university committee: he will not misuse language to violate the integrity of his erotic experience. Visiting his daughter Lucy (one thinks of Wordsworth's 'Strange Fits of Passion') makes matters worse because he disapproves of her sexual orientation (she is lesbian) and of her compliant relationship with her black neighbour Petrus, who the hero considers insolent. He has gone to visit her, interestingly enough, to complete an opera entitled 'Lord Byron in Italy', a period that treats Byron's own struggle for erotic freedom. David Lurie, whom Coetzee casts as a kind of atavistic Byronic hero, believes his absurd opera (complete with a tinny banjo to accompany the part of Teresa Guiccioli) will be 'a meditation on love between the sexes in the form of a chamber opera' (p. 4). One day, during his visit to his daughter, she is raped (perhaps by friends of her neighbour), and he is helpless to stop the marauders. As he stumbles into one disgrace after another, the reader realises that it is the disgrace of middle age that Coetzee finds most compelling. Faced with a series of diminishing sexual options, Coetzee's hero refuses to surrender this last and most sacred form of liberty. He has an assignation with an unattractive woman, a friend of his daughter's, who is in charge of euthanising dogs, Bev Shaw. 'Let me not forget this day, he tells himself, lying beside her when they are spent. After the sweet young flesh of Melanie Isaacs, this is what I have come to. This is what I will have to get used to, this and even less than this' (p. 150).

David Lurie's self-pity destroys both himself and others. Yet Lurie, lurid and alluring (the allurement of egotism?) as his name implies, is also 'all too human'. Portrayed as a virtual rapist in some reviews of the book – one who comes to equate his own actions with those of the assailants of his daughter – he is also embarrassed, like Narbonne and Conrad, by *eros*.[29] What could be more human than that? Byron, Staël, and Arendt were all political exiles whose public postures were undermined by their erotic attachments: to Annabella Milbanke, to Napoleon, and, in the case of Hannah Arendt, to Martin Heidegger. By failing to mention Napoleon's accomplishments in *Corinne* and *On Germany*, Staël revenged herself on the French Emperor for his brusque sexual dismissal of her ('No doubt', he said on one occasion, inspecting her décolletage, 'you have nursed your children yourself?');[30] Byron's attacks on Annabella Milbanke were also determined, in part, by her rejection of his first marriage proposal and public separation from him (as well as the sexual scandal which ensued); Hannah Arendt's fascination with Adolf Eichmann, a man who could not think, seems to be one response to her affair with Martin Heidegger, who compromised his own reputation for philosophical thought by serving as Rector of Heidelburg University. Arendt's affair with Heidegger was the defining moment of her life, according to her close friend Mary McCarthy. The loss of this erotic freedom is bemoaned by Byron in *Don Juan*, and David Lurie in *Disgrace*: 'No more, no never more can be, thou, my heart, my sole universe', the narrator of *Don Juan* declares (*CPW*, 5, 1, 215); 'I will have to get used to this; and even less than this', David Lurie complains (p. 150). One can attribute Adolf Eichmann's actions to the 'banality of evil', as Arendt did; dismiss Byron as a member of the Satanic circle, as Southey did; refer to Staël as an hermaphrodite, as George Canning did; or attack Castlereagh as an intellectual eunuch, as Byron did. But such charges, whether they come from the political left or the right, from eloquent poets or bungling speakers, reveal that language is itself a tool of the passions: it is morally neutral and can be used for 'good' or 'bad' purposes. Why mistake such Juvenalian satire for an independent moral view? Why assume a necessary connection between linguistic and political corruption? For freedom is not just a matter of words, clichéd or otherwise. Erotic freedom, that oxymoron, conditions political freedom, and we have the erotic attachments of Arendt, Staël, and Byron to remind us of this and to complicate our understanding of their abstract pronouncements on political affairs. Language, like passion, is always interested, or, as Hume put it in his *Treatise of Human Nature*, 'Reason is, and ought only to be, the slave of the passions' (2.3.3.4).

Notes

1   Hannah Arendt, *Eichmann in Jerusalem: A Report on the Banality of Evil* (New York: Penguin Books, 1963), p. 48; henceforward *EJ*.

2   Hannah Arendt, 'Lying in Politics', in *Crises of the Republic, Lying in Politics, Civil Disobedience on Violence, Thoughts on Politics, and Revolution* (New York: Harcourt Brace Jovanovich, 1972), p. 3.

3   Mme de Staël, *Considerations of the Principal Events of the French Revolution*, 3 vols (London: Brandon, Cradock, and Joy, 1818), 3, 570.

4   Joanne Wilkes, *Byron and Madame de Staël: Born for Opposition* (Aldershot: Ashgate, 1999), p. 184.

5   *CPW*, 5, 262. 'Modesty has fled from hearts and taken refuge on lips. The more depraved our conduct is, the more guarded words become; we believe we can regain with words what we have lost in character.' See *Lettre de M. Eratou A M. Clocpitre, Aumonier de S.A.S. M. le Landgrave, Œuvres de Voltaire*, ed. by Louis E. D. Moland (Paris: 1877–1885), X, 499.

6   Thomas Gustafson, *Representative Words: Politics, Literature, and the American Language, 1776–1865* (Cambridge: Cambridge University Press, 1992), p. 6.

7   Paul Johnson, *Intellectuals* (New York: Harper & Row, 1988), p. 69; J. M. Coetzee, *Disgrace* (New York: Viking, 1999), p. 1.

8   Friedrich Nietzsche, *Beyond Good and Evil: Prelude to a Philosophy of the Future*, trans. by Walter Kauffmann (New York: Vintage, 1966), p. 81.

9   Alan Schom, *Napoleon Bonaparte* (New York: HarperCollins, 1998), p. 193.

10 J. Christopher Herold, *Mistress to an Age: A Life of Madame de Staël* (New York: Harmony, 1958), p. 179.

11 The book in which this remark appeared is *On the Present Circumstances Capable of Ending the French Revolution*, written in 1799 but unpublished until 1906. See Herold, *Mistress to an Age*, p. 183.

12 Wilkes, *Byron and Madame de Staël*, p. 19.

13 Edward Tangye Lean, *The Napoleonists* (Oxford: Oxford University Press, 1972).

14 Wilkes, *Byron and Madame de Staël*, p. 80.

15 Staël pursued several liaisons during her unhappy marriage to the Baron de Holstein. Her affair with Narbonne, was perhaps the most influential, however, for it influenced the chapter on 'Love' and indeed the entire composition of Staël's

'Treatise on the Passions'; it is also the leitmotif of almost every other work of fiction and non-fiction she penned. Staël's purpose in *Treatise on the Passions* was to relate the happiness of individuals to the happiness of nations. As she was living in England for six months in the company of Narbonne she had little cause to look further than her own heart for the answer to her questions.

16 Wilkes, *Byron and Madame de Staël*, p. 12.

17 Herold, *Mistress to an Age*, p. 94.

18 Herold, *Mistress to an Age*, p. 94.

19 Herold, *Mistress to an Age*, p. 94.

20 Béatrice W. Jasinski, *Correspondance Generale. Lettres Inédites à Louis de Narbonne* (Paris: Chez Jean-Jacques Pauvert, 1960), 2, 36.

21 Herold, *Mistress to an Age*, p. 95.

22 Herold, *Mistress to an Age*, p. 95.

23 Émile Dard, *Un Confident de l'Empereur: Le Comte de Narbonne, 1755–1813* (Paris: Librairie Plon, 1943), p. 124.

24 Herold, *Mistress to an Age*, p. 123.

25 Linda Kelly, *Juniper Hall: An English Refuge from the French Revolution* (London: Weidenfield & Nicholson, 1991), pp. 40–2, 128–9. See also volumes ii and iii of *The Journals and Letters of Fanny Burney, 1791–1840*, ed. by Joyce Hemlow (Oxford: Oxford University Press, 1972–1984).

26 Isaiah Berlin, 'Two Concepts of Liberty', in *The Proper Study of Mankind: An Anthology of Essays*, ed. by Henry Hardy and Roger Hausheer (London: Pimlico, 1998), pp. 191–242. Originally published in *Four Essays on Liberty* (New York: Oxford University Press, 1969).

27 Wilkes, *Lord Byron and Madame de Staël*, p. 48, n. 62, quotes these lines and cites Willis W. Pratt, *Byron's Don Juan*, vol. IV: *Notes on the Variorum Edition* (Austin, TX: University of Texas Press, 1957), p. 45, on the resemblance. I have not been able to find this translation, but Mme de Staël, *On the Passions* (London, 1798), p. 152, reads, 'Men have but one object in love, while the permanence of the sentiment is the basis on which the happiness of the woman depends.'

28 Coetzee, *Disgrace*, p. 1.

29 'He acted on erotic impulse', Joseph McElry states in the *The Nation* 270:9 (6 March 2000), pp. 30–4, adding, perceptively, that sex has 'engendered a certain charity in him' (p. 34). James Wood of *The New Republic* 221:25 (20 December 1999), pp. 42–6, is most critical of Lurie's conduct towards Melanie, calling his act a 'virtual rape', while Michael Gorra of the *New York Times* states that 'what Lurie has in some sense done to another man's daughter is trebly visited on his own' (p. 7). Yet Lurie pre-empts moral critique by indicting himself: 'not rape [he admits concerning his seduction of Melanie], not quite that, but undesired to the core'. Most reviewers of the book find Lurie unsympathetic, though they admit he is (at times) demonised by the climate of political correctness that can stultify all aspects of academic life. See Michael Gorra, Review of *Disgrace*, *The New York Times Book Review* (28 November 1999), p. 7; *The New York Review of Books* 47:1 (2000), p. 23; Elizabeth Lowry, *The London Review of Books* 21:20 (1999), p. 12; Katie Grant *et al.*, *The Spectator* (10 July 1999), p. 34; Ranti Williams, *Times Literary Supplement* 5021 (1999), p. 23.

30 Herold, *Mistress to an Age*, p. 228.

Uncircumscribing Poetry: Byron, Johnson, and the Bowles Controversy

TONY HOWE

Byron's writings defy as much as they define British literary Romanticism. His radical looking forward as a poet is difficult to separate from his insistence upon looking back. In articulating and defending his own poetics, as well as in attacking those of what he described as the 'tone of the time', he often drew from the Augustan literary tradition. Critics have explored these borrowings and adaptations, focusing mainly on the influence of Pope and Dryden, which makes sense given Byron's clear admiration for Dryden, and repeated claims that Pope was his favourite poet.[1] This is, however, only part of the story, for it is to overlook one of Byron's most important eighteenth-century intellectual relationships. In this essay I will suggest that any account of Byron as a thinker and poet would be deficient without bringing into view Samuel Johnson, a figure in many ways strongly contrasted with the Byronic persona, but one that fascinated and rubbed off on Byron in often surprising ways.[2] The Johnsonian personality, a composite of moral rigour, reflexive curmudgeon, great humour, and high style, is uniquely infectious.[3] His admirers often pick up on his mannerisms and Byron was no exception to this. Leigh Hunt reported that 'He liked to imitate Johnson, and say, "Why, Sir," in a high mouthing way, rising, and looking about him.'[4]

But my concern is less with this influence than with trying to understand Byron's creative engagement with a historically specific critical debate, one that centred with varying degrees of admiration on the enduring legacy of Johnson, and that remains in its larger structures central to any understanding of literary history. It was as a serious thinker about the nature of poetic writing and his own dissenting place in its recent transformations that Byron turned to Johnson's authority, although often with far-from-Johnsonian results. As an early, sceptical commentator on the rise of Romanticism and on the corresponding reaction to the Augustan ideal, particularly as represented by Pope, Johnson became one of the pivots of

Byron's mature thought and, along with Pope, Sterne, and Montaigne, one of the most important background presences in *Don Juan*. By exploring Byron's consciously Johnsonian scepticism as a literary critic in prose and verse towards some of Romanticism's more culturally totalitarian voices, I hope to gain fresh insights into Byron's poetics and politics and to show how they were shaped by one of the major literary controversies of his day.

Byron's engagement with Johnson is most obvious during his involvement in the 'Bowles controversy' of the early 1820s. William Lisle Bowles is best remembered as a sonneteer and for his apparently enthusiastic reception by Coleridge. He was also a copious editor and literary commentator, and in 1806 sparked a controversy over the status of Pope (one that would stretch into the early 1820s) by publishing a new and far from complimentary edition of the poet, one tied to the kind of imperative Romantic aesthetics against which Byron had set himself. Bowles's anti-Popean sentiments provoked some barbed lines in Byron's *English Bards and Scotch Reviewers*, which was begun as early as 1807. Several years later, after the controversy had been resurrected by Thomas Campbell, they also spurred Byron into his brief spell as a literary critic in prose, a period that covers late 1820 and early 1821.[5] In the *Letter to John Murray* Johnson is the major critical presence: he is described variously as a 'great Moralist' and, in a rare moment of national pride, 'the noblest critical mind which our Country has produced' (*CMP*, 125, 138). Byron also apparently told Thomas Medwin that 'I have been reading "Johnson's Lives", a book I am very fond of. I look upon him as the profoundest of critics, and had occasion to study him when I was writing to Bowles.'[6]

It was this study of Johnson that brought Byron into contact with the history of the debate into which he himself was now entering. But what did Byron learn from his study? The most obvious critical assumption common to both writers is that the activity of writing should be continuous with, rather than divorced from, the other processes of life. For Johnson, experience stands in a legitimising relationship with literature: if the poet does not collide with the world, and his poetry lacks the texture of those impacts, then he has little claim to be a poet. His Horatian preoccupation with lived experience as a literary virtue pervades the *Lives of the English Poets*. In the *Life of Cowley*, for instance, he wrote that 'the basis of all excellence is truth: he that professes love ought to feel its power'.[7] On similar grounds he criticised Matthew Prior's 'Amorous Effusions' as 'the dull exercises of a skilful versifier resolved at all adventures to write something about Chloe, and trying to be amorous by dint of study' (*Lives*, II, 2).

Without the informing voices of the world, literature degenerates into literary convention. The comparison with Byron is easy to draw: inexperienced poets, who have 'always more or less of the author about them' (*BLJ*, 5, 192), were frequent targets of his well-travelled scorn. 'I could not write upon any thing', he asserted, 'without some personal experience or foundation' (*BLJ*, 5, 14). Or, as he put it in his own *Hints from Horace*, the

> poet claims our tears; but by his leave,
> Before I shed them, let me see him grieve.

(143–44)

Johnson's disdain for inexperienced literature found a particular focus in his attack on incipient Romantic literary theory, most notably in the *Life of Pope*, where he appears to be indirectly calling in question his Literary Club fellow and enthusiastic champion of the new wave, Joseph Warton.[8] In this case, however, inexperience produces something more troubling than 'dull exercises'; it forms the basis of a mistaken, restrictive, philosophy. Warton claimed in the initial volume of his *An Essay on the Writings and Genius of Pope* (1756) that 'true poetry' is produced by a 'creative and glowing IMAGINATION', and that 'the sublime and the pathetic are the two chief nerves of poetry'.[9] He distinguished between on one hand a 'MAN OF WIT' and on the other a 'TRUE POET', implying that Pope should be placed in the former category by asking 'what is there transcendentally sublime or pathetic in POPE?'[10] Johnson's riposte to this queried not just Warton's assessment of Pope, but also his entire approach to literary criticism. Warton was in Johnson's view overly prescriptive and too reliant on a modish and unsubtle brand of rhetoric, which for Johnson were the textual signs of an immature life of the mind:

> It is surely superfluous to answer the question that has once been asked, Whether Pope was a poet? Otherwise than by asking in return, If Pope be not a poet, where is poetry to be found? To circumscribe poetry by a definition will only shew the narrowness of the definer, though a definition which shall exclude Pope shall not easily be made.

(*Lives*, III, 251)

Warton believed that he championed a poetry of boundless imagination over the narrow scope of manners and artificial life. Johnson, however, saw such boundlessness as a rhetorical construct, a simplifying imposition onto a far more complex reality. This was 'the cant of those who judge by principles rather than perception' (*Lives*, III, 248), a style of critical writing devoid of nuance and subtlety, drastically at odds with its object, and thus inappropriate to the task of discussing poetry. For Johnson inexperience could be diagnosed textually, through a process of close reading that revealed the shortfall of critical prose in relation to its object.

The antidote to the circumscribing tendencies of critical cant was a very different form of critical practice, one that for Johnson was represented by Dryden. Johnson's description of Dryden's criticism emphasises not his principles (which he certainly had), but his stylistic abundance and energy, his sheer *literariness* as a critic:

> It will not be easy to find in all the opulence of our language a treatise so artfully variegated with successive representations of opposite probabilities, so enlivened with imagery, so brightened with illustrations. ... the criticism of Dryden is the criticism of a poet; not a dull collection of theorems, nor a rude detection of faults, which perhaps the censor was not able to have committed; but a gay and vigorous dissertation, where delight is mingled with instruction, and where the author proves his right of judgement by his power of performance.
>
> (*Lives*, I, 412)

Two psychologies of critical rule-making are distinguished: one characterised by the dullness of the theorem maker, the other 'variegated', 'enlivened', and 'brightened' by the mind of the poet. But the difference exists not in mere decoration: critical 'principles' must be sensitive to the qualities of what they seek to explain; there must be a vital alignment of judgement and performance in which the skill of the latter validates the authority of the former. The poetic aspects of Dryden's criticism play a central rather than secondary role in the creation of its meaning and in its success as a means of describing literature. This *literary*-critical mode was for Johnson the antithesis of the pseudo-scientific cant of Warton. It also turns the Augustan-Romantic debate, as conventionally conceived, on its head: freedom of poetic expression is located firmly in the Augustan tradition; stuffiness, restriction and poetry by rules are the characteristics of the newcomers. It was Romanticism's polemical charge – its attempt to bring the artful variegations of the literary under the banner of the non-literary – that for Johnson signalled its threat and predicted its ultimate failure.

Johnson's notoriously complex prose stylistics – his relentless checks, balances, pivots, and turns – constitute, in themselves, a form of argument against the kind of critical straitjacketing he objected to in those like Warton. Byron, it appears, recognised the significance of this unshackling through style. We get a clue here from Byron's disapproval of Bowles' own use of Johnson, which involved sifting out the negatives in the *Life of Pope* from the more positive views that coalesce in Johnson's densely textured prose:

> If the opinions cited by Mr. Bowles, of Dr. Johnson *against* Pope, are to be taken as decisive authority, they will also hold good against Gray, Milton, Swift, Thomson, and Dryden: in that case what becomes of Gray's poetical, and Milton's moral character? even of Milton's *poetical* character, or indeed of *English* poetry in general? for Johnson strips many a leaf from every laurel. Still Johnson's is the finest critical work extant, and can never be read without instruction and delight.
>
> (*CMP*, 150)

Byron read Johnson's *Lives* not as a series of detachable opinions but as intricate fabrics of praise and censure. He appreciated that Johnson's biography, with all its nuance and complexity must be read as a whole, not dissected and rearranged. He recognised that style was central to Johnson's opposition to the critical systemising of Warton and as such was relevant to his own attack on Bowles.

Byron was well aware of the controversy's history. He knew of the ideological continuity between Warton and Bowles (Bowles was a pupil at Winchester when Warton was a Master) and noted 'the unjustifiable attempts at depreciation begun by Warton – & carried on to & at this day by the new School of Critics & Scribblers who think themselves poets because they do *not* write like Pope' (*BLJ*, 6, 31).[11] He was right that Bowles' edition of Pope, and its tacit theoretical commitments, were strongly influenced by Warton: the edition retains Warton's ideal of 'true poetry', his distinction between 'natural' and 'artificial' subjects, and restates his wish to exclude Pope from the highest echelons of poetic excellence. It is also clear that Byron imagined his war with contemporary literary 'system' as an extension of English Augustan polemic: 'As to Johnson and Pope ... had they lived now – I would not have published a line of anything I have ever written' (*BLJ*, 9, 68). Byron seems to have been self-consciously replaying the dispute between Johnson and Warton, placing himself in the role of his 'great Moralist', in opposition to the inheritor of a cultural cant that had now become fashion.

But it was not just Byron who was reading Johnson: the latter seems to have been at the centre of a wider sceptical refutation of Bowles of which the *Letter to John Murray* was only one part. It was the 1819 publication of Thomas Campbell's *Specimens of the British Poets* (published by Murray and sent out to Byron in Italy) that resurrected the controversy by returning to Bowles's edition of 1806. Campbell took Bowles to task for his levering

apart of nature and artifice, and did so with a decidedly Johnsonian gesture
of inclusiveness: 'Nature, in the wide and proper sense of the word, means
life in all its circumstances.'[12] The same year Bowles replied with his
uncompromisingly titled *The Invariable Principles of Poetry*, a pamphlet that
reiterated his aesthetic principles and their consequences for Pope's reputation. The pamphlet provoked several responses, including a *Quarterly
Review* article by Isaac D'Israeli.[13] D'Israeli also looked back to Johnson and
refers in his review to the *Life of Pope* and notably quotes the anti-Wartonian
sentences on circumscribing poetry, which, if he was not already thinking
of them, would have alerted Byron to their relevance.[14] Mixing Johnson's
attack on Warton's 'narrowness' with a slug of Byronic vitriol, D'Israeli
complained that 'it has frequently been attempted to raise up such arbitrary standards and such narrowing theories of art; and these "criterions"
and "invariable principles" have usually been drawn from the habitual
practices and individual tastes of the framers; there is a sort of concealed
egotism, a stratagem of self-love.'[15] Literary art is beyond the range of
linguistically crude 'criterions' which can only reduce and restrict it; such
modes of criticism result from the personal limitations and 'egotism' of
critics enmeshed in a kind of category error whereby criticism becomes not
an elucidation but an enslavement of the literary. Radically different forms
and styles of critical writing to those of Bowles were therefore essential if
the traditions of poetry were to remain free to develop their unique
perspective on the world. These were the beliefs common to the neo-John-
sonian critics, including Byron, who opposed some of Romanticism's most
determined campaigners.

For Byron, however, these problems were not restricted to the sphere
of literary criticism; Bowles's cant was only one facet of a broader social,
political and ethical malaise:

> The truth is that in these days the grand 'primum mobile' of England is *Cant* –
> Cant political – Cant poetical – Cant religious – Cant moral – but always *Cant*
> – multiplied through all the varieties of life. – It is the fashion – & while it lasts
> – will be too powerful for those who can only exist by taking the tone of the
> time. – I say *Cant* – because it is a thing of words – without the smallest influ-
> ence upon human actions – the English being no wiser – no better – and much
> poorer – and more divided amongst themselves – as well as far less moral –
> than they were before the prevalence of this verbal decorum.
>
> (CMP, p. 128)[16]

Cant 'poetical' was more than an attempt to monopolise poetry, it was
symptomatic of a prevalent linguistic style that Byron associated with polit-

ical oppression. Bowles's characteristic manner of critical discourse, a style Byron saw as inscribed in the very theoretical foundations of Romanticism, was cut through with (for him) objectionable politics. It was part of a simplification of the world that was for Byron the primary means through which repressive governments divided, demoralised, and overpowered those they governed. By demanding the critical objectification of the literary and thus dismissing its potent resistance to verbal formulation, Bowles' brand of Romanticism was complicit with these very processes. Byron's response to this was a politicised version of Johnson's insistence that criticism must respect poetry's shadowy and elusive magnificence and not attempt to circumscribe it with 'definition', which in these terms becomes an act tantamount to tyranny. It was in its resistance to such ordering voices and their totalitarian echoes that poetry for Byron found its modern moral function; and it was in the *Letter to John Murray* that he put forward this view most directly: 'In my mind the highest of all poetry is Ethical poetry – as the highest of all earthly objects must be moral truth' (*CMP*, p. 143). The ethical end of poetry is to attack, undermine, and over-write the demoralising cant of public discourse. What was disastrous about Bowles was that he was working in the opposite direction by rewriting poetry as cant, and thus disabling it as a useful political force.

To understand Byron's notion of 'Ethical poetry', which is in turn one of the clues to understanding *Don Juan*, we need to look at his engagement with the central examples over which Campbell and Bowles fought. Campbell had attempted to refute Bowles by introducing instances of (mainly non-literary) 'poetic' spectacles from 'artificial' life, stressing their inherent poetic qualities. The 'artificial' spectacle that generated most interest was a 'ship of the line' at sea, which Campbell invoked as an instance of 'the sublime objects of artificial life': if the ship is both 'artificial' and poetic, Campbell argued, then it stands to reason that Bowles's argument must be faulty.[17] Bowles replied to this in the *Invariable Principles* as follows:

> Let us examine the ship which you have described so beautifully. On what does the poetical beauty depend? Not on *art*, but NATURE. Take away the *waves*, the *winds*, the *sun*, that, in association with the streamer and sails, make them look so beautiful! take all poetical associations away, ONE will become a strip of blue bunting, and the *other* a piece of coarse canvas on three tall poles!![18]

His response was to break down the prospect into its component 'associations' in line with his 'natural'/'artificial' dichotomy. He argued that the poetry comes only from the 'natural' 'associations', a fact that will become evident if we take them away. Campbell and Bowles were locked into a binary argument, each ranging his forces on the side of 'artificial' and 'natural' respectively, a method of debate that Byron was keen to keep at a distance: 'Mr Campbell has no need of my alliance' (*CMP*, p. 129).[19] He knew that by merely reversing Bowles's terms Campbell was, however much he disagreed with his conclusions, in fact endorsing Bowles's method, which was exactly what Byron wanted to call into question:

> Mr. B. asserts that Campbell's 'Ship of the Line' derives all its poetry not from '*art*' but from '*Nature.*' – 'Take away the waves – the winds – the Sun &c. *one* will become a stripe of blue bunting – and the other a piece of coarse canvas on three tall poles.' – Very true – take away the 'waves' – 'the winds' and there will be no ship at all – not only for poetical – but for any other purpose – & take away 'the Sun' and we must read Mr. B's pamphlet by candle-light. – But the 'poetry' of the 'Ship' does *not* depend on the 'waves &c.' – on the contrary – the 'Ship of the line' confers it's own poetry upon the waters – and heightens *theirs* … the poetry is at least reciprocal.
>
> (*CMP*, pp. 129–30)

Byron's jokes parody the logic chopping of Bowles: they gesture out to what exceeds the narrow bounds of his opponent's mode of argument. Poetry, Byron argued, cannot be dismantled and examined piece by piece, as if criticism were a kind of scientific experiment. This would be to miss the whole point of what poetry is, to overlook it. Poetry exists for Byron in the connections between human situations and the natural world: it is 'reciprocal', and it is in its reciprocities that we find poetry's ethical basis in its resistance to simple categorisation. For Byron what Bowles calls the 'artificial' 'confers' poetry onto the 'natural' and vice versa; and it is in this process that we are shown something important about the world and our place within it as human beings. In breaking rather than maintaining these reciprocal relationships with his crudely imposed lexical binaries, Bowles was not, as he thought, cutting to the essence of poetry, but was dismembering the very situations in which poetry inheres. 'If this is not "minute moral anatomy" – I should be glad to know what is? – It is dissection in all its branches' (*CMP*, p. 166).[20] By arguing for a poetic ideal which was not reciprocal but one-sided, Bowles risked divorcing poetry from its central and traditional role as a means of showing us (not the same as telling) the reciprocities of life and language that constitute our world, but that defy the kind of explanation to which Bowles tried to make them submit. By deploying a critical lexis that establishes exclusive categories ('natural' versus 'artificial'), he failed to capture poetry's essential quality, its reciprocity, its existence in the movement between what the scientific mindset encourages us to see as static and separable.

Here we are as close as we are likely to get to an affirmative Byronic poetics, one that was formed in opposition to some of the rhetorical trends of Romantic self-definition. In the *Letter to John Murray* Byron locates the value of poetry precisely in its capacity to speak about those processes of life that cannot be brought into line by linguistic bullying of the kind he attributed to Bowles.[21] Most likely drawing from his knowledge of the controversy's history, especially Johnson's critique of Warton's proto-Bowlesian rhetoric, Byron understood that in order to respect the dynamic processes that were the representational domain of the literary, critical writing must itself be alive to the reciprocal and seek to maintain it within its own language. As Johnson emphasised in his *Life of Dryden*, criticism must perform rather than dissect. Byron's most successful moment as a literary critic in these Johnsonian terms is his final word on the question of the 'ship of the line'. As if tired of the pedestrian nature of the argument, he suddenly launched into a vivid personal recollection of a storm in the spring of 1810 when the ship he was travelling in was anchored off Cape Sigeum:

> What seemed the most '*poetical*' of all – at the moment – were the numbers (about two hundred) of Greek and Turkish Craft – which were obliged to 'cut and run' before the wind – from their unsafe anchorage – some for Tenedos – some for other isles – some for the Main – and some it may be for Eternity. – The Sight of these little scudding vessels darting over the foam in the twilight – now appearing – and now disappearing between the waves in the cloud of night – with their peculiarly *white* sails (the Levant sails not being of '*coarse canvas*' but of white cotton) skimming along – as quickly – but less safely than the Sea-Mew which hovered over them – their evident distress – their reduction to fluttering specks in the distance – their crowded succession – their *littleness* as contending with the Giant element – which made our stout 44.'s *teak* timbers (she was built in India) creak again, – their aspect – and their motion – all struck me as something far more 'poetical' than the mere broad – brawling – shipless Sea & the sullen winds could possibly have been without them.
>
> (*CMP*, pp. 131–2)

This was a brilliant contribution to what was otherwise a rather flat debate about the 'nature' or 'essence' of poetry. But there is more to it than Byron wearying of the narrow disputatious grind: his *literary* criticism is also making a historically sanctioned point about the whole endeavour of writing about poetry.[22] His double-voiced critical prose speaks to the terms of the debate but also addresses the limitations of those terms by opening them out to the category-resistant workings of imaginative writing. With its ceaseless sense of movement, its emphatically connective dashes, and its deeply felt response to the situation described, Byron's prose establishes its own reciprocities, between human life and its natural element as well as between critical argument and poetic meaning. In so doing his criticism remains true to those processes that were for Byron the basis of ethical life, but that seemed to be falling prey to the contemporary dissecting tendencies represented most mercilessly by Bowles' 'invariable' principles.

It is a short step from this style of poetic criticism to some of the critical poetry that punctuates *Don Juan*, and that extends the attack on Bowles to the contemporary literary scene as a whole. These stanzas were written shortly before Byron's involvement in the Bowles controversy, but clearly share its thinking:

And Wordsworth, in a rather long "Excursion"
(I think the quarto holds five hundred pages)
Has given a sample from the vasty version
Of his new system to perplex the sages;
'Tis poetry – at least by his assertion,
And may appear so when the dog-star rages –
And he who understands it will be able
To add a story to the Tower of Babel.

You – Gentlemen, by dint of long seclusion
From better company, have kept your own
At Keswick, and through still continued fusion
Of one another's minds, at last have grown
To deem as a most logical conclusion,
That Poesy has wreaths for you alone:
There is a narrowness in such a notion,
That makes me wish you'd change your lakes for ocean.

(*Don Juan*, 'Dedication')

Like Johnson in the *Life of Pope*, Byron attacks what he saw as an attempt to circumscribe poetry through a distinctly Romantic rhetoric that is in turn related to the 'narrowness' of the definers, a word that directly recalls Johnson's *Life*. But what Byron developed out of his Johnsonian study was more than a piece of neo-Augustan satire; he implies here a positive anti-Wordsworthian poetics that reasserts in its own language the vital but elusive complexity that Byron saw as being bypassed by Romantic aesthetics. In response to Wordsworth's systematising of poetry, Byron unleashes the potential of poetic language to defy such an imposition. Wordsworthian rhetoric, so often characterised by its suggestions of vastness and comprehensiveness, is under the pressure of Byron's stanzas reduced to one way of talking about poetry, a 'version', which despite its assertiveness to the contrary, has no claims to objectivity. Wordsworthian cant is confronted by a very different kind of language, one that foregrounds the sheer difficulty of describing poetry by subtly pressurising words into a confession of their own limitations, while at the same time revealing their extraordinary capacities. Vast becomes 'vasty', the mere addition of a letter pushing the word out of its sublime register into a rather lower range ('nasty'/'gusty'). The drawn-out pseudo-Wordsworthian seriousness of 'still continued fusion' also makes us voice a markedly different possibility: 'con-fusion'. Coleridgean organicism sprouts up everywhere, but it is an unhealthy, inbred kind of growth (own/grown/alone), a nature spawned in isolation that also chimes with Byron's remarks on Keats.[23] Byron's language is everywhere aggressively corrective, aimed at reasserting the ethical basis of writing by collapsing system and its suspect politics. It may well have left the great critic of eighteenth-century England speechless, but it was Johnson as much as Pope that was behind this new and potent questioning of the Romantic imperative.

Notes

1   See for instance the excellent collection of essays *Byron: Augustan and Romantic*, ed. Andrew Rutherford (London: Macmillan, 1990).

2   For a wide, comparative survey of the writers, see Joel Allan Dando, 'The Poet as Critic: Byron in His Letters and Journals. Case Studies of Shakespeare and Johnson' unpublished doctoral thesis, Harvard University, 1985.

3   Byron was of course well acquainted with the Johnson canon. He owned editions of the *Dictionary*, the *Lives of the English Poets*, and Boswell's magnificent biography. The 1816 sale catalogue of Byron's books also contains almost complete collections of the poems and periodical essays.

4   *His Very Self and Voice: Collected Conversations of Lord Byron*, ed. by Ernest J. Lovell, Jr (New York: Macmillan, 1954), p. 328.

5   Byron's *Letter to John Murray*, which addresses the question of Pope's status and surveys the contemporary literary scene more generally, was published on Saturday, 31 March 1821.

6   *Medwin's Conversations of Lord Byron*, ed. by Ernest J. Lovell, Jr (Princeton, NJ: Princeton University Press, 1966), p.198.

7   *Lives of the English Poets*, ed. by G. B. Hill, 3 vols (Oxford: Clarendon Press, 1905), I, 6. All subsequent references are to this edition and are incorporated in the text.

8 There is a likely biographical dimension to the disagreement. Johnson's brief Oxford sojourn is well documented, as is his subsequent immersion in London life. Warton, by contrast, led a sheltered existence, moving between Winchester, Oxford, and various clerical positions, a difference of which Johnson was highly conscious and which may have contributed to tensions between the two men. For an account of the friendship between Johnson and Warton and its breach, see John Wooll, *Biographical Memoirs of the Late Revd. Joseph Warton* (London: Cadell, 1806), p. 98 and *passim*.

9 Joseph Warton, *An Essay on the Genius and Writings of Pope*, 2 vols (London, 1806), I, iii, vi.

10 Warton, *Essay* I, ii, vi. For a fuller account of Warton's aesthetics see Joan Pittock, *The Ascendancy of Taste: The Achievement of Joseph and Thomas Warton* (London: Routledge, 1973).

11 For a more detailed account of the various controversies over Augustan literature in Byron's day, see Upali Amarasinghe, *Dryden and Pope in the Early Nineteenth Century* (Cambridge: Cambridge University Press, 1962), p. 22 and *passim*.

12 Thomas Campbell, *Specimens of the British Poets; with Biographical and Critical Notices, and an Essay on English Poetry*, 7 vols (London: John Murray, 1819), I, 264.

13 Isaac D'Israeli, *Quarterly Review* XXIII, no. xlvi (July 1820), art. v, pp. 400–34. For Byron's reading of D'Israeli, see James Chandler, 'The Pope Controversy: Romantic Politics and the English Canon', in *Critical Enquiry* 10, no.3 (March 1984), pp. 498ff. It seems likely that Byron read the review as he refers to D'Israeli in a contemporary letter in relation to the Bowles controversy (see *BLJ*, 8, 237).

14 D'Israeli, *Review*, p. 408.

15 D'Israeli, *Review*, p. 410.

16 Christopher Ricks has linked Byron and Johnson as haters of cant (and lovers of the word). See *Allusion to the Poets* (Oxford University Press, 2002), pp. 121–2.

17 Campbell, *Specimens*, II, 265.

18 William Lisle Bowles, *The Invariable Principles of Poetry: In a Letter addressed to Thomas Campbell, Esq; Occasioned by some Critical Observations in his Specimens of British Poets, Particularly relating to the Poetical Character of POPE* (London: Longman, 1819), p. 11.

19 In this respect Hazlitt's parody of Byron ('You see, my dear Bowles, the superiority of art over nature') was a little unfair. Hazlitt's review of the controversy appeared in the *London Magazine* (June 1821) and is reprinted in *The Complete Works of William Hazlitt*, ed. by P. P. Howe, 21 vols (London: Dent, 1930–1934), XIX (this quotation p. 63).

20 The comment recalls Byron's insistence that he would not change *Don Juan* to fit in with John Murray's conservative tastes: 'I will have none of your damned cutting & slashing' (*BLJ*, 6, 105).

21 I disagree here with Claude Rawson who has remarked that 'Byron's famous letters on Pope … are not very interesting or distinguished documents, more preoccupied with a tedious and self-important wrangle with Bowles than with a genuine understanding of Pope.' 'Byron Augustan: Mutations of the Mock Heroic in *Don Juan* and Shelley's *Peter Bell the Third*', in *Byron: Augustan and Romantic*, ed. by Rutherford, pp. 82–116, pp. 82–3.

22 Also see also Paul M. Curtis, 'The Bowles–Pope Controversy: Polemics and Paradox', in *Byron and the Mediterranean World*, ed. by Marius Byron Raizis (Athens: Hellenic Byron Society, 1995), pp. 141–52, p. 144.

23 'Such writing is a sort of mental masturbation – he is always f–gg–g his *Imagination. –* I don't mean that he is *indecent* but viciously soliciting his own ideas into a state which is neither poetry nor anything else but a bedlam vision produced by raw pork and opium' (*BLJ*, 7, 225).

Free Quills and Poetic Licences:
Byron and the Politics of Publication

TIMOTHY WEBB

Whatever his later reputation, and however much he may have been celebrated as a 'freedom-fighter' or an inspiring force in more than one struggle for national liberty, Byron himself was recurrently sceptical and unsentimentally realistic about the operations of 'freedom' in practice. In English contexts this freedom was often linked with freedom of expression, though Byron's own experience, both in politics and especially as a writer, convinced him that the absolutes of desire were often necessarily qualified by the compromises demanded by the real world of politics and publication. This ambivalence, or mature recognition of practical realities, can be identified both in and behind many of his major poems.

Beppo, for example, may seem at first sight to be troublingly complacent when it allows itself, and its readers, to enjoy a traditional excursus on the alternative pleasures of England and Italy (Italy, stanzas 41–6; England, stanzas 47–9). The disproportionate emphasis on the attractions of Italy indicates where the narrator ('A broken Dandy lately on my travels') places his preference, which is further underlined by the negative catalogue of English pluses that constitutes stanza 49 (including the plurally possessive but teasingly paradoxical, 'Our little riots just to show we are free men').

Yet among the virtues which the broken dandy narrator associates with England are the following:

> I like to speak and lucubrate my fill;
> I like the government (but that is not it);
> I like the freedom of the press and quill;
> I like the Habeas Corpus (when we've got it);
> I like a parliamentary debate,
> Particularly when 'tis not too late.

The list is continued in the following stanza until it reaches a naively patriotic climax in 'I like all and every thing'. Behind these apparent simplicities and seemingly unironical endorsements there is a political philosophy, and a rhetoric, which insists on qualifications and complications. For example, Byron himself had, briefly, taken advantage of the opportunity provided by the 'parliamentary debate' to express his views on Irish Catholicism and frame-breaking, and the celebration of this and other freedoms, however qualified, has left its mark on the passage;[1] but even here the positives sometimes turn out to be fragile. The narrator declares his satisfaction with the present arrangements which allow him both to think freely and to express his thoughts ('to speak and lucubrate my fill') which are encoded in a national system which allows liberty of printed expression ('freedom of the press and quill'); yet this is immediately followed by another item, which in spite of its seeming jocularity, suggests that freedom of the individual citizen is not necessarily guaranteed: 'I like the Habeas Corpus (when we've got it)'. Habeas Corpus had been suspended in England on 4 March 1817 and the suspension was not repealed until 31 January 1818. *Beppo* was actually written during the period of suspension and was published on or shortly before 24 February 1818.[2] The apparently light-hearted tone conceals the fact that, even though he was not living in England at the time, Byron was evidently concerned by the possibly restrictive implications of this measure.

The troubling possibilities of this legislation for the future of the English reputation for freedom are raised in the final paragraph of the prose dedication of the fourth canto of *Childe Harold's Pilgrimage* (this canto finally appeared on 28 April 1818). Here, as in *Beppo*, the occasion is a comparison between Italy and England, and here again Byron administers a reproof to self-satisfied national complacency: 'What Italy has gained by the late transfer of nations, it were useless for Englishmen to enquire, till it becomes ascertained that England has acquired something more than a permanent army and a suspended Habeas Corpus: it is enough for them to look at home.'[3]

As it stands, the passage carries its own importance but archival evidence indicates that even the right to make this objection in print had to be fought for. William Gifford, editor of the *Quarterly Review* and chief adviser to John Murray, Byron's publisher, deleted the reference to Habeas Corpus in the original. Byron, however, was not prepared to concede. Firmly, he directed that the cancelled words should be reinstated and indicated his frame of mind on the proof: 'I won't give up "ould Apias Korkus" it was not repealed when I wrote – & if it had – it shouldn't spoil my periods – Oons!'[4] The bantering tone of this and its joky intimacy (compare Ezra

Pound's assumption of epistolary voices, especially when writing to T. S. Eliot) may indicate some embarrassment, or perhaps the simulation of embarrassment; it might also be read as one of the many moments at which Byron tries out a comical tone of voice, often by drawing on the convenient example of an allusion. Here, as Andrew Nicholson points out, the reference is to Smollett's *Humphry Clinker*, where Winifred Jenkins writes to Mrs Mary Jones on 14 June and commits the solecism which Byron absorbed, even if he slightly adjusted or misremembered the original: 'if master had not applied to Apias Korkus, who lives with the ould bailiff'. In this case, the basic confusion about the facts is compounded by the transforming properties of a Welsh accent as represented by Smollett.[5] His correspondence with Hobhouse is often marked by this friendly experimentation and by this sense of a shared set of literary touchstones and a shared vocabulary (see, for example, his use of 'holpen' and of 'oons').[6] Yet we should not be deflected by this, nor by the recourse to stylistic arguments ('it shouldn't spoil my periods') into neglecting the fact that Byron is sticking to his original choice and rejecting the intervention of a trusted adviser; this contentious issue involves much more than the choice of words or the run of a sentence.

This example illustrates the fact that Byron's desire to express his own views on freedom, and especially on freedom in England, sometimes found itself in opposition to those very tendencies it was designed to expose. On this occasion, he was victorious and the choice on which he insisted was supported by the publisher; but this was not always the case, and there were occasions on which Byron acceded to other opinions, or compromised, just as there were occasions when (to Byron's indignation) John Murray took his decisions without consulting the author. The broken dandy may have liked 'the freedom of the press and quill' but, for Byron as a writer, freedom was not so much an abstract ideal as a difficult practicality which had to be scrutinised regularly and shrewdly. Whatever his views on liberty in Italy, Greece, or America, Byron continued to work with a publisher who was based in London, and he had to convince both the publisher and the group of advisers who stood between him and the poet that what he had written was suitable for publication. Unlike Shelley, his works were not refused by the publisher or suppressed and, unlike Shelley, he profited from the continuity and the mutual trust generated by working with one publisher for much of his writing life. But his closeness to John Murray and his commitment to the persuasive medium and self-gratifying currency of publication ensured that he was often faced with difficult choices; on occasion, he even seems to have anticipated the restrictions to his own freedom of expression which Murray or others might have imposed or suggested. Frequently, too, the issue is confused for us by the difficulty involved in distinguishing between choices which have been conditioned by purely aesthetic factors and others which seem to admit a wider and less easily categorised set of factors. Yet, one way or another, it is hard not to conclude that, at times, Byron imposed his own form of self-censorship.

From the time of *Childe Harold's Pilgrimage* when the first connection was arranged by Robert Charles Dallas till near the end of his writing career, when he finally transferred publishing responsibility to John Hunt, Byron entrusted his work to John Murray. His engagement with Murray was continuous, energetic, sometimes argumentative, and often suspicious. Although John Hunt's brother Leigh (who had been introduced to Murray through the offices of Byron) reported in 1816 that Murray had liberated himself from the pressures of political allegiance,[7] there can be no doubt that (like many publishers) he often displayed a prudential or conservative tendency, which infuriated Byron. At first sight, the Tory publisher Murray might not seem to be the kind of man with whom the Whiggish Byron would have been expected to associate; there are also times when, as a 'tradesman', he falls easy victim to Byron's aristocratic scorn. Yet, clearly, there was something in the relationship which was substantial and enduring – in a way which was often suggestive and helpful, too, through an involvement with Murray and a range of advisers whom Byron characterised as Murray's 'Synod' or *'the knowing ones'*.[8] For a start, Byron could test his strength against the possibility of hostile reaction. Proofs and correspondence provide fascinating evidence of the ways in which this operated, as does the record of publishing history, though much research still remains to be done.

A few examples are indicative. The text of *Childe Harold's Pilgrimage* was scrutinised at various times by a number of experienced eyes, including those of Dallas, Gifford, Scrope Davies, and Hobhouse. Like Murray, Gifford (the notoriously waspish editor of the strongly Tory *Quarterly Review* which Murray had initiated) might seem an improbable authority figure for such a man as Byron; yet Byron continued to hold him in high esteem, especially in literary matters, even if he often resisted his suggestions or interventions. On 15 February 1817 Byron reminded Murray that Gifford had been a friend 'through thick & thin – in despite of differences of years – morals – habits – & even *politics*'; later, he was characterised as a '*literary* father' to Byron's '*prodigal* Son'. In spite of disagreements, the respect was enduring. On 20 September 1821 Byron registered how seriously he took Gifford's disapproval of 'my new dramas': 'I regret his demur the more that he has always been my grand patron and I know no praise which would compensate me in my own mind for his censure.' His correspondence reveals that he was prepared to flatter and that he was apparently gratified by Gifford's 'kindness' in his approval of Canto 3 of *Childe Harold's Pilgrimage* and his role 'as my Editor'. Gifford's opinion was recurrently important to Byron over a number of years: for instance, his authority was invoked for the *Siege of Corinth*, *Sardanapalus*, *Werner*, and the *Lament of Tasso*.

But, although Byron sought his approval, and was pleased to receive such authoritative endorsement, he was always prepared to ignore Gifford's criticisms or reservations if he thought they were misplaced (as in the case of *Cain*).[9] Byron wrote on one of the proofs to Canto 4 of *Childe Harold's Pilgrimage*: 'I have attended to most of Mr. G's suggestions, and I am obliged to him for them – others I have left, partly from the passage of time – and partly from unwillingness – or laziness – or what you will – the truth is best.'[10] Again, in a letter of 5 March 1818 to Hobhouse he responds at greater length, indicating very precisely how he attended thoughtfully to Gifford's suggestions on aesthetic grounds, and offering a more extended tribute to his editorial virtues:

> I am … greatly obliged by G[ifford]'s suggestions which are well meant & generally well grounded – & surely good natured as can be – & one ought to attend to the opinions of a man – whose critical talents swept down a whole host of writers at once – I don't mean from *fear* – but real respect for the sense of his observations.

On this occasion, though, and in spite of this almost biblical sense of awe before the mighty effects of Gifford's critical powers, he has preferred the argument put forward by Hobhouse and instructs him accordingly:

> You are right – & I am right – *restore* '*the*' for '*some*' – which I had altered against my creed – to please G[ifford] – what other alterations I made according to his wish are I think properly made – as I am mostly of his opinion except as to '*some*' – & 'past Eternity' which last I have not altered as I think with Polonius '*that's good*' – [11]

As this shows, Byron may have been prepared to be influenced by Gifford's advice but he did not always accept it. He also defiantly tells Hobhouse: 'I can't give up Nemesis – my great favourite – I can't, I can't'.

This was in direct resistance to Gifford's stylistic reminder in his note to 4, 781, 'Recollect you have Nemesis again'. On the proof itself Byron responded: 'I *know* it – and if I had her ten times would not alter once – she is my particular belief and acquaintance – and I wont blaspheme against her for any body'.[12] Again, one of Gifford's annotations to the Dedication to Canto 4 was a not-unjustified query concerning the word 'death': 'Would any other word serve? – to prevent ill-natured stupidity from growing witty.' Byron responded: 'Let them be witty and be damned – we'll be witty too.'[13] The exchange is characteristic since it illustrates a tension between Gifford's anxiety of reception and Byron's more confidently assertive, more riskily daring, approach. It was perhaps this same contested anxiety which caused Gifford to cancel the reference to Habeas Corpus, and Byron to restore it. Byron wrote to Hobhouse on the back of the proofs:

> I hope that you or Mr. Gifford will do me the favour to cast an eye to the proof & press of this [*Childe Harold's Pilgrimage*] as well as of '*Beppo*'. I find some Italian words most damnably '*strappazzate*'. I hate the sight of a proof – for God sake send me no more but correct at your own good pleasure – only *don't omit* for I want to be as tedious as need be – why leave out '*ould Apias Korkus*' it was not restored when I wrote – and the Ministers may be damned for repealing it & spoiling my period.[14]

Of course, the last part of these remarks is a more formal version of what Byron had written on the proof; 'ould Apias Korkus' was a point of reference to which Byron recurred with particular personal relevance when Hobhouse himself was later prosecuted and imprisoned in Newgate for writing a pamphlet.[15]

These instructions remind us that, whatever his reservations, after his departure from England in 1816 Byron was dependent on the good will, the literary instincts, and the sharp eyes of friends and advisers who were closer to home and more directly in contact with Murray; the fact that he lived abroad for most of the years of his literary fame strengthened this dependency. For example, Gifford acknowledged discomfort with the lines, 'temple of all gods, / From Jove to Jesus' (4, 1307–8): '*From Jove to Jesus* may perhaps displease – and the sense is perfect without those words.' Byron replied in a way which combined stylistic considerations with a supporting sense of literary tradition: 'This is true – but the Alliteration – I cannot part with it – I like it so – besides it's no worse than Pope's "Jehovah – *Jove* – or Lord".'[16] When Gifford, who insisted on grammatical correctness, expressed concern about the phrase 'there let him lay' (4, 1620) ('I have doubt about *lay*') Byron responded: 'So have I – but the *post* and *indolence* and *illness*!!' As he put it in a letter to Hobhouse: '– The wicked necessity of rhyming retains "lay" – in despite of sense & grammar.'[17] It is characteristic of Byron that he submitted to this 'wicked necessity' without making any attempts at adjustment. Again, Gifford was not satisfied with 'Thy waters washed them power when they were free' (1632), noted 'There seems some error in the verse', and replaced Byron's 'washed them power' with 'wasted them'. Byron asked Murray what these lines meant and reminded him pointedly: 'Consult the M.S. *always*.' The pattern here is quite clear (*'that is not me'*).[18] However much he admired Gifford, or was flattered by Gifford's attentions to his 'majestic march' (not least his admiration for Canto 3 by which he was 'infinitely delighted' and later for the purity of diction in *Marino Faliero*),[19] Byron retained a strong intellectual independence and the capacity to stick firmly, sometimes even obstinately, to the dictates of his own judgement.

Sometimes this led to friction with Murray, acting either directly on his own behalf or at the suggestion of advisers such as Gifford. In the published text of *Childe Harold's Pilgrimage* Murray had printed:

> And thou, who never yet of human wrong
> Lost the unbalanced scale, great Nemesis.
>
> (IV, 1180–1)

Byron corrected 'Lost' to 'Left'st' and added a fierce annotation: 'Mr. J. Murray is a careless Blockhead, and forgets that in addressing the Deity a Blunder may become a Blasphemy. Venice Septr 23rd 1818.'[20] The following day he reinforced the point in a letter to the publisher. Murray should have printed 'Left' (a slight variation), not 'Lost': '– which is nonsense – as what *losing* a scale means – I know not – but *leaving* an unbalanced scale or a scale unbalanced is intelligible. – Correct this – I pray – not for the public or the poetry – but I do not choose to have blunders made in addressing any of the deities – so seriously as this is addressed.–' After making a few other points, he returns to his original complaint with a vehemence which is both revealed and emphasised by the repetition:

> – In referring to the mistake made in stanza 132 I take the opportunity to desire that in future in all parts of my writings relating to religion you will be more careful – & not forget that it is possible that in addressing the deity a blunder may become a blasphemy – & I do not choose to suffer such infamous perversions of my words or of my intention. – I saw the Canto by accident. –[21]

Byron's insistence on his personal values and his fierce rejection of any editorial intrusion reminded Murray (as it reminds us) that whatever the personal genialities, Byron did not forget what he saw as the appropriate relationship between the creative writer and the merely mechanical, banausic publisher.

On occasion, though, he was prepared to listen, especially to the advice of those whom he regarded as his friends. For instance, he provided the following note to the last two lines in Canto 2: 'If Mr D[allas] wishes me to adopt the former line [the received text] so be it. I prefer the other I confess, it has less egotism – the first sounds affected.'[22] Against his own inclinations, he followed the advice of Dallas. Another good example is a passage in the draft Dedication to Canto 4 in which, without naming names, Byron regrets his performance in *English Bards and Scotch Reviewers* ('the premature attacks of an undistinguishing moment of blind anger and boyish vivacity') and the 'undeserved satire' of his attacks on 'the literary men who practised such forebearance' (perhaps Jeffrey and Moore, among others). Scrope Davies counselled him to drop the passage, and Byron complied: 'But I bow to Scrope's alteration of the preface, and I request that it be adopted forthwith.'[23] Another instance is the stanza which originally followed 1215 in the manuscript and which clearly referred to Byron's feelings for Caroline Lamb but without naming her specifically. On 6 January 1818 Byron directed that these lines should be left out. He annotated one version of the text more explicitly: 'There was another stanza which followed the above in the MSS, which was omitted at the request of some of those to whom the work was shewn previous to publication.'[24] These unidentified 'friends' probably told Byron that, even if Caroline Lamb was not named in the stanzas, the identification was all too easy to make; perhaps, too, the directly personal tone of these lines seemed too gratingly intrusive or betrayed a troubling complexity of feeling in the poet which was better restrained.

Similar practices may have operated in the omission from the first canto of the stanza about the fate of William Beckford (270–78) though in this case Byron's motivation has been disputed. On the manuscript he gave unequivocal directions: 'If ever published I shall have this stanza omitted. Byron. February 1st, 1811. I would not have this about Beckford.'[25] Louis Crompton, who is concerned to demonstrate Byron's homosexual tendencies and practices, interprets this omission in terms of what the lines might have revealed about Byron's sympathies, had they been published. Crompton claims that: 'He had also intended to include the following stanza on Beckford' but it was 'suppressed and not published until 1833'. For all their apparently collusive homophobia (or perhaps even because of it), these lines 'show how fully Byron was aware of the social sanctions visited on homosexuals and bisexuals by English society and how little wealth, talent, and position availed to protect any man who was once suspect'.[26] Here Crompton's choice of words seems to imply that Byron was a victim of greater forces, but the evidence might allow a more complicated model in which Byron himself seems to have anticipated some of the possible public effects of his description of 'unhappy Vathek'.

Whatever the cause, or causes, for the deletion of this stanza, the facts suggest again that, in preparing *Childe Harold's Pilgrimage* for publication, Byron was aware, or made aware, that even this seeming freedom had its own limitations. This difficult case seems to shade into others where the text of *Childe Harold's Pilgrimage* omits several stanzas which appear in manuscript: most notably, perhaps, the description of the henchman-page (after I, 63), the extended account of the Convention of Cintra (after I, 287), the satirical passage on travel-writing (after I, 890), and the attack on Grecian antiquarians (after II, 117).[27] These passages are characterised by Spenserian diction and a sometimes laborious periphrastic reluctance to name names but what marks them even more obviously is the way in which they admit into the poem a collection of figures who are unmistakably contemporary and clearly identified by name: 'Hew / Dalrymple', 'By vaunting Wellesley or by blundering Frere', 'Dark Hamilton and sullen Aberdeen', 'Elgin', 'digging Gell'. Even here, there is some generic tension between the poem's Spenserian objectives and its growing satirical propensities. Byron's public reticence on the subjects of Caroline Lamb and of Beckford may be related, in part at least, to the tendencies expressed in these passages.

These examples make it clear that, in the extended process of writing *Childe Harold's Pilgrimage* and preparing it for the press, Byron had already begun to encounter the difficulties and the pressures of pragmatic choices which would feature even more prominently in some of his later work. Take, for example, the note on Napoleon which he had originally intended to provide a commentary on *Childe Harold's Pilgrimage*, IV, 1629. This note includes a discussion of the facts of Waterloo and the different objectives of nationalistic myth-making. Byron writes:

> For assuredly we dwell on this action, not because it was gained by Blucher or Wellington, but because it was lost by Buonaparte – a man who, with all his vices and his faults, never yet found an adversary with a tithe of his talents (as far as the expression can apply to a conqueror) or his good intentions, his clemency or his fortitude.

> Look at his successors throughout Europe, whose imitation of the worst
> parts of his policy is only limited by their comparative impotence, and their
> positive imbecility.[28]

In the proof Byron instructed: 'Erase this passage – after the words: lost
by Buonaparte.' In fact, whether by negligence, misinterpretation, or deliberate editorial policy, the whole note was erased, with the effect that this
Byronic commentary disappeared from the record until it was restored by
E. H. Coleridge as a footnote at the bottom of the page but with no explanation of its complicated and suggestive history. A fuller account is now
provided by Jerome McGann but his edition prints the text of Byron's note
together with a history and explanation at the back of the book so that it
is not materially part of our experience of encountering the poem.

Such latitude was scarcely what Byron had intended. Certain freedoms
were conceded to Murray; so, for example, after suggesting an improve-
ment to a line in *Beppo*, Byron proposes that the case be referred to Gifford
and Hobhouse, '& as they think so let it be – for though repetition is only
the "soul of Balladsinging" … yet anything is better than weakening an
expression – or a thought'.[29] Sometimes, too, he presented Murray with
alternatives and suggested that he should use whichever version he
preferred: for instance, he annotates *Don Juan* I, 1552, 'Take that which of
these three seem[s] to be the best prescription' or, again, opposite *Don Juan*
II, 1208, he writes: 'To the Publisher. Take of the variations what is thought
best – I have no choice.'[30] This slightly surprising renunciation of autho-
rial privilege may have been designed to provide Murray with the illusion
of editorial licence; yet Byron watched sharply over his own rights and was
prepared to be outraged when they were ignored.

Perhaps the most powerful indication of what could be involved in this
sort of issue is provided by Murray's decision (apparently taken on
Gifford's advice) to cut Manfred's last line: 'Old man! 'tis not so difficult
to die.' Byron was shocked and infuriated by this omission which, in his
view, seriously weakened the effect of the play. He expressed his reactions
in a letter of 12 August 1817 to Murray:

> You have destroyed the whole effect & moral of the poem by omitting the last
> line of Manfred's speaking – & why this was done I know not. – Why you
> persist in saying nothing of the thing itself I am equally at a loss to conjecture
> – if it is for fear of telling me something disagreeable – you are wrong – because
> sooner or later I must know it – & I am not so new nor so raw nor so inexpe-
> rienced – as not to be able to bear – not the mere paltry petty disappointments
> of authorship – but things more serious – at least I hope so – & that what you

may think irritability is merely mechanical – & only acts like Galvanism on a dead body, – or the muscular motion which survives sensation. — If it is that you are out of humour because I wrote to you a sharp letter – recollect that it was partly from a misconception of your letter – & partly because you did a thing you had no right to do without consulting me – [31]

At the centre of this passionate complaint is Byron's recognition not only that a cut has been made to the detriment of *Manfred* but that Murray had not referred the matter to him nor even mentioned it. What compounds this lapse in good relations is Byron's earlier compliance with the advice from Gifford which had been transmitted by Murray. He had even told Murray that he could burn the play, 'if you like – & Gifford *don't* like'. When Murray had conveyed Gifford's criticism, Byron had expressed his gratitude and acknowledged the 'absurdity of this same overt act of nonsense' which was 'unfit for publication or perusal'. 'I won't', he said firmly, 'have any part published'. As a direct result, he rewrote much of the third act and sent the 'reformed' version to Murray with the injunction that Gifford should correct the proofs.[32] Not surprisingly, a shocked and disillusioned Byron now emphasises how this ultimate lack of consultation concerning the omission of Manfred's crucial last line embodies a highly damaging failure of trust between publisher and poet. He also leaves Murray in no doubt that this omission carries serious literary consequences. Gifford and Murray may well have been troubled by the adversarial effect of Manfred's insistence to the abbot that he would not submit to the comforts of an orthodox code but preferred the existential challenges of his own philosophy – what Francis Jeffrey called his 'firmness' and his 'tremendous solitude'. Byron recognised the importance of this issue and the value of the single line which had been omitted. In his letter to Murray he argued that to leave out this line was to destroy 'the whole effect & moral of the poem'.

If, as Andrew Nicholson has suggested,[33] Manfred's last words bear a strong resemblance to the words which Napoleon was recorded to have uttered (in French) when he attempted to commit suicide, the force of this heroic preference for a personally selected fate would have been richly complicated; yet, even if this is no more than a striking coincidence, the parallel with Napoleon suggests that what is at stake is not so much stylistic as the deeper significance of *Manfred* itself. Murray restored the line in later editions but the disagreement shows clearly how Byron could not trust his own publisher and how he needed to exert constant vigilance in order to ensure, whenever possible, that he was granted freedom of utterance.

Many of these issues featured in the production and publication of Byron's later work, notably in the case of *Don Juan* where the poet, the publisher and their advisers were recurrently reminded of the balance which had to be maintained between the satirist's freedom of expression and the constraints of the law (as interpreted or anticipated by Murray or by Byron himself). Suggestively and symptomatically, Byron defends his practice by invoking those very legal systems and institutions of the state which he might have seemed to be challenging but which, if properly acknowledged, provided a framework which sanctioned his enterprise:

> Why Man the Soul of such writing is it's licence? – at least the *liberty* of that *licence* if one likes – *not* that one should abuse it – it is like trial by Jury and Peerage – and the Habeas Corpus – a very fine thing – but chiefly in the *reversion* – because no one wishes to be tried for the mere pleasure of proving his possession of the privilege.[34]

It is no accident that Byron invokes Habeas Corpus here: earlier he had insisted on his right to mention it as a guarantee of basic democratic rights and now it is adduced as one of those features of the arrangements of the State which one should neither take for granted nor abuse. Where the naive visitor in *Don Juan* celebrates 'inviolate' laws, Byron himself equates the laws of literature with the laws of the land, which must be properly respected; his insistence on 'the *liberty* of that *licence* if one likes' reminds Murray that freedoms need to be exercised carefully and with a proper sense of the privileges involved. This kind of 'licence' derives its force from a recognition of boundaries (*'not* that one should abuse it') and an understanding that its value arises from its agreed lack of restraint in a system based on restraints. The phrase 'no one wishes to be tried' has its meaning within the analogy Byron has established but here, as elsewhere in the comparison, the legal terms serve to remind Murray that *Don Juan* and its author and publisher can continue unprosecuted if they observe carefully the limitations of the liberties which they assume for themselves.

The history of how this 'licence' was maintained in practice and at what cost (Byron eventually transferred publishing responsibilities to John Hunt) is too detailed and too complex to be explored here. What is worth noting is the way in which the very form of *Don Juan* allows Byron to enact the struggle between liberty and constraint with which the poem itself is often engaged, and which frequently marked the history of its publication. Regularly, and unmistakably, the poet draws the attention of his readers to the inescapable dilemma which he has created for himself by selecting the demanding form of ottava rima. The initial choice had been an open one but, once it had been made, the apparently arbitrary had become absolute. Where 'the wicked necessity of rhyming' may have troubled the poet of *Childe Harold's Pilgrimage*, the seeming absurdity but inflexible inexorability of its demands offered a subject from which the poet of *Don Juan* creatively profited. In this way, Byron in *Don Juan* consciously, and self-consciously, *performs* that very struggle between freedom and constraint which is the explicit concern of so much of his writing.

Notes

1 For the full texts of Byron's speeches and suggestive annotation, see *CMP*, pp. 28–43, 289–311.
2 For the text, see *CPW*, 4, 129–60.
3 *CPW*, 2, 124.
4 *CPW*, 2, 319, corrected from the Murray proof (by courtesy of John Murray and Andrew Nicholson).
5 Personal communication from Andrew Nicholson. Byron refers to Smollett and specifically to *Humphry Clinker* on a number of occasions, in letters to Moore, Murray and Kinnaird (*BLJ*, 4, 156; 5, 253; 8, 237; 9, 209 in which Kinnaird is instructed to read to Murray the bookseller's letter to the Welsh clergyman in the introduction to *Humphry Clinker*).
6 See, for example, *BLJ*, 21, 132.
7 *Leigh Hunt: A Life in Letters*, ed. by Eleanor M. Gates (Essex, CT: Falls River Publications, 1998), p. 76.
8 *BLJ*, 7, 85; 8, 198; 6, 25.
9 *BLJ*, 5, 169; 11, 117; 8, 218; 3, 63–4; 5, 105, 113, 158; 8, 156; 10, 42; 11, 190; 9, 103.
10 *CPW*, 2, 315.
11 *BLJ*, 6, 20.
12 *BLJ*, 6, 21; *CPW*, 2, 330.
13 *CPW*, 2, 318.
14 *BLJ*, 6, 16.
15 *BLJ*, 7, 49.
16 *CPW*, 2, 338.
17 *CPW*, 2, 340; *BLJ*, 6, 21.
18 *CPW*, 2, 341; *BLJ*, 6, 71.
19 *BLJ*, 8, 136; 7, 175.
20 *CPW*, 2, 336.
21 *BLJ*, 6, 70–1.
22 *CPW*, 2, 291.
23 *CPW*, 2, 122, 318; *BLJ*, 6, 21.
24 *CPW*, 2, 337.
25 *CPW*, 2, 276.
26 Louis Crompton, *Byron and Greek Love: Homophobia in 19th-Century England*

(Berkeley, CA: University of California Press, 1985), p. 120.

27 *CPW*, 2, 10–11, 19–20, 41–2, 48–9.
28 *CPW*, 2, 340–1.
29 *BLJ*, 6, 26–7.
30 *CPW*, 5, 680, 691.
31 *BLJ*, 5, 257.
32 *BLJ*, 5, 193 (see also 170), 212, 219.
33 Private communication.
34 *BLJ*, 6, 208.

Index

Note: page numbers in **bold** refer to illustrations.

absolutism 81, 82, 84
action, dramatic 119–28
Adélaïde, Mme 198
Aeschylus 51, 56
aesthetics 117–28
    aesthetic dialectics 123, 124
    grammatical errors and 172
Age of Reptiles 152–3, 158
agency
    denial of 24, 27
    political 24, 32
Ahriman (Arimanes) 65–6, 67
Ahura-Mazda 66
Allies (against Napoleon) 184
alliteration 224
ambition 76–7, 82
America 221
Amis, Kingsley 167
amor fati 39
ancien régime 47
Anglo-Saxon law 6–7
animus 196, 198
Anstey, Christopher 106
Anti-Jacobin, The 7
anti-trinitarianism 133, 141
archaism 166, 167
Arendt, Hannah 193–5, 197, 203–4
aristocratic class 8, 88–100
    debauchery of 91
    enmeshment in 89–93
    exotic 109–10
    freedom from 89, 94–5, 97–100
    ideals and values 89, 91–4, 95–6, 98–100
    political ideology 128
    power of 92–4, 97–100
    representation of 83
    satiety of 91–2, 95
    turning away from/betrayal of 88–92,
        93–100
    see also elites
Aristotle 119–20, 123
Arnold, Matthew 168, 169
art
    disillusionment with 44–5
    and objectification of the artist's lived
        experience 118
'artificial' versus 'natural' 210–14
Assyria 117–18
Aston Hall 20
atonement, doctrine of 142
Auerbach, Eric 118
Auerstadt 185, 188
Augustan literary tradition 206–7, 209, 210,
    215
Augustan-Romantic debate 209
Austerlitz 185
Austria 185
authority
    based on care and respect 79–80
    political 74, 77–80, 82, 84
    unfeeling 79

Bacchus 123
Bacon, Francis 147
Bakhtin, Mikhail 120, n15 130
Baldwin, William 21
Balzac, Honoré de 188
Bankes, William 15
Beatty, Bernard 106, 133
Becher, Revd. J. C. 5, 11, 13
Becker, Ernest 189–90
Beckford, William 226, 227
Beethoven, Ludwig van 184, 187
Being, Chain of 61, 62, 65
'being looked at' 8, 23
Berlin 188
Berlin, Isaiah 50, 56, 57, 58, 177, 201
betrayal 103, 105, 107–8, 112
Bible 141
Biblical literalism 7, 147, 151, 160

biographical function, of grammatical errors
171–2
Blackwood's 118
Blake, William 55, 125, 132–3, 135
Blessington, Lady 197
Blucher, Gebhard Leberecht von 227
Blumenthal, Friedrich 136
body
    control over 78
    female 25
    and gender performance 25, 26–7
    male 25–7
    rebellion against the mind 83
    as site of resistance 27
Bollmann, Erich 199–200
Bonnivard, François de 1, 2, 6
Bowles, William Lisle 207, 209–15
'Bowles controversy' 196, 207, 209–15
boyhood love, laments on the passing of 14
Britain 22
    see also England; Scotland
Broderip, William 153, 158
Brougham, Henry 15
Brown, William Wells 106
Buckland, William 147–8, 149–51, **150**,
    152–3, 159
Burke, Edmund 7
Burney, Fanny 200
Butler, E. M. 187
Butler, Dr George 16
Butler, Judith 24, 27, 32, n13 35
'Byromaniacs' 152, 159
Byron, Lady Anne Isabella Noel 133, 181,
    189
Byron, George Gordon
    affairs
        at Southwell 11–12, 13
        Augusta Leigh 20, 21, 181
        Lady Caroline Lamb 20, 58, 226, 227
        Lady Oxford 20, 21
    ambivalence regarding his social status
        100
    and the aristocracy 8, 88–100
    attitude to his public 118, n6 129
    autobiographical nature of his works 117,
        118, 128
    bisexuality 197
    and the 'Bowles controversy' 207, 209–
        15
    character 189
    and the emancipation of geology 147–60

and England 17, 56
exile 56, 203
fraudulent nature 13
and the gaze 8, 22–7
and Gifford 222–5, 228, 229
and grammatical freedom 165–77, 224–5
homoerotic/homosexual tendencies 14,
    195, 196, 226–7
humour 220–1
and the 'Inkle and Yarico' fable 103–15
and John Murray 221–6, 228–30
and Johnson 206–10, 212, 214, 215–16
and Keats 216
and Milton 132–43
and Napoleon 181–4, 186–91, 196–7,
    227–9
notoriety 152, 158–9
obsessions 181–3, 190
ottava rima poems 4, 17, 230–1
poetry for private perusal 10, 14–15
politics 8, 21–2, 31, 34, 46, 47, 90–1, 128,
    194–5, 197–8, 203–4
    withdrawal form active 21–2
and the politics of publication 219–31
goes public with his poetry 15
public persona 118
radicalism 90
and religion 133, 141–2, 155–6, 160, 220
scepticism 207
self-censorship 10, 222
sexual satiety 14
Southwell days 5, 11–13, 15–17
in Venice 1, 3, 17
works and writings
    Alpine Journal 56
    Beppo 1, 12, 94–5, 118, 219–20, 224,
        228
    Cain 7, 8
        and the Bible 141
        criticisms of 148–50, 152, 159
        and freedom 139, 143
        and geology 147, 148–60
        and Gessner's *The Death of Abel* 135–
        6, n23 145
        grammar 166, 167
        and Milton's *Paradise Regained* 132,
        134–43
        moral plague 148
        structure 138
    Childe Harold's Pilgrimage 1, 8, 37–48,
        118, 152

and aristocratic modes of thinking
  and being 88, 91–2
Canto I 88, 91–2, n17 130, 167
Canto II 88, 91–2, 166, 167, 226
Canto III 37–42, 44, 46, 48, 120, 156,
  158, 160, 174–6, 190, 197, 223
Canto IV 37, 39, 41–3, 45–8, 156,
  158, 160, 165, 176–7, 223–4, 227
freedom 37–41, 43–8, 220, 222–7
grammar 165, 166, 167, 174–7
rhyming 231
satire 227
turns and counter-turns 40
Childish Recollections 13–14, 15, 16
Don Juan 1, 3–7, 15, 17, 45, 56, 78, 81,
  83, n8 87, 128, 189, 194–5, 197,
  203, 212, 215
aristocratic modes of thinking and
  being 88, 95–9, 100
blind faith in leaders 80
Canto I 228
Canto II 228
Canto III 109, 172
Canto IV 103
Canto V 103, 173
Canto VI 171, 195
Canto VII 76, 170
Canto VIII 76
Canto XII 170
Canto XIII 97, 170
Canto XIV 97, 172
Canto XV 97, 170
Canto XVI 169
Canto XVII 98
freedom 103, 228, 230–1
geology 147, 150, 156
grammar 166, 168, 169–73, 176,
  n25 179
humour 12
and the 'Inkle and Yarico' fable 103,
  106, 108–15
and Johnson 207
Juan-Haidée relationship 103, 106,
  108–15
love 201–2
militarism 76
and Milton 132
moral plague 148
reviews 118
rhyming 230–1
Eastern/Oriental Tales 73, 77, 78, 83,

85
English Bards and Scotch Reviewers 15, 207
Fugitive Pieces (volume) 10–12, 13, 15
author's cuts to 11, 12
misprints 12
Morgan copy 12
Hours of Idleness, a Series of Poems.
  Original and Translated 10, 15, 16
Lament of Tasso 223
Lara 74, 198, 199, 201
Letter to John Murray 207, 210, 212, 214
'Lines to a Lady Weeping' 31
Manfred 7, 8, 37, 50–9, 60–71, 123,
  124, 228–9
Astarte 52–5, 57, 60, 61, 63, 64, 65,
  67–70
death 60, 62–5, 67–8, 70–1
freedom 50–2, 54–9, 67, 70–1
negativity 50–9
Marino Faliero
and aristocratic modes of thinking
  and being 88–100
grammar 168
misconceived failure of 126
Mazeppa 72, 74–86, 120
ambivalence of Mazeppa 81, 84–6
central narrative 81, 83
contradictions 84–6
framing narrative 75, 76–80, 81, 84
narrative structure 75–6
transitional narratives 75–6, 81–3, 84
Newark volumes 10, 12, 16
'Ode to the Framers of the Frame
  Bill' 31
Oscar of Alva 15
Poems Original and Translated 16
Poems on Various Occasions 12–15
Sardanapalus 3, 8, 74, n10 87, 117–28,
  223
aesthetics 117–28
freedom 117–19, 121–6, 128, n5 129,
  n9 129–30
Siege of Corinth 223
The Blues 106–8, 171–2
The Bride of Abydos 8, 20–34
dedication 21–2
freedom 27–31
gaze 22–7, 31–4
gender identity 23–7, 29, 32, n10 35
impetus for 21
resistance 21, 22, 27, 31–3

surveillance 24, 25, 27–8, 32–3
The Corsair 73, 78, 167, 199, 200–1
'The Dream' 158
The Island 74, 88, 92–4, 103, 113–14
'The Isles of Greece' 166
The Prisoner of Chillon 1, 2–3
The Prophecy of Dante 38–9
'The Vision of Judgement' 1–2
Werner 223
Byronic hero 72–9, 81–6, 103, 143
  doomed 93
  and freedom 72–4
  political role 72–3
  tensions of the 72
Byronic heroine 136, 138, 143
Byronism, rejection 152

Cain 63
Calvin 2
Campbell, Thomas 207, 210–11, 212–13
Canning, George 203
cant 194–5
  Cant 'poetical' 211–12
Carbonari 34
Carlile, Richard 148, 150
Carlyle, Thomas 50
Casimir, John 74, 79, 81, 82, 84
Castlereagh, Viscount 194–5, 196, 203
Catholicism 97–8, 100, 160, 220
Censor 2
censor deputatus 3
censorship *see* self-censorship
Certeau, Michel de 31
Chain of Being 61, 62, 65
Charles XII, King of Sweden (fictional
  portrayal) 74, 75, 76–85
Chateaubriand, François René de 184
Chaucer, Geoffrey 5, 63
Chaworth-Musters, Mary 11
Chew, Samuel 70–1
Child, Lydia Maria 106
Christensen, Jerome 40, 41
Christian liberty 132, 135, 143
Christianity 61, 63, 67, 68–71, 133–4
  and geology 149, 151, 159
  see also Catholicism; Protestant theology
Church 148
  negation of the commonplace wisdom of
  55
civilisation, dependence on its own
  barbarism 47

class 103, 109–11
  barriers 91
  lower classes 90
  merchant class 110
  see also aristocratic class
clauses 174–6
Clubbe, John 7
Cobourne, Mrs 11
Cochran, Peter 176–7
coercion, gaze as vector of 22, 25, 26, 31, 32
Coetzee, J. M. 196
  Disgrace 202–3
Coleridge, E. H. 166, 167, 228
Coleridge, Samuel Taylor 4, 133, 184
Coleridgean organicism 216
Collyer, Mary 136
Colman, George the Younger 106, 114
colonialism 112, 114
compulsion, language of 39
Comus 3
confinement 27–31, 33
conservatism 91
Constant, Benjamin 50, 58–9, 202
constitutional monarchy 81
Conybeare, William 149, 150, **150**
Corbett, Martyn 126, n5 129
Corneille 120
Corns, Thomas 133
cosmology 61, 151, 152
Creation mythology 151, 160
creativity 45
  limits of 47
Crompton, Louis 226–7
Cromwell, Oliver 3, 133
Cuvier, Georges 147–8, 152

daimonisch (daimonic) 187
Dallas, Robert Charles 222, 226
dangling participle 165, 174–7
Dante 38–9, 159
Darwin, Charles 160
Davies, Scrope 222, 226
De Forest, John William 104
De la Beche, Henry **155**, 157–8, **157**
de Man, Paul 174
De Quincey, Thomas 160
de Staël, Mme 184
death 60, 62–5, 67–8, 70–1, 190–1
  freedom of 117
debauchery 91
decadence 91

Dedalus, Stephen 165, 177, n2 177
Delacroix, Eugène 1, 2, 6
democracy 55, 62, 81, 86
demons 70
Denmark 76
dependence, rebellion against 40
despair 37–8, 41, 43
Destinies 65, 66–7
devil 139, 153
    see also Lucifer; Satan
dialectics
    aesthetic 123, 124
    drama-poetry 119, 121–6, 128
dialogic texts 72, 74, 120, n15 130
dinosaurs 152–5, **155**, **156**, 157–8, **157**, 159
D'Israeli, Isaac 211
dominant order 28, 30, 31, 32–3
Dostoevsky, Fyodor M. 188
drama 119–28
    and poetry 119–26, 128
dramatic action 119–28
Dryden, John 122–3, 127, n10 130, 206,
    209, 210
dualism 60–1, 65–6, 70
'dull life', reaction against 43

earthly forces/demons 62
earthly nature 43
Eden myth 114
Edinburgh Review 15, 184
Edleston, John 14
effeminacy 25–7, 118, 127
Ehrlichmann, John 193
Eichmann, Adolf 193–4, 195, 197, 203
Eliot, T. S. 118, 221
elites 22
    see also aristocratic class
Ellis, George 171
Elphinstone, Margaret Mercer 58
emancipation
    of geology 147–60
    see also freedom; liberty
emasculation 25–6, 127, 201
emotional freedom 73–4, 82, 86
emotional repression 73–4
England 181, 219–21
England, A. B. 99
enjambment n25 179
equality 3
Erdman, David 118
Erfurt, Congress of 185

eros 195, 197–8, 203
erotic freedom 203–4
erotic politics 194–204
Ethical poetry 212–13, 215, 216
evil
    freedom from 71
    and good 61, 65–6
    resistance to 67–8
evolution 160
Examiner, The (journal) 7
exile 56, 203
exotic settings 117–18
Eywood 20

Faliero, Marino 3
fatality 44, 57, 92–4
fate 42–4, 63, 66
    overcoming 39
Felsensen, Frank 104–5, 114
female body 25
feminine
    faith in 93–4
    unity 127
femininity 26
    performance 25
feminist criticism 128
Fichte, Johann Gottlieb 186
Fielding, Henry 4, 5
Fitzgerald, Edward 159
Flahaut, Comte de 58
Flood mythology 151
forgetfulness, search for 64
fossil record 149–51, 154, 157–8
Foucault, Michel 33
France 181, 182, 184, 199
Frankenstein, Victor 154
Franklin, Caroline 97, 112, 114
fraudulence 13
Frederick William IV of Prussia 184
free will 44
freedom 7–8, 72–4
    aesthetic 117–19, 121–6, 128, n5 129, n9
        129–30
    ambivalence towards 86
    in *Cain* 139, 143
    in *Childe Harold's Pilgrimage* 37–41, 43–8,
        220, 222–7
    civil 132
    and constraint 230–1
    of death 117
    domestic 132

in *Don Juan* 103, 228, 230–1
emotional/psychological 73–4, 82, 86
erotic 203–4
fantasy of 30
fleeting sense of 27–31
'for' 177
'from' 41, 56–7, 59, 177
from the aristocratic class 89, 94–5, 97–100
of geology 147–60
grammatical 165–77
of the hero 72–4
inner 139
intellectual 132, 139–40
in *Manfred* 50–2, 54–9, 67, 70–1
mental 100
Napoleon and 191
and negativity 50, 51–2, 54–9, 177
of outlaws 85
perilous nature 47
personal 51–2, 56, 58
political 80, 81, 86, 121, 140, 204
as political abstraction 46
positive 56, 57, 177
in practice 219–31
religious 132, 133–4, 135, 140, 143
in *Sardanapalus* 117–19, 121–6, 128, n5
    129, n9 129–30
simulcrum of 30
textual 118
in *The Bride of Abydos* 27–31
see also emancipation; liberty
French Revolution 7, 46, 58, 184–5, 199
    Tree of Liberty 3
Freud, Sigmund 189, 190

Gambs, Pastor 199
Gance, Abel 188
Gardner, Helen 169
gaze 8, 22–7
    'being gazed at' 8, 23
    fatal 23, 31, 33
    mutual 22
    as pathway of desire 22
    politics of the 23, 32
    preoccupied/misplaced 22–3, 31, 33
    regulation of 23–4
    and resistance 32–4
    as vector of coercion 22, 25, 26, 31, 32
    see also looking
gender identity

disruption 32
    as performative 24–7, 29, n10 35, n13 35
    and social control 23–4
gender roles
    and liberty 202
    reversal 111
Genesis, Book of 147
Geneva 2, 58
gentlemanliness 196
Gentz, Friedrich von 186
geology
    catastrophe geology 148
    emancipation of 147–60
    heroic age of 147
    poetical 151–2, 155, 159–60
    scriptural 160
George III 1, 6, 7
George IV (Prince Regent) 22
Germany 184, 186, 187
Gessner, Salomon, *Der Tod Abels/The Death
    of Abel* 132, 135–6, n23 145
Gibbon, Edward 140
Gifford, William 21, 51, 168, 220, 222–5,
    228, 229
Gleckner, Robert 45
Glenbervie, Lord 58
Glorious Revolution 1688 22
God
    conceptions of 155–6
    and Creation 151, 160
    the Father 133, 142
    Old Testament 155
    the Son 133, 141, 142, 143
    worship of 133–4
Goethe, Johann Wolfgang von 51, 61, 169,
    184–8
    Faust 51, 61–2, 63, 185, 188
good, and evil 61, 65–6
grammatical errors 165–77
    antagonistic effect 172
    biographical function 171–2
    'careless' carelessness 165–9, 173
    dangling participle 165, 174–7
    defamiliarising effect 172
    'deliberate' carelessness 165, 167–8, 169–73, 177, n3 178, n21 178–9
    ironic 172
    performative 173
    printing/copying errors 169
    vivifying effect 172
Granville, Countess Harriet 148

Gray, Thomas 6, 150, 210
Greece 182, 221
Greek translation 15
Greer, Germaine 10
Guiccioli, Teresa 136
guilt 61, 63, 65–6, 68, 128

Habeas Corpus 220, 224, 230
Hades 153
Haldemann, H. R. 193
Hamlet 40, 60
Hampden Club 20
Hardy, Thomas 188
harems 23–4, 26, n9 35
Harrow 16, 182, 197
Hawkins, Thomas 153, 154, **156**, 159–60
Hayley, William 132–3
Hazlitt, William 45, 46–7, 135, 184, 188, 197
heaven, women and 29
Hegel, Georg Wilhelm Friedrich 188
Heidegger, Martin 195, 203
Heine, Heinrich 184, 188
Hell, as state of mind 63, 69
Helvetian Republic 55, 59
Hemans, Felicia 47–8
heroes
    Weberian 72
    see also Byronic hero
heroism 190
Herold, J. Christopher 187, 196, 198–9, 200
Hobhouse, John Cam 181, 221, 222, 223,
    224, 225, 228
Holland, Lord 21–2
Homer 193
Homeric tradition 108
homo-social poetry 15, 16
homoeroticism/homosexuality 10, 14–15,
    184, 195–6, 226–7
homophobia 226–7
honourable conduct 92–3
Hope, Thomas 186
Horace 12, 45
horse-rider relationship metaphor 78–80,
    83, 85
House of Lords 21
Hugo, Victor 188
Hume, David 140, 204
humour 5, 12
Hunt, John 169, 222, 230
Hunt, Leigh 197, 206, 222
Hunter, William 133, 134

Huxley, Aldous 186

'I', autonomy from the text 40
idealism, noble 94
ideals, aristocratic 89, 91–4, 95–6, 98–100
identity
    super personal 57
    see also gender identity
imagination 183, 188, 190
immortality 62, 69
    of the soul 70
individual, engagement with the world 140
'Inkle and Yarico' fable 103–15
    revisions 103, 104, 105, 111
Irish Catholicism 220
irony 81
Islamic society 23–4
Italy 182, 219, 220, 221

Jamison, Kay Redfield 189, 190
Jefferson, Thomas 186
Jeffrey, Francis 167–8, 226, 229
Jena 185, 188
Jesus 141–2, 143, 195
    passion of the Christ 142
    temptation in the wilderness 138–9
Jews 193
Johnson, Paul 195
Johnson, Samuel 173, 206–10, 212, 214,
    215–16, n8 217
Joseph, M. K. 90

katharsis 119, 120
Keats, John 4, 119, 128, 216
Keatsian readings, Sardanapalus 121–3, 125,
    128
Kelsall, Malcolm 22, 91, 95–6
Kennedy, Dr 133, 141
Kinnaird, Douglas 50, 140, 181
Kirkdale Cave hyenas, Yorkshire 149–51,
    150
Knight, G. Wilson 125
knowledge 61–2
Kolbrener, William 134

Lake School 2
Lamartine, Alphonse de 188
Lamb, Lady Caroline 20, 58, 226, 227
language 203–4
language rules 193–5
Lansdown, Richard 119, 126

Las Cases 186
Latin translation 12, 15
leadership 72–3, 74, 76–8, 80–1, 83–5
    blind faith in 80
    honourable/noble 92, 93
    military 76
Lean, Edward Tangye 197
Leigh, Augusta 20, 21, 181
Lewalski, Barbara 134
Lewis, Mr 51
Liberal, The 22
libertarians 72
liberty 1–8, 72, 140, 201–3
    Christian 132, 135, 143
    comparative 32–3
    and constraint 201–2, 230–1
    in *Don Juan* 103
    and erotic constraint 201–2
    'for' 201
    'from' 201
    from Byron's public persona 118
    and gender roles 202
    limited 28–9
    Napoleon and 191
    narrative 4–5
    political 202
    psychological 202
    simulacrum 29
    taking a liberty 4–5
    see also emancipation; freedom
licence 1–8
    poetic 3–5, 72, 173, 177, 219–31
    sexual 3–4, 5, 8
lies, political 193–4
Ligon, Richard 103, 104
literalism, Biblical 7, 147, 151, 160
Literary Club 208
literary-critical mode 209
lived experience, objectification of the
    artist's 118
Locke, John 58, 140
Lodi, battle of 182
Long, Edward 15
looking 22–3, 25–6, 32–3
    see also gaze
Louis XV 198
Louis XVI 7
love
    boyhood 14
    fate of 112–13
    and slavery 103–9, 111–15

    time as foe to 112–13
    unrequited 200
love poems
    heterosexual 10–12, 13–14, 15, 22
    homosexual 10
lower classes 90
Lucifer 137–40, 141–3, 148, 149, 150, 152,
    153–4, 159
    see also devil; Satan
Luddites 34
Lyell, Charles 147, 154, 156–8, **157**

Magna Carta 6
malapropisms 170
Malcolm, Janet 189
male body 25–7
male self-interest 107–8
male-for-male passion 15
    see also homoeroticism/homosexuality
man, dualism of 60–1
Manet, Édouard 6
manic depression 189
Manichaeism 65–6, 70
Mantell, Gideon 152, 153, 154, **155**, 156,
    157
Marchand, Leslie 117
Marlowe, Christopher 51, 63
    Faustus of 50–1, 61
Martin, John 154–5, **156**
Martz, Louis 136
masculinity 32
    performance of 25–7
    shift from 93
Mayne, Ethel C. 168
Mazzini, Giuseppe 7
McCarthy, Mary 203
McGann, Jerome 10, 14, 21, 37–8, 74–5, 79,
    81, 83, 85–6, 106, 114, 134–5, 139, 169,
    171, 198, 228
McLachlan, H. John 140
Medwin, Thomas 134–5, 136, 207
Melbourne, Lady 20, 21, 181
mental freedom 100
metaphysics 61, 63
militarism, attack on 76, 80, 81, 84–5
military leaders, attack on 76
Mill, John Stuart 58
Millbanke, Annabella 203
Milton, John 2, 3, 63, 132–43, n10 144, 154,
    159, 210
    De Doctrina Christiana 132, 133–4, 140, 141

Paradise Lost 134, 135, 136, 137, 139, 149, 153
Paradise Regained 132, 134–43
mind, power of the 47–8
mind-body relations 83
mixed marriages 107
monarchy, constitutional 81
monologic texts n15 130
Montaigne 207
Moore, Thomas 20, 181, 184, 226
Morris, Governor 198
Moses 147, 148, 155
Mozart, Wolfgang Amadeus 187
Murray, John 50, 88, 151, 154, 220, 221–6, 228–30
myth
    Creation 151, 160
    Eden 114
    Flood 151
    Napoleon and 188
myth-making, nationalistic 227–8

Napoleon Bonaparte 7, 38, 44, 46, 76, 181–91, 195–7, 203, 227–9
Napoleonic constitution 59
Narbonne-Lara, Comtesse de 198
Narbonne-Lara, Louis Vicomte de 198–201
narrative momentum 128
    retarding of 120, 123, 125, 128
narrative structure
    Mazeppa 75–6
    'story within the story' 75
narratives
    central 81, 83
    framing 75, 76–80, 81, 84
    ironic 81
    linear 126
    transitional 75–6, 81–3, 84
narrators 4–5
nationalistic myth-making 227–8
natural theology 159–60
'natural' verses 'artificial' 210–14
nature worship 41–2
Nausikaa 108
Nazi ideology 193–4
negativity 50–9, 177
Nemesis 66, 67, 68
neo-classicism 120, 123, 125–6
    unities 125–6
Neoplatonism 61, 62, 65, 67, 70
New Yorker magazine 193

Newcombe, Thomas 136
Newey, Vincent 37, 43
Newgate prison 224
Newman, John Henry 147, 159
Newstead Abbey 10, 15, 20
Newton, Isaac 140
Nicholson, Andrew 221, 229
Nietzsche, Friedrich Wilhelm 39, 40, 188, 195
Nisus and Euryalus 12–13, 14, 15
Noah 151
noble conduct 92–4
'nurturing native' figure 109

objectification, of the artist's lived experience 118
Ocean 48
Odysseus 108
Old Testament 155
order, dominant 28, 30, 31, 32–3
organicism 216
original sin 141, 142
Ormazd 66, 67
Ortega y Gasset, José 189
Orwell, George 195
ottava rima 56, n21 178–9, 230–1
outlaws, freedom of 85
Oxford, Lady 20, 21, 22
Oxford, Lord 20, 22

pacing, of the verse 128
Paglia, Camille 127, 168
panopticism 24
Parma, Duke of 198
Pasha, Ali 183
passion 182–3, 202–4
    male-for-male 15
    sexual 202–3
pathetic fallacy 175–6
Paul, St 3
personal failure 37
Peter the Great 76
Petronius 105
    'The Ephesian Matron' 105
Pickstock, Catherine 175
Pigot, Elizabeth 12, 14
Pigot, John 11, 12
poetic control 40–1
poetic licence 3–5, 72, 173, 177, 219–31
Poland 76
political authority 74, 77–80, 82, 84

political failure 37
political ideology, aristocratic 128
political lies 193–4
political oppression 211–12
politics 22
    Byron and 8, 21–2, 31, 34, 46, 47, 90–1,
        128, 194–5, 197–8, 203–4
    and the Byronic hero 72–3
    of the gaze 23, 32
    of publication 219–31
    of resistance 34
Poltava, Battle of 75, 76, 77
Poole, Gabriele 7, 120
Pope, Alexander 21, n5 129, 172, 196, 206–
    7, 210–11, 216, 224
positivism 147
Pound, Ezra 220–1
power
    aristocratic 92–4, 97–100
    collective 58
    distribution of 77
    harems and 23–4
    political 82
Pratt, Mary Louise 109, 112, 114
Pratt, Willis 11
present perfect constructions 173–4
Price, Richard 7, 104, 114
Priestley, Joseph 140
Prior, Matthews 207
Prometheus 56, 154, 183, 191
prophecy 45, 99–100
Protestant theology 160
Prussia 185
Prussian troops 184, 187–8
psychological freedom 73–4, 82, 86
publication, politics of 219–31
Pulci 4
Pushkin, Alexander 188

Quarterly Review 152–3, 220, 222

race 103, 107–14
Racine 120
radicalism 90–1, 148, 150, 152
rapidity, sense of 168, 172
Reign of Terror 3
religion 133, 140–2
    and the aristocracy 97–100
    freedom of 132, 133–4, 135, 140, 143
repression 73–4
reptiles 152–5, **155–7**, 157–9

Reptiles, Age of 152–3, 158
resistance 21, 22, 31–4, 40, 55
    body as site of 27
    simulacrum 27, 31
rhyme 42–4
    b 42
    ottava rima 56, n21 178–9, 230–1
    triple 40
Ridenour, George 169
Ridges 12, 15, 16
    see also S. and J. Ridge of Newark
risqué humour 5, 12
Rogers, John 134
Romanticism 47, 117, 120, 185, 206–9, 211–
    12, 214–16
Rostand, Edmond 188
Rousseau, Jean Jacques 183
Ruskin, John 177
Russell, Bertrand 72
Russia 76, 185

S. and J. Ridge of Newark 10
    see also Ridges
St Helena 182, 188
Sardou, Victorien 188
Satan 137–9, 141, 143, 153, 154
    see also devil; Lucifer
satire 106–7, 148, 149–50, 171–2, 227
scepticism 207
Schom, Alan 196
Schulz, Max F. 113
science 160
Scotland 181
Scott, Sir Walter 2, 46, 168, 183, 184, 186,
    188
sea-dragons 154–5, **156**, 157, 159
Seaham 3
self, capacity to endure 38
self-censorship 10, 222
self-deception 193, 194
self-interest, male 107–8
self-mastery 57
self-satire 171–2
self-torture 69, 70
sensual pleasure, disdain for in the Byronic
    hero 73, 86
sentimental travel-writing 109, 112, 113
sexual licence 3–4, 5, 8
sexual passion 202–3
sexuality 195–8
Shakespeare, William 133, 135, 165, 183

Sheldon, G. A. 166
Shelley, Mary 169
Shelley, Percy Bysshe 3, 4, 45, 46, 118–19, 133, 135, 150, 221
  The Cenci 119, 123
sin, original 141, 142
Six Mile Bottom 20
slavery, and love 103–9, 111–15
Smollett, Tobias George 4, 221
social change, class barriers to 91
social control 21, 23–4
social status 100
Socinianism 132, 133, 134, 135, 140–2, n10 144
Socrates 195
Socratic questioning 136
Sollors, Werner 104, 114
Sophocles 120
soul, immortal 70
Southey, Robert 1–2, 3, 4, 198, 203
Southwell 5, 10–12, 13, 15, 16–17
Sozzini, Fausto 140–1
'Spasmodics' 159
spectacle 126
Spectator 103, 105, 106
Spenserian stanzas 42
spirits 53–5, 57, 61–6, 67–8, 70, n2 71
Staël, Albert de 199
Staël, Auguste de 199
Staël, Mme de 8, 58, 194, 195, 196–204
Stedman, John 104, 106, 114
Steele, Richard 103–12, 114
Stendhal 184
Sterne, Laurence 4, 207
subjection 73
submission 80
suicide 57
Suliotes 34
Sumner, Charles 133
superiority, sense of 90, 92, 95, 97
superlatives 172–3
supernatural 53–7, 60, 61–8, 70, 154
Superreaders n9 129–30
surveillance 24, 25, 27–8, 32–3
Sweden 199
Swift, Jonathan 210
Switzerland 55–6, 59, 181–2
syntax 174–6, 177
systems 189

Talleyrand, Charles Maurice de 196

Tennyson, Lord Alfred 159
text, as vehicle 41
theology 159–60
Thomson, James 210
Thorwaldsen, Bertel 135
thought 39–40
thwarted lives 45
Tocqueville, Alexis de 58
Toland, John 133
Tolstoy, Leo 188
Tragedies 117, 119–21, 124, 126, 127
transcendental aspiration 42–3
transference 189–90
translations 12, 15
travel-writing, sentimental 109, 112, 113
tyrants 23, 31, 33

uncertainty 121, 124, 125
underworld 53–4
Unitarians 141

Valmy, battle of 184
values, aristocratic 89, 91–4, 95–6, 98–100
veiling 24, n10 35
Venice 1, 3, 17, 47, 94–5
Verdi, Giuseppe 7
Vienna, Congress of 1815 55–6, 59, 194
Vietnam 193
Vigny, Alfred de 188
Virgil 15
vitality 37–8
Voltaire 76, 140, 185, 195

war 81
Ward, Geoffrey 120
Warton, Joseph 208, 209, 210, 214, n8 217
Washington, George 198
Waterloo, battle of 227
Watson, Bishop 141
Weberian hero 72
Webster, Lady Frances Wedderburn 20, 21
Webster, Noah 195
Weimar 185
Wellington, Duke of 195, 227
West, Paul 172
Whewell, William 154
Whigs 6–7, 22, 58, 89, 95–8
  decline 91, 7 101
Wilkes, Joanne 1, 194, 197
Wilkinson, Henry 148–9
will 8, 44, 56, 66

Winegarten, Renée 72
Wittreich, Joseph 132–3
women, intellectual 106–7
Wordsworth, William 3, 132–3, 135, 168, 172, 173–4, 176, 215–16
Wordsworthian poetics 41–2, 215–16

Yeats, W. B. 189

Zeus 56
Zoroastrianism 61, 65–8